Merry Christmas Dad / Gramma 2015
& Bree, Ronny & Gab

The King's Grave

Also by Michael Jones

The King's Mother
Bosworth 1485: Psychology of a Battle
Agincourt 1415: A Battlefield Guide
Stalingrad: How the Red Army Triumphed
Leningrad: State of Siege
The Retreat: Hitler's First Defeat
Total War: From Stalingrad to Berlin

The King's Grave

---

*The Discovery of Richard III's Lost Burial Place
and the Clues It Holds*

PHILIPPA LANGLEY AND MICHAEL JONES

St. Martin's Press ❦ New York

Maps drawn by Rodney Paull

www.stmartins.com

Library of Congress Cataloging-in-Publication Data

Langley, Philippa.
    The king's grave : the discovery of Richard III's lost burial place and the clues it holds /
Philippa Langley and Michael Jones.—1st U.S. edition.
        p. cm.
Includes bibliographical references and index.
    ISBN 978-1-250-04410-5 (hardcover)
    ISBN 978-1-4668-4270-0 (e-book)
1. Richard III, King of England, 1452–1485—Death and burial. 2. Excavations (Archaeology)—
England—Leicester. 3. Leicester (England)—Antiquities. I. Jones, Michael K. II. Title.
    DA260.L34 2013
    942.046092—dc23

                                                                                                2013030043

    St. Martin's Press books may be purchased for educational, business, or promotional use.
    For information on bulk purchases, please contact Macmillan Corporate and Premium Sales
    Department at 1-800-221-7945, extension 5442, or write specialmarkets@macmillan.com.

    First published in Great Britain by John Murray (Publishers), an Hachette UK Company

                            First U.S. Edition: October 2013

                    10 9 8 7 6 5 4 3 2 1

To all those who saved the Dig, and to all those whose researches have illuminated Richard III as man and king

Contents

CONTENTS

Maps

Preface

O N 22 AUGUST 1485 two armies faced each other at Bosworth Field in Leicestershire. King Richard III, of the House of York, lined up in battle against his rival to the throne, Henry Tudor – a clash of arms that would determine the fate of England. It was Tudor who won the victory. Richard was cut down after leading a cavalry charge against his opponent and killed in savage fighting, after being only a few feet away from Henry himself. He was the last English king to die in battle.

That year marks a pivotal date in our history books: the ending of the Middle Ages and the beginning of the modern era. The House of Tudor became one of our most famous ruling dynasties – and its 118-year triumph culminated with William Shakespeare's history plays. Within them, Richard III emerged as one of England's most consummate and appalling villains, a ruthless plotter, an outcast from his own family, deformed in body and nature, who murdered his way to the throne. The most horrifying of these crimes was the killing of the young nephews placed in his care, the Princes in the Tower. In Shakespeare's *Richard III*, the king's own death at Bosworth is powerfully portrayed – alone, with no means of escape and surrounded by his enemies, Richard calls out: 'A horse! A horse! My kingdom for a horse!' His despairing cry is not heeded and he is overpowered and slain. It is the judgement of God upon his wickedness.

Shakespeare's drama was based on a series of Tudor histories that progressively blackened Richard's name. The principal charge against him in the reign of Henry VII was that he had seized the throne by killing his nephews. That ghastly accusation – believed by many – should have been enough to consign him to the scrapheap of history. But by the reign of Henry VIII he had already been accused of a number of additional crimes, including disposing of his brother, George, Duke of Clarence, in the most startling fashion, drowning him in a large vat of malmsey wine. By the reign of Elizabeth I it was commonly believed that he had poisoned his own wife. It is striking how the Tudors kept adding to Richard's tally of victims. Alongside this was an almost compulsive need to distort his appearance. A physical characteristic, where one shoulder was raised higher than the other, was deliberately exaggerated in a succession of Tudor portraits to depict the king in increasingly sinister fashion.

By the time of Shakespeare this propaganda had reached its zenith. Richard had now become a crouching hunchback, whose bent and distorted body mirrored the hideous depravity of his crimes. By then, the king's actual body, buried hastily in Leicester in the aftermath of the Battle of Bosworth, had disappeared from view. It was widely believed that the disgraced monarch's humble grave, in the Church of the Greyfriars, had been lost at the time of Henry VIII's Dissolution of the Monasteries – its contents even emptied into the River Soar. With the king's remains seemingly absent, the Tudors further twisted his historical reputation. He grew into a dark Machiavellian figure, an outcast from all sensibility – whose life and death provided a terrible moral warning.

It was a damning indictment - yet some were suspicious. Early in the reign of James I a number of attempts were made to present an alternative, redeeming portrait of the vilified king. Such efforts have persisted to this day, with the founding of the Richard III Society, determined to present a more human and sympathetic picture of Richard as man and monarch. More recent academic studies have modified the Tudor legend in some respects. Yet, despite all these efforts, Shakespeare created a play so sinister and darkly seductive that it still remains the portrait most are drawn to. Shakespeare's powerful and unsettling depiction, of a man beyond the moral pale, gained new currency when it was transformed into the Sir Laurence Olivier film in 1955. It has been long recognized that only a discovery as important as Shakespeare's drama is compelling would provide a counterpoint to the Tudor villain the playwright portrayed. Now – in a municipal car park in Leicester – that discovery has been made. The grave of Richard III has been found – with the king's body still within it. It is one of the most significant archaeological discoveries of recent history.

This book reveals the remarkable series of events that led to this astonishing find. It tells of a search for Richard's remains – and also, accompanying it, the search for his real historical reputation. For, before the remnants of his body were uncovered, permission was obtained by Philippa Langley for them to be laid to rest – in a proper and fitting reburial – in Leicester Cathedral. Here at last was an opportunity to step beyond Shakespeare and make peace with the most vilified of our rulers. Not to condemn him, nor to sanitize his actions, but to place him firmly back in the context of his times.

As Richard's bones were painstakingly examined, it was found that he had scoliosis, a curvature of the spine that would have left one shoulder higher than the other. It also quickly became apparent that his body was racked with battle injuries. A time capsule had been opened, showing the last moments of Richard's bloody fight at Bosworth: the king's head shaved by the glancing blows from a halberd or sword, the back of his skull completely cleaved off by a halberd – a two-handed pole weapon, consisting of an axe blade tipped in a spike. And then, as his face was powerfully reconstructed from the skeletal structure around it, we at last had the opportunity to see him as he really was.

This is the story of one of history's most infamous kings – now restored to us – and the man behind the Tudor myth.

Philippa Langley and Michael Jones
July 2013

The Houses of York and Lancaster

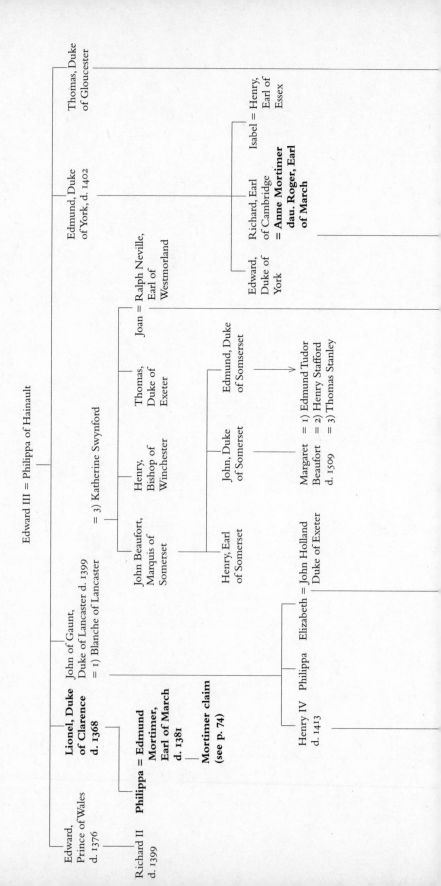

Edward III = Philippa of Hainault

Edward, Prince of Wales d. 1376

Richard II d. 1399

Lionel, Duke of Clarence d. 1368

Philippa = Edmund Mortimer, Earl of March d. 1381

Mortimer claim (see p. 74)

John of Gaunt, Duke of Lancaster d. 1399
= 1) Blanche of Lancaster
= 3) Katherine Swynford

John Beaufort, Marquis of Somerset

Henry, Bishop of Winchester

Thomas, Duke of Exeter

Joan = Ralph Neville, Earl of Westmorland

Henry, Earl of Somerset

John, Duke of Somerset

Edmund, Duke of Somerset

Margaret = 1) Edmund Tudor
Beaufort = 2) Henry Stafford
d. 1509 = 3) Thomas Stanley

Henry IV d. 1413

Philippa

Elizabeth = John Holland Duke of Exeter

Edmund, Duke of York, d. 1402

Edward, Duke of York

Richard, Earl of Cambridge
= Anne Mortimer, dau. Roger, Earl of March

Isabel = Henry, Earl of Essex

Thomas, Duke of Gloucester

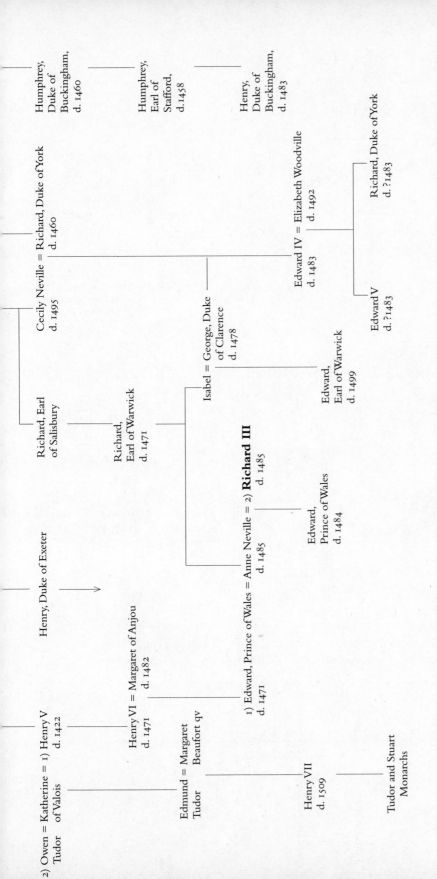

The House of York's claim to the throne rested on its descent through the female line from the Mortimers, and Edward III's second surviving son, Lionel, Duke of Clarence. Henry Tudor's Beaufort descent was from Edward III's third son, John of Gaunt, and his liaison with Katherine Swynford. When Gaunt finally married Katherine the Beauforts were legitimated, but subsequently barred from succession to the throne.

The House of York

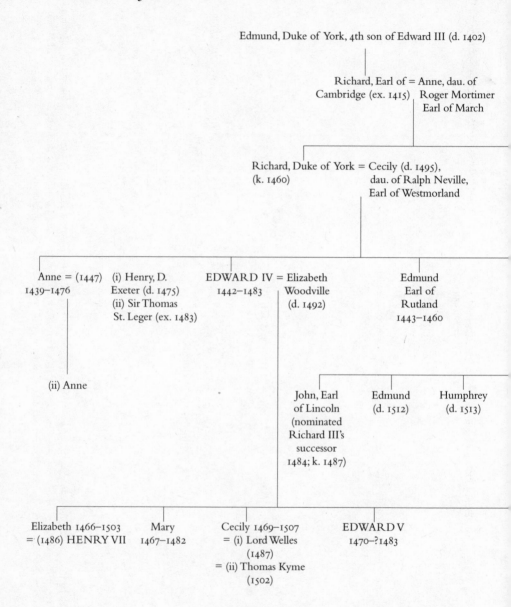

Edmund, Duke of York, 4th son of Edward III (d. 1402)

Richard, Earl of = Anne, dau. of
Cambridge (ex. 1415) Roger Mortimer
Earl of March

Richard, Duke of York = Cecily (d. 1495),
(k. 1460) dau. of Ralph Neville,
Earl of Westmorland

Anne = (1447) (i) Henry, D.
1439–1476 Exeter (d. 1475)
(ii) Sir Thomas
St. Leger (ex. 1483)

EDWARD IV = Elizabeth
1442–1483 Woodville
(d. 1492)

Edmund
Earl of
Rutland
1443–1460

(ii) Anne

John, Earl
of Lincoln
(nominated
Richard III's
successor
1484; k. 1487)

Edmund
(d. 1512)

Humphrey
(d. 1513)

Elizabeth 1466–1503
= (1486) HENRY VII

Mary
1467–1482

Cecily 1469–1507
= (i) Lord Welles
(1487)
= (ii) Thomas Kyme
(1502)

EDWARD V
1470–?1483

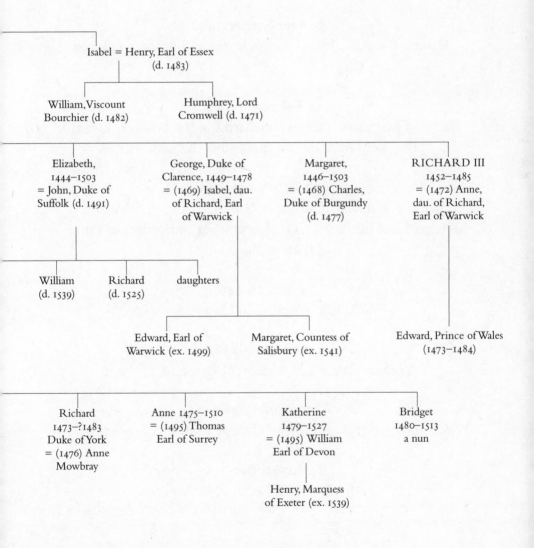

Isabel = Henry, Earl of Essex
(d. 1483)

William, Viscount
Bourchier (d. 1482)

Humphrey, Lord
Cromwell (d. 1471)

Elizabeth,
1444–1503
= John, Duke of
Suffolk (d. 1491)

George, Duke of
Clarence, 1449–1478
= (1469) Isabel, dau.
of Richard, Earl
of Warwick

Margaret,
1446–1503
= (1468) Charles,
Duke of Burgundy
(d. 1477)

RICHARD III
1452–1485
= (1472) Anne,
dau. of Richard,
Earl of Warwick

William
(d. 1539)

Richard
(d. 1525)

daughters

Edward, Earl of
Warwick (ex. 1499)

Margaret, Countess of
Salisbury (ex. 1541)

Edward, Prince of Wales
(1473–1484)

Richard
1473–?1483
Duke of York
= (1476) Anne
Mowbray

Anne 1475–1510
= (1495) Thomas
Earl of Surrey

Katherine
1479–1527
= (1495) William
Earl of Devon

Bridget
1480–1513
a nun

Henry, Marquess
of Exeter (ex. 1539)

Chronology of Richard's Life

2 October 1452

Richard born at Fotheringhay, Northamptonshire

↓

12 October 1459

Richard's father goes into exile after his defeat at Ludford

↓

30 December 1460

Battle of Wakefield. Richard's father and brother Edmund
killed

↓

2 February 1461

Battle of Mortimer's Cross. Richard's oldest brother, Edward,
Earl of March, victorious against the Lancastrians

↓

17 February 1461

Earl of Warwick defeated at Second Battle of St Albans.
Richard and his brother George sent for protection to Philip,
Duke of Burgundy

↓

4 March 1461

Edward IV proclaimed king in London

↓

29 March 1461

Yorkists defeat Lancastrians at Battle of Towton

↓

12 June 1461

Richard and his brother George return to England

↓

1 November 1461

Richard created Duke of Gloucester

↓

May 1464

Edward IV marries Elizabeth Woodville

↡

September 1465

Richard resident in household of Earl of Warwick

↡

January 1469

Richard returns to court

↡

June 1469

Warwick's rebellion starts

↡

26 July 1469

Battle of Edgecote. Henry Tudor's guardian, William, Lord Herbert, Earl of Pembroke defeated by rebels and subsequently executed

↡

17 October 1469

Richard made Constable of England

↡

12 March 1470

Warwick rebels again. Battle of Losecote Field. Warwick and Clarence flee to France and ally themselves with the Lancastrians

↡

2 October 1470

Warwick invades; collapse of Edward IV's authority. Richard accompanies Edward into exile in Burgundy. Readeption (Restoration) of Henry VI

↡

March 1471

Edward IV and Richard return from exile and land in Yorkshire

↡

14 April 1471
Earl of Warwick is defeated at the Battle of Barnet

☦

4 May 1471
Margaret of Anjou and the Lancastrian Prince Edward are
defeated at Tewkesbury

☦

21 May 1471
Henry VI is murdered in the Tower of London, almost
certainly on Edward IV's orders

☦

Spring 1472
Richard marries Warwick's daughter Anne Neville, starts to
fight for a share of the Neville inheritance and begins to build
up a northern affinity

☦

29 August 1475
Edward IV and Louis XI meet at Picquigny, ending the English
invasion of France. Richard shows his displeasure by absenting
himself from the agreement

☦

18 February 1478
Richard's brother, George, Duke of Clarence, convicted of
treason and executed in the Tower of London

☦

24 August 1482
Richard invades Scotland. Berwick recaptured

☦

9 April 1483
Death of Edward IV; succession of Edward V

☦

29–30 April 1483

Richard and Buckingham arrest Rivers, Grey and Vaughan at Northampton and Stony Stratford and secure custody of Edward V

4 May 1483

Richard and Edward V enter London: George Neville, Duke of Bedford dies and Richard loses hereditary right to the Neville lands

10 June 1483

Richard appeals for help from northern supporters against the Woodvilles

13 June 1483

Execution of Lord Hastings and arrest of Morton and Archbishop Rotherham at council meeting

22 June 1483

Richard's right to the throne proclaimed in a sermon by Ralph Shaw

26 June 1483

Richard becomes king

6 July 1483

Coronation of Richard III

29 August 1483

Richard arrives in York on royal progress

10 October 1483

Rebellion flares up in southern England

2 November 1483
Execution of the Duke of Buckingham at Salisbury

23 January 1484
Richard's only parliament meets at Westminster

April 1484
Death of Richard's son, Edward of Middleham

7 December 1484
Richard's first proclamation against Henry Tudor

16 March 1485
Death of Richard's queen, Anne Neville

9 June 1485
Richard arrives in Nottingham to await Henry Tudor's landing

23 June 1485
Richard's second proclamation against Henry Tudor

7 August 1485
Henry Tudor lands at Milford Haven

22 August 1485
Battle of Bosworth. Richard III killed; Henry Tudor (Henry VII) succeeds him

History of the Church of the Greyfriars, Leicester

1230
House in existence on Greyfriars site

1255
Church of Greyfriars first mentioned

1402
Rebellion: number of greyfriars executed by Henry IV

25 August 1485
King Richard III buried in the choir of the Greyfriars Church

1495
Tomb and epitaph erected over burial by Henry VII

1538
Dissolution of the Monasteries. Greyfriars expelled and priory and church closed. Sold to John Bellowe and John Broxholme to remove roof lead and timbers

1540s
Greyfriars priory and church become ruins. Site sold to Sir Robert Catlyn
(superstructure of King Richard's tomb removed)

1600
Site sold to Robert Herrick. Mansion house and gardens built

1611
John Speed reports King Richard's grave lost and his bones dug up at the Dissolution

1612

Christopher Wren records a 'handsome stone pillar' marking
the site of King Richard's grave in Herrick's garden

✝

1711

Herrick's descendants sell land to Thomas Noble. New Street
laid out with houses

✝

1759

Herrick's mansion house sold to William Bentley

✝

1914

Land and gardens sold to Leicestershire County Council who
erect offices around it

✝

1930s–40s

Land and gardens tarmacked to become car parks

✝

1968

Site passes to Leicester City Council, Social Services
Department

Looking for Richard project, Leicester

2004–5
Philippa Langley visits car parks. Dr John Ashdown-Hill
discovers Richard III's mtDNA

☙

2007
University of Leicester Archaeological Services (ULAS) digs in
nearby Grey Friars Street but uncovers no trace of Greyfriars
Church

☙

2008
Ashdown-Hill refutes River Soar story. Annette Carson in
Richard III: The Maligned King asserts the king's grave is probably
in the Social Services car park

☙

21 February 2009
Langley and Ashdown-Hill meet. Langley begins Looking for
Richard (LFR) project at Cramond Inn, Edinburgh

☙

September 2010
Leicester City Council supports LFR project

☙

January 2011
Langley obtains TV rights to John Ashdown-Hill's book, *Last
Days of Richard III*

☙

March 2011
Langley commissions ULAS for LFR project

☙

June 2011
Langley receives permission from Leicester City Council for
Ground Penetrating Radar Survey and archaeological
investigation of Social Services car park

†

28 August 2011
Langley carries out Ground Penetrating Radar Survey of the
three car parks

†

March 2012
April dig cancelled

†

July 2012
International Appeal saves dig

†

25 August 2012
Two-week dig begins. Leg bones discovered beside letter 'R'

†

31 August 2012
Langley instructs exhumation of remains found beside letter
'R'. ULAS applies for licence to exhume up to six sets of
remains of persons unknown

†

3 September 2012
Discovery of Greyfriars Church. Exhumation licence received
from Ministry of Justice. Dig extended into third week by
Leicester City Council

†

4 September 2012
Exhumation of remains beside letter 'R' begins

†

5 September

Full set of remains exhumed (minus feet). Discovery of choir of
church

✝

12 September 2012

Announcement of discovery of the remains thought to be those
of Richard III

✝

6 December 2012

Carbon-14 dating analysis confirms remains are late fifteenth
century

✝

16 January 2013

Facial reconstruction revealed to Langley

✝

3 February 2013

DNA match confirmed between remains and Michael Ibsen
(living relative of Richard III)

✝

4 February 2013

University of Leicester confirms remains found on 25 August
2012 are those of Richard III. Channel 4 and Darlow Smithson
Productions premiere *Richard III: The King in the Car Park*

Introduction

The Inspiration

I SUPPOSE I had always known about Richard. Shakespeare's villain must have registered somewhere in the recesses of my mind, but he didn't strike a chord with me. When I was growing up in the northern market town of Darlington, history had been my favourite subject. We had studied the Viking period through to 1066, our teacher bringing history vividly to life, and I'd revelled in the characters that formed our island nation. Oddly enough, we were never taught about Richard III and the Wars of the Roses, the conflict that tore the country apart. And there was another mystery that I discovered years later: Richard, Duke of Gloucester's home at Middleham Castle lay a short drive away yet there had been no school trips to see the history right on our doorstep.

I began to take an interest in Richard after I read Paul Murray Kendall's biography, *Richard III*, in which he questioned Shakespeare's interpretation of the king, proposing a different character altogether. Kendall drew on the testimonies of those who had known Richard intimately, such as the city fathers of York who, the day after Richard's death at Bosworth, had written: 'King Richard, late mercifully reigning upon us . . . was piteously slain and murdered, to the great heaviness of this city . . .' noting he was 'the most famous Prince of blessed memory'. Richard's life had everything: politics, power, romance, intrigue, mystery, murder, self-sacrifice, loyalty and incredible acts of bravery. I was intrigued to know more about the man and why it had been so necessary for the Tudors to rewrite his story.

As I learned more about him I was puzzled as to why Richard had always been represented one-dimensionally on screen. The malevolent, crooked, Shakespearean figure has been rolled out since the dawning of the film industry with Hollywood portraying a tyrant in its first-ever full-length feature film, *Richard III*, in 1912. No one seemed interested in rendering a more complex, nuanced portrait while, perversely, Tudor history has been extensively filmed, television companies favouring exciting modern dramas about the Tudor monarchs who succeeded Richard III. *The Six Wives of Henry VIII*, starring Keith Michell, was screened in 1970, quickly followed by Glenda Jackson's *Elizabeth R* and many other similar programmes. It would seem that little has changed today. HBO's critically acclaimed *Game of Thrones* is loosely based on the Wars of the Roses but is a fantasy, and the BBC has a forthcoming modern, glossy series about the women of this period, *The White Queen*, adapted from Philippa Gregory's trilogy, with Richard sidelined to a supporting role. Cinema, too, has recounted almost every story concerning the Tudors, but has yet to bring the actual Richard to life.

I was baffled by the industry's apparent desire to avoid putting King Richard III's more subtle persona centre-stage on the screen. Was this because of a general lack of interest in the character or something more profound? Perhaps Richard was too complex, and it was too difficult to find his voice. Or perhaps the establishment was happy to maintain the Tudor version of his story, in which case there was little need to reinterpret his life. After all, Shakespeare had already presented the Tudor account. Many modern works claiming to reveal the real King Richard were simply rehashes of the Tudor Richard. Villains sell.

Some independent voices, using contemporary sources who had known Richard, described a different man but they were lost among the Tudor histories. However, I was persuaded by the evidence for the real, human Richard. By now I had joined the Richard III Society, the oldest and largest historical society in the world. Its Ricardian statement of intent resonated with the 'many features of the traditional accounts of the character and career of Richard III' being 'neither supported by sufficient evidence nor reasonably tenable'. Since 1924, its work has provided the platform for leading research on the man and his times. Moreover, the view of the society's patron, the Duke of Gloucester, and his moving dedication address in 1980 in defence of 'something as esoteric and fragile as reputation' captivated me.

I started to write my own screenplay about Richard but, try as I might, I couldn't make the Richard I'd found in all the primary sources square with all the deeds he was supposed to have done. I could portray Richard, the loyal, dutiful son and brother living happily in the north, undertaking the tasks he is known to have performed there – and this matched what I knew about his character – but I couldn't make the quantum leap of propelling him on to the throne. I was confronted by a giant jigsaw puzzle where many pieces fitted together easily, reflecting Richard's character, but the key moments remained opaque. King Richard III was an enigma. I was by no means the first writer to have this problem. There are many accounts of historians being unable to understand his actions at important points, particularly in 1483 when he took the throne. But I was approaching him from a different perspective. I had to be familiar with his character before I could put into context the many challenges of his life, rather than the other way round. The later events of Richard's life did not define him; his character had been formed before they took place.

I wasn't interested in creating a saintly, one-dimensional

figure; that would have been as nonsensical as the sinister person presented to us for so long. And yet I couldn't make sense of the jigsaw before me.

I was about to give up when a new book on Richard was published: *Bosworth 1485: Psychology of a Battle* by the historian Michael Jones (and co-author of this book). It was acclaimed as a seminal work on the battle itself and on Richard's character, placing him in the context of his family, unlike Shakespeare and the Tudor writers who had separated him from it. But what changed everything for me in *Bosworth 1485* was the startling new evidence relating to Richard and his family, and new insight into the battle that would come to define him. The jigsaw of Richard's life and its key moments were beginning to come together.

By this time I had formed the Scottish Branch of the Richard III Society and was keen to meet this writer to hear about his research and his new evidence. When we met we discovered that we shared a similar view of Richard and the pivotal events of his life. With Michael Jones's book underpinning my screenplay, I immersed myself in the world of Richard III, devouring all I could on the king, visiting every place that had held meaning for him. In May 2004, my initial research complete, I travelled to the site of the Battle of Bosworth, which was both affecting and fascinating. The lie of the land in this small corner of Leicestershire seemed to suggest a battle fought over a much wider area than previously realized.

After Bosworth, I headed to Leicester. I wanted to explore the city and see it as Richard might have done. To view the remains of the castle, visit the site of the Blue Boar Inn, walk the Western Gateway and cross Bow Bridge over the River Soar, returning via Richard's statue and the cathedral and, finally, to the New Street car park, where it was rumoured that Richard's grave might once have been from a fragment of medieval wall that remained there. After visiting the cathedral, and laying my Yorkist white rose on the ledger stone to his memory in the choir, I wandered over to New Street, a small lane opposite. As I crossed St Martin's the street names around it bore witness to the friary precinct that had once existed nearby: Richard had reputedly been buried in the Church of the Greyfriars in 1485; Friar Lane ran along New Street's southern end, with Grey Friars Street running off to the east.

New Street car park is a tarmacked expanse of wasteland accommodating a hundred or so vehicles. That warm afternoon it lay almost empty and quiet, giving me the opportunity to walk its length and ponder what might lie beneath the unpromising surface. As I approached the parking attendant's hut by an old beech tree, I could see the section of medieval stonework lodged in the wall. I tried to get a feel for what it would have been like in Richard's day, how it might have looked, but nothing remained here of the past. I felt no resonance with Richard's life, or death.

Leaving New Street to head home, I spotted another car park almost directly opposite. I hadn't noticed it before, but I'd been so intent on getting to the first car park that I must have walked straight past it. This one had high green gates with a barrier over the entrance and a sign marked 'Private'. I was going to move on but experienced an overwhelming urge to enter. I slid around the barrier and into the car park which, again, was pretty much deserted apart from a few scattered vehicles. It was a large open space for seventy or more vehicles, surrounded by Georgian buildings with a large red-brick Victorian wall running north to south straight ahead of me. I found myself drawn to this wall and, as I walked towards it, I was aware of a strange sensation. My heart was pounding and my mouth was dry – it was a feeling of raw excitement tinged with fear. As I got near the wall, I had to stop, I felt so odd. I had goose-bumps, so much so that even in the sunshine I felt cold to my bones. And I knew in my innermost being that Richard's body lay here. Moreover I was certain that I was standing right on top of his grave.

Back home and trying to comprehend what I had experienced, friends and family told me not to dismiss it. A year later, after completing the first draft of my screenplay, I returned to the car park, questioning if what I had felt that day had been real. As I walked to the same spot and looked at the Victorian wall, the goose-bumps reappeared. I stared down at my feet. Slightly to my left, on the tarmac, there was something new – a white, hand-painted letter 'R', denoting a 'reserved' parking spot, but it told me all I needed to know.

My return visit to a Leicester car park was intended to mark the end of my investigation into Richard's story but would now mark the beginning of an entirely new search to uncover the real Richard III.

My quest for the king's grave had started.

I

The Road to the Dig

IF MY GUT instinct was correct, how did the medieval Greyfriars
Church become a modern car park? Most historical sources
agreed that following his death in 1485 at the Battle of Bosworth,
King Richard III had been buried at the Church of the Greyfriars
in Leicester, and ten years later Henry VII had paid for a tomb.
Further investigation revealed that in 1538 at the Dissolution of
the Monasteries the church was closed and fell into ruins. By
1611, the map maker John Speed reported the place was 'overgrown with nettles and weeds' and King Richard's grave 'not to
be found'. But it is also known that Robert Herrick, a former
Mayor of Leicester, had bought part of the Greyfriars site and
built himself a mansion. In 1612 Christopher Wren, father of the
famous architect, noted that in Herrick's garden there was 'a
handsome stone pillar', three feet tall, inscribed with: 'Here lies
the body of Richard III some time King of England'. The
Greyfriars site subsequently passed through several owners until,
in the early twentieth century, it was tarmacked over to become
car parks. Later, part of it was sold to Leicester City Council
Social Services Department and it had been in its car park that I
had had my unsettling experience.

As I continued to flesh out Richard's character for revised
drafts of my screenplay, the conclusion to his story started to
frustrate me. He was the last English warrior king, but had no
known grave. Any search for that grave would be fanciful and

irrational, particularly since stories abounded about his bones being removed at the Dissolution of the Monasteries and thrown into the River Soar. There was also the question mark over the Greyfriars Church: where was it? Furthermore, supposing human remains were found, how could they be identified as those of Richard III?

Then, everything changed.

Dr John Ashdown-Hill, historian, genealogist and member of the Richard III Society, made a most remarkable discovery. Having traced an all-female line of descent from Richard's elder sister, Anne of York, to Joy Ibsen, an elderly lady living in Canada, he identified King Richard's mitochondrial DNA sequence. It was a rare one. Only 17 per cent of the population had haplogroup 'J' for Jasmine, but, further, only 1.5 per cent had this particular haplotype, J1c2c.

The science was compelling. Female mitochondria are the most plentiful DNA in the human body. Deoxyribonucleic acid (DNA) is the hereditary material present in all cells of living organisms and the main ingredient of our chromosones, giving us our distinctive genetic characteristics. We each receive our mtDNA from our mother but it is only passed on through the female line, from mother to daughter. Having the mtDNA sequence of Richard III was crucial, since it represented the best opportunity for the survival of DNA within ancient remains because of its quantity, and also offered the greatest potential for a positive identification. The fact that it was a rare type of mtDNA was an added bonus. In addition, the female line of descent is generally considered more trustworthy than the male, because the official, named mother of a child is usually the child's authentic biological mother.

But how, and why, had the DNA discovery come about? Ashdown-Hill had been working with leading DNA expert Professor Jean-Jacques Cassiman at the Centre for Human

Genetics, University of Leuven, Belgium, to try to establish whether bones found in Mechelen in the mid-twentieth century could be the remains of Margaret of Burgundy (1446–1503), an elder sister of Richard III. In the mid-twentieth century, three sets of bones had been discovered and Ashdown-Hill's research had concluded that one of these might be those of Margaret. He now needed to compare Joy Ibsen's mtDNA with that in the ancient bones; a match would confirm the remains as those of Richard's sister. There was only one problem: some time in the past, one set of bones had been coated with varnish as a preservative, making it impossible to isolate DNA, while the other sets may have been contaminated by handling over the years.

Although Ashdown-Hill was unable to extrapolate the ancient mtDNA from the Mechelen bones to identify them, it was a game-changing discovery. I now knew that if we did go in search of King Richard's body, we would be able to identify him. In autumn 2005 I contacted Ashdown-Hill, and suggested he write to *Time Team*, the archaeological TV show, proposing a search for Richard's grave in the Social Services car park. *Time Team* replied that their three-day dig format was not compatible with a search of such a large area. Of course, I couldn't tell them (or Ashdown-Hill) why I felt that three days might just be enough.

Then, in late summer 2007, an archaeological excavation took place in Grey Friars Street in Leicester where a small single-storey 1950s extension at the NatWest/Pares Bank site was being demolished to make way for a block of flats. Undertaking the archaeology was University of Leicester Archaeological Services (ULAS), and what they discovered or, more precisely, what they did not discover, changed my plans irrevocably.

The dig was in the Greyfriars area, but the only find that suggested there might have been a medieval church in the vicinity was a fragment of a stone coffin lid found in a post-medieval drain. The dig was dismissed locally as of little importance, but I disagreed. It suggested that the Greyfriars Church was located further to the west of the Greyfriars area than had been assumed, away from the heavily developed eastern part towards the car parks, open spaces ripe for archaeological investigation.

I wrote to Leicester City Council's archaeologist, Chris Wardle, requesting further information on the dig, but received no response. However, after I encouraged the Richard III Society to make contact, Wardle was persuaded to write an article for the society's *Ricardian Bulletin*, which gave me a much clearer picture of the Greyfriars area.

It had previously been asserted that Richard might have first been buried in the Church of the Annunciation in the Newarke in Leicester, but in 2008 John Ashdown-Hill found more evidence to support the Greyfriars Church burial. And in her book *Richard III: The Maligned King*, Annette Carson examined sources contemporary with Richard III (i.e. pre-Tudor) with the aim of uncovering the man behind the myth, and proved that it was possible to discover the king's real character. *The Maligned King* suggested that the king probably still lay undisturbed where he was originally buried in the Greyfriars Church, which was most likely situated under the private car park of the Department of Social Services. It was the first book I had read to make this claim.

The next piece in the jigsaw once more came from John Ashdown-Hill. While researching Richard's burial, he discovered that it was John Speed who had started the story about the removal of Richard's remains, as a means of explaining why he could find no trace of Richard's grave. But Speed's map showed that he had been looking for the grave in the wrong place. He had been looking in the Blackfriars (Dominicans) site, not the Greyfriars (Franciscans), and it was the Blackfriars site he had reported as overgrown with nettles and weeds. Ashdown-Hill concluded that the body of Richard III had not been dug up in 1538 and was therefore still at the Greyfriars site.

So the question remained: where was the Greyfriars Church? The street names and the recent dig in Grey Friars Street appeared to confirm my instinct that the burial place was on the northern side of the Social Services car park where I had had my experience. But I needed evidence, without which no one could be expected to take me seriously.

Then, researching in the Richard III Society's archives, I found a copy of a medieval map from Leicestershire County Council records. This showed the Greyfriars Church opposite St Martin's Church (now Leicester Cathedral) at what is now the northern end of the Social Services car park. I had my smoking gun (see map on p. 12).

In February 2009 I invited Ashdown-Hill to Edinburgh to give a series of talks to the Scottish Branch of the Richard III Society about his mtDNA discovery and the history of Richard's burial place in Leicester. His research into priory churches, particularly mendicant orders reliant upon begging such as the Greyfriars, showed their churches were located alongside major roads. The Greyfriars Church must, he said, be on the northern side of the Social Services car park.

We broke for lunch at the Cramond Inn where I announced my intention to search for King Richard's grave. I would need the permission of Leicester City Council (LCC), the car park landowners, and would have to commission, and pay for, a Ground Penetrating Radar (GPR) survey that would use radar pulses to locate subsurface anomalies, and the archaeological dig to follow. Dr Raymond Bord, the branch's treasurer, had a contact in Leicester, while Dr David and Wendy Johnson had details for one of the key *Time Team* members. I also urged John Ashdown-Hill to write to ULAS, the local archaeological team.

Time Team confirmed their lack of interest, and ULAS didn't respond. It was a blow, but I was undaunted. As Ashdown-Hill left to take up a university post in Turkey, the recession hit hard.

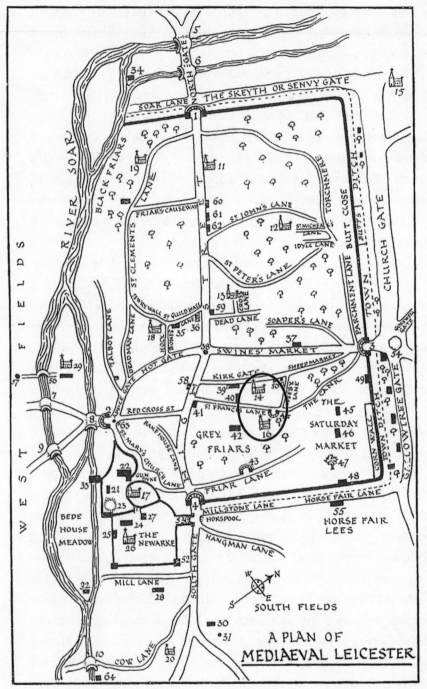

Philippa Langley's smoking gun. The Church of the Greyfriars (16) is depicted directly opposite St Martin's Church (14), now Leicester Cathedral, in what is the northern end of the Social Services car park.

My priority had to be to get LCC behind a search for the grave. I needed some powerful means of persuasion: I needed television.

By September 2010, having sounded out the TV industry, I approached Dr Bord's Leicester contact (retired lawyer Paul Astill) who put me in touch with local councillor Michael Johnson, and through him I contacted Sheila Lock, LCC's chief executive. I proposed a TV documentary special, *Looking for Richard: In Search of a King*. UK archaeological units had confirmed that archaeological practice was to reinter as close as possible to the point of discovery, so Leicester Cathedral (situated directly opposite the projected area of exploration) was proposed in the pitch as the place for reburial. Within weeks, Lock had written to confirm LCC's interest.

I now commissioned the Johnsons, founding members of the project from its inception at the Cramond Inn and who were supporting my search, to design a tomb for Richard. Historian David and his artist wife Wendy had over forty years' experience in researching Richard III. My own research now widened to include the law on burials and exhumation, the Ministry of Justice (MoJ) policy, and the funeral customs of medieval kings. I would be searching for the mortal remains of an anointed King of England, an unprecedented goal, for which no guidelines existed. I would use desk-based research to underpin what principles I could, together with advice from the relevant authorities.

The law on the exhumation of named individuals with living relatives sets out the decency and privacy with which the exhumation must be carried out. Exhumations of, and archaeological reports on, dead soldiers from the two world wars, for example, carry an important prohibition: archaeologists are not free to publish photographs of the remains unless surviving relatives give their permission. However, there is no law protecting the remains of named individuals dating from more than 100 years ago. The only case that gave any clues as to seemly conduct was the discovery of the remains of Anne Mowbray, Duchess of York and Norfolk, who died in 1481 aged eight. Her coffin had been discovered by workmen clearing the site of a church in east London in 1964 and an archaeologist began an investigation of the remains, but without obtaining any proper consent. After questions in the House of Lords, Mowbray's relatives closed the investigation, but their action came too late to stop pictures of the remains being published in the newspapers. It was a lesson in what not to do, as I pointed out to the authorities.

The Reburial Document was ready. Drawn up by Dr David and Wendy Johnson, its purpose was to convince potential partners that the Looking for Richard project was serious and viable. Its eleven pages, together with the pitch document, set out the ethos behind the project, which would have two main aims:

• to search for the grave of Richard III, and, if found, honour him with a reburial and tomb;
• to attempt to bring to life the real man behind the myth.

I wanted my project to be a unique attempt to get to the truth. Furthermore, the search for an anointed King of England was incredibly sensitive, in Richard's case particularly so. After the Battle of Bosworth, his naked body had been slung over a horse, taken into Leicester, and placed on public display. In the retelling of his story, I did not want Richard III subjected to public humiliation again.

The project would also honour Richard with a tomb, and the Reburial Document included the first sketches of the design. Two ceremonies were proposed: a solemn Vespers for the Dead at the reinterment, followed by a later Service of Celebration.

All this was jumping the gun. We still didn't know the precise site of the Greyfriars Church, but there was one key fact in our favour. Research had yielded only seven other potential named burials inside the church, of which only one, Sir William Moton of Peckleton, could be said with any certainty to have been buried there. It seems the vow of poverty taken by the Greyfriars (followers of St Francis of Assisi) and a treasonous rebellion by some of the order in 1402 against Henry IV might have kept the burials inside the church to a minimum, and so reduced the likely number of graves.

I had obtained the TV rights to John Ashdown-Hill's book, *The Last Days of Richard III*, which provided the research behind the project, to protect it from acquisitive producers. Now I put in a confidential call to Dr Phil Stone, chairman of the Richard III Society, who offered whatever help the society could provide. Over the coming months he would become my mentor and guide, his quiet determination adding a backbone of steel to the project's endeavours. Dr Stone suggested that he take me to the office of the society's patron, since he thought that Richard, Duke of Gloucester might be interested in a search to find the grave of his medieval namesake. At the meeting, it was confirmed that I would be the nominated point of contact for the duke for the project and keep his office informed of any developments.

The Reburial Document was given to the MoJ, Leicester City Council and Leicester Cathedral, who were all satisfied that the precautions set out in the document would protect Richard's honour and dignity. At the MoJ, we discussed the Anne Mowbray case and how an exhumation would ensure that all decency be afforded King Richard upon discovery of his remains. The concerns of relatives (as with those of any other remains having known living relatives) would be taken into account in the drafting of the Exhumation Licence. However, the MoJ warned that it could not act in this by itself, and the protections and protocols I required for the remains should be inserted into my agreements with the local authorities.

In Leicester it had been agreed that the Looking for Richard project would receive LCC's support and backing through the office of its CEO, and the council would work directly with me as the originator/client. However, due to the recession, it would not be able to provide any direct funding, but would act as the project's main facilitator. This would allow me access to the council's experts, including their museum services who would advise on all aspects of the dig, with particular reference to the care of ancient artefacts, and the highways department who would reinstate the car parks, and also offer introductions to local businesses and funding bodies. LCC also confirmed that it would give me permission to dig in its car park on the understanding that, if found, King Richard III would be reburied in the nearest consecrated ground, Leicester Cathedral.

To have any hope of getting the project under way, I now needed funding, and a recognized archaeological team willing to do the dig, as well as the costing. Finding the right team would be crucial. The UK archaeological teams I had contacted had been sceptical about the search, and didn't know the terrain. However, LCC had recommended a local archaeologist with whom it had worked: talented and sensitive, Richard Buckley, co-director of ULAS, might be just what the project needed, and his colleague, Harriet Jacklyn, was an equally experienced osteologist. I recognized the ULAS name immediately as the team that had undertaken the Grey Friars Street dig but hadn't responded to Ashdown-Hill's previous proposal to search for Richard III's grave. They were a leading archaeological unit with a considerable reputation and wouldn't want to be seen setting off on any wild-goose chase so it would be a difficult sell. In January 2011 I telephoned Richard Buckley, who was intrigued by the project, but not convinced. He knew where the sizeable Greyfriars precinct was and the potential the car parks offered, but said he would have to do further research and only if this came up with anything would he be interested in taking matters further. I duly sent him the pitch and Reburial Document. In March 2011 I met Sarah Levitt, Head of Arts and Museum Services and lead on the project for LCC. She understood the sensitivities surrounding the search for the remains of a named individual and would be happy to include protections within our agreement. An agreement, however, was a long way off. Once we had archaeologists on board (she also recommended Buckley) she would help with introductions to local funding bodies.

At an on-site meeting at the Social Services car park I spent time with Councillor Michael Johnson whose enthusiasm for the project had opened the door to LCC. Walking with me towards the northern end of the car park, he asked where I believed the church might be. As I told him about the GPR survey I planned to commission to attempt to reveal its walls beneath the tarmac, we walked on to the same spot where I had my intuitive feeling, and I experienced the same powerful reaction once again.

Much rested on my next meeting, at ULAS, where Richard Buckley had agreed to meet me. If I could get him on board, the project would have a chance of securing the local funding it desperately needed. Buckley quickly put me at my ease; he had done his research and wanted to show me something. In one of their finds rooms, on a wooden table stretching almost the full length of the room, was a series of maps. Buckley started at one end with a map from 1741 by Thomas Roberts, and pointed to the 'Gray Fryers' area marked on it: it looked like an orchard, and was situated directly opposite St Martin's Church (Leicester Cathedral), right where the car parks are now.

On the south side of the 'Gray Fryers' was the outline of a building that Buckley said looked like a gatehouse, and could be a marker for the remnants of Herrick's mansion house. As I looked, I could see a formal garden to the north with four pathways leading to a central area. I couldn't believe my eyes. Could

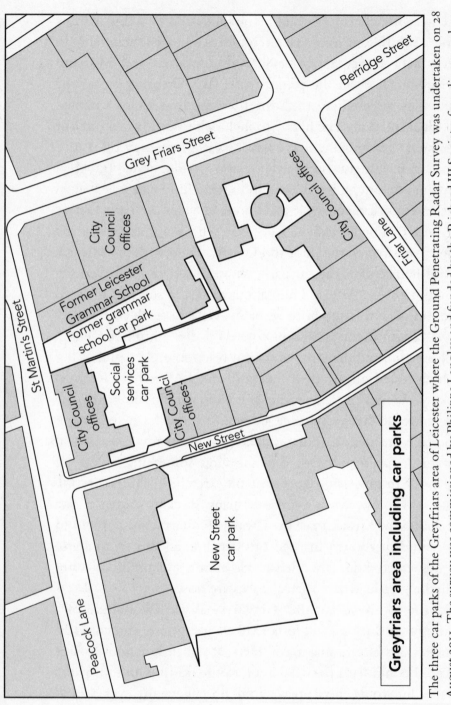

Greyfriars area including car parks

The three car parks of the Greyfriars area of Leicester where the Ground Penetrating Radar Survey was undertaken on 28 August 2011. The survey was commissioned by Philippa Langley and funded by the Richard III Society, founding members of the *Looking for Richard* project, members of the Scottish Branch and private investors.

this central area be where Herrick's stone pillar had stood? I put forward my theory. My reasoning was simple enough: if you have the grave of a king in your garden and erect a 'handsome stone pillar' to mark it, wouldn't you lay out your paths to lead towards it? It seemed logical to me. However, Buckley was focused on working through the ages, showing me on each map how the land use had changed over time. After the Dissolution, the 'Gray Fryers' land was gardens, but was finally covered with tarmac to become car parks in the 1930s–40s. It was archaeologically virgin ground, only built on at its outer edges and never investigated.

But it was clear Buckley wasn't convinced. 'Archaeology is not about going in search of a famous person, it's not what we do,' he said. For one thing, there was the story of Richard's bones being thrown into the River Soar. As I explained that this had been refuted by John Ashdown-Hill's researches, I knew I was losing him: the River Soar tale was just too powerful. What about the Greyfriars Church, might that be of interest? I brought out my copy of the medieval map showing the Greyfriars Church opposite what was now the cathedral, and told him why I thought this would be at the northern end of the Social Services car park.

Buckley dismissed the map, asserting that medieval maps are notoriously vague, but he nonetheless sat up. Finding the Greyfriars Church would be of interest to him, because he could learn so much about medieval Leicester and the layout of these friary churches from it. As I pushed for my preferred site, using Ashdown-Hill's research into mendicant priories' locations beside major roads, Buckley agreed it was a possibility. After discussing the Christopher Wren report on Herrick's garden and its marker column, then the open car park spaces, ripe for archaeological investigation, and the GPR survey, Buckley declared he would be happy to look for the Greyfriars Church.

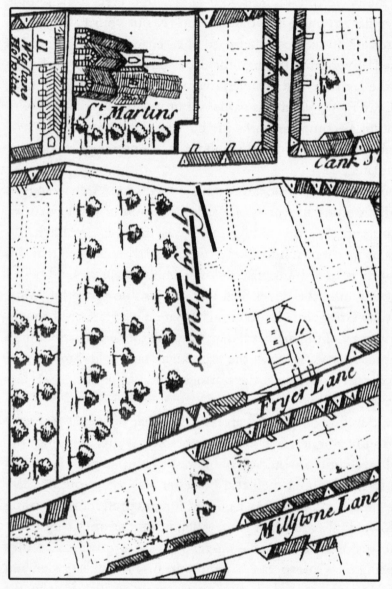

Thomas Roberts's map of 1741 with modern overlay of trenches. A formal garden is visible to the east of the three trenches, thought to be the garden of Alderman Robert Herrick.

So it was settled that, while he searched for the church, I would search for the grave of a king. Unlike Buckley, I had no reputation to lose. I asked how he rated our chances of success. He said, 'Fifty–fifty at best for the church, and nine to one against finding the grave.' He was a glass half empty kind of guy, while I was the glass half full kind of girl. He asked what I thought the chances were: I replied, 'Nine to one on for finding them both.' He laughed, asking what had driven me to this search. I told him about my screenwriting, and hopes of seeing Richard's real story brought to life. I didn't tell him about my intuitive feeling. But it didn't matter, because Richard Buckley was on board and beaming and I wanted to hug him. The Looking for Richard project had taken a giant leap forward.

However, there was still the urgent need to find funding. Buckley mentioned Leicester University and its not insubstantial research budgets. ULAS, though an independent body hiring its offices from the university, worked closely with it. Buckley called Richard Taylor, the university's Deputy Registrar and Director of Corporate Affairs, who thought the project had merit, and understood that the ULAS academic research would be in quest of the church. He asked what might be required of the university. Hesitant to bring in such a powerful player on the funding side, I asked for their specialists and expertise to be made available to the project free of charge. Taylor quickly confirmed that I had only to let him know what I needed, so I immediately mentioned the DNA unit and Professor Mark Lansdale, Head of the Psychology Department. Taylor agreed and said that if I needed extra funding once the dig was under way, the university would help. I asked how much. 'If you find the Greyfriars Church, the wallet will open,' he replied.

In March 2011, on Buckley's advice, I commissioned ULAS to undertake the Archaeological Desk-Based Assessment (DBA). This is the preliminary research document drawn up to determine the archaeological viability of a site. It would be based on historical research, including detailed map regression, and analysis of any potential ground disturbance, together with the location of gas mains and electric and fibre-optic cables. The DBA would provide me, as the client, with the necessary professional green light to enable the dig to go ahead. I gave ULAS what information I had on the Leicester Greyfriars site. The cost of the DBA was £1,140, so I called Phil Stone because the Richard III Society had a bursary fund for original research to which I could apply. The joint secretaries, Sue and David Wells, helped prepare the request document, which Phil Stone gave to the Executive Committee who passed it immediately.

In April 2011, with the DBA completed, I asked ULAS where it intended to dig the first trenches. Richard Buckley explained that in order to pick up any trace of the east–west church walls beneath the surface, two overlapping thirty-metre trenches would run north–south which he hoped would bisect the walls. The trenches would also have to be positioned to maximize the remaining parking on site to help with costs. I pressed again for the northern end of the car park and Buckley confirmed that Trench One would cover the exact area I wanted; it ran right over the letter 'R'.

The greatest expense of the dig was going to be the reinstatement work, turning the site back into a car park. I also had to find, and fund, interim parking for the Social Services for the duration of the dig, which we agreed would last for two weeks. Richard Buckley assured me it would be possible to dig three trial trenches in that time. I proposed the dig should take place over the Easter holiday period, April–May 2012, as this would give me time to get the funding, and broadcaster, on board. It would also reduce the cost of the off-site car parking. But in the meantime I had to raise an estimated £35,000.

Sarah Levitt told me that I would need permission from the

team at the Greyfriars Social Services for the dig and the disruption it would cause. Their consent was vital; Levitt would not be able to overrule them if they refused. I was tense for my meeting with Mick Bowers, Head of Greyfriars Property Services. Bowers understood the dig would cause major headaches, but he'd spoken to his team, who were willing to take on the extra workload involved because, they said, the search for Richard was a worthy one. Bowers would be in charge of matters at their end. It was a huge relief, and I thanked him. 'Not a problem,' he said, and smiled. I later discovered his wife was a Ricardian.

The next priority was to finalize the TV programme. The first-ever search for the grave of an anointed King of England was a good story, so someone would bite. It just so happened I had a certain someone in mind.

I had been a big fan of the documentary filmmaker Julian Ware for many years. He insisted on meticulous research, a sensitive approach and top production values. He was joint creative director of the award-winning Darlow Smithson Productions (DSP), which had just made *WW1: Finding the Lost Battalions* (July 2010), about amateur historian Lambis Englezos's search for the lost graves of the 1916 Battle of Fromelles in France. Ware confirmed his interest in the Looking for Richard project, to be headed up by DSP's Acting Head of Development, Simon Young, an archaeologist who had produced *Finding the Lost Battalions*.

A few weeks later, however, the project's future was up in the air again. Sheila Lock (CEO of LCC) was ill, Chris Wardle, the City Archaeologist, was not convinced of its viability, and to cap it all Leicester was about to vote for its first elected mayor, the person who would then run LCC and therefore be able to kill the project stone dead.

Or not. In May 2011 Sir Peter Soulsby was elected Leicester's mayor. He valued history and heritage (it was in his manifesto), so it was with some relief that a few weeks later Sarah Levitt confirmed he'd given the Looking for Richard project the green light. We were back on.

At the cathedral, the dean, the Very Reverend Vivienne Faull, welcomed the Reburial Document and expressed the cathedral's readiness to accept the remains of King Richard into its care, should he be found. Taking me to the sanctuary, the dean proposed that the tomb should be close to its northern wall. As I looked at the great east window dedicated to the fallen in battle, I felt her suggested place would be a fitting tribute and final resting place for England's last warrior king.

But I still had to raise the necessary funds. Sarah Levitt put me in touch with Martin Peters, Managing Director of Leicestershire Promotions Ltd (LPL), responsible for marketing the county and city. With DSP on board, and a TV special in the offing with Channel 4, Peters understood the venture's potential, and so agreed to fund the Looking for Richard project.

By early August 2011, with the £35,000 I needed, I had agreed terms with LCC as the landowner and ULAS as the contractor. As the client, my agreements repeated the Reburial Document's ethos for the project: if we discovered Richard III's remains, the science and analysis would be completed at the earliest opportunity. The two partners were aware that I was searching for a named individual with living relatives, and even though he had been dead for over 500 years, I wanted him granted the same decency and privacy as is laid down by the law governing exhumations of those who died less than a hundred years ago.

The agreement also made it clear that as named custodian of the remains after identification, I would take Richard to a Catholic place of sanctity and rest where he would be prepared for his reburial in the (Anglican) cathedral. It was important that this should be in a spiritual environment and the king's faith taken into consideration if he were finally to be laid to rest.

Everything appeared to be going well but there was a clock ticking. I had commissioned a GPR survey from Stratascan to cover the three car parks: New Street, the Social Services and, crucially, the former grammar school site, which was immediately adjacent to the Social Services. But the former grammar school was up for sale for redevelopment. A new owner might not give us permission to dig, yet if John Ashdown-Hill's research (and my intuition) and Richard Buckley's maps were correct, it could be critical to the success of the project. Buckley told me to take heart. In a recession there might not be a developer interested in buying the grammar school.

I asked Buckley about the potential of the GPR survey. Having previously undertaken three on city centre sites, he was sceptical, since all had proved inconclusive and failed to reveal any structures that later digging had uncovered. In this case, however, with it being virgin ground, he felt it might be worth a go. However, he warned me that the church might be in the south of the precinct, and if this were the case it would be game over for my search because the south was heavily developed, which meant that King Richard's grave would be under a building. The cost of the survey (just over £5,000) would be met by the Richard III Society and founding members of the Looking for Richard project.

On Sunday, 28 August 2011 Stratascan began the GPR survey, using a powerful MIRA scanner. Annette Carson, an international award-winning copywriter as well as a biographer, had helped put together a short promotional script for DSP to film. She understood that the prospect of major media attention might keep the local authorities on board in difficult times. Richard Buckley, Phil Stone and John Ashdown-Hill (back briefly in the UK) were to be interviewed along with Carson, whom, at last, I finally met. Also coming along were local Richard III Society members Sally Henshaw, secretary of the Leicestershire Branch, and Richard Smith, their chairman, who had both been helping the project with research. Giving up his time on the bank holiday weekend too was Assistant Mayor, Councillor Ted Cassidy, representing LCC in Sir Peter Soulsby's absence and who spoke powerfully to camera. With filming under way, the assembled team asked why I was so determined to search for Richard's grave. I pointed to the 'R' on the tarmac, and told them my story.

DSP were filming in the cathedral as I again met the Reverend Faull, together with Dr John Ashdown-Hill. The dean repeated her view that the tomb would be best situated in the sanctuary. Later, Dr David and Wendy Johnson showed her the first detailed computer-generated images (CGI) of the tomb design, its imagery of the boar, white rose of York and cross of St Cuthbert displaying what had been important to Richard, both as duke and king.

A few weeks later, Richard Buckley's scepticism of the GPR survey proved justified. The results were inconclusive, and alarming. A layer of apparent 'made' ground, or demolition debris, close to the surface had skewed the results, or was hiding the archaeology beneath. We couldn't see any walls, and only with my prompting could Stratascan identify two or three potential gravesites, none of which was in the northern end of the Social Services car park near my 'R'. The survey was a disaster for the project. Channel 4 was wavering, which meant Martin Peters at LPL was too, with his budgets constrained in straitened times. By March 2012, without the guarantee of a TV documentary, and with deep regret, LPL pulled its funding. The Easter dig was cancelled.

Despite these setbacks, I couldn't give up now. Sarah Levitt had offered us new dates in 2012: the August bank holiday weekend would work for LCC. Phil Stone, at the Richard III Society, told me to grab them, saying we couldn't afford to lose another opportunity and we would make the new dates work. He offered to give £5,000 to kick-start the new funding round. Martin Peters was next. He said that, if we could guarantee a film for his website, LPL would put in up to £15,000, while Michael Johnson gave £500 from Leicester Adult Schools.

By the end of April 2012, I considered re-mortgaging my home. Phil Stone had confirmed that we were too late to launch an appeal in the society's *Ricardian Bulletin*, so I rang Leicester University. After some negotiation, Richard Taylor agreed the university would put in £10,000, plus £2,000 VAT (if needed) and a further £2,000 if Richard III was found (to cover the cost of the coffin and pall). Now Richard Buckley and I worked to reduce the cost of the dig. Thanks to his carefully revised layout for the first two trenches, allowing for more parking during the dig, I managed to shave over £2,000 from the cost of the off-site parking for the Social Services staff. The August dig could go ahead without my desperate re-mortgaging plan. Sarah Levitt confirmed the deadline of 1 August for all monies to be paid into the ULAS account. Miss it, and the dig was over.

With a few weeks to go before the deadline, LPL gave us devastating news. Due to problems with their own funding, they could only put in £5,000. They would secure this funding, but I was £10,000 short. I trawled every local business and worthy to make up the shortfall. Martin Peters at LPL stepped in to help as did Martin Traynor, Group CEO of the Leicestershire Chamber of Commerce. It was a valiant effort, but in the worst recession in living memory local businesses could not see any investment potential in an archaeological dig; even one that was in search of a king. Further, the research grant I had hoped for from Leicester Archaeological and Historical Society was refused. The society said it couldn't support an archaeological project in search of King Richard's grave, citing the River Soar story as evidence of its likely outcome. At my request, John Ashdown-Hill put together a two-page document outlining his research repudiating the story, to no avail. The search for Richard would be cancelled. In desperation I called Phil Stone, who authorized an immediate appeal to the membership of the Richard III Society – worldwide. Annette Carson agreed to design and write a two-page International Appeal leaflet.

The appeal went out by email. Within moments, pledges of money were pouring in from the USA, Canada, Australia, New Zealand, Brazil, Germany, Austria, the Netherlands, Belgium and throughout the UK. Some who contacted me were out of work and struggling to feed their families but wanted to give what they could. The response was overwhelming, moving me to tears. In three weeks, the appeal raised just under £13,000 and gave the Looking for Richard project its mandate. The donors told us:

'Search for him. Find him. Honour him.'

On 1 August 2012 all monies were paid into ULAS's account (see full funding below).

Looking for Richard: In Search of a King – Two-Week Dig

	£	%
Richard III Society and members	17,367*	52.84
University of Leicester	10,000	30.43
Leicestershire Promotions Ltd	5,000	15.21
Leicester Adult Schools	500	1.52
Total	32,867	100

* Includes £100 donation from the Society of Friends of Richard III in York, and donations from some members of the Richard III Foundation Inc.

The remaining funding of £716 from the International Appeal was paid to ULAS at the end of the dig for costs including the exhumation.

The tomb designers, Dr David and Wendy Johnson, had brought in graphics specialist Joseph Fox from Lost in Castles. With the tomb design nearly ready, Fox was working on the final renders, while award-winning local sculptor Graeme Mitcheson was interested in taking on the tomb commission. And Michael Ibsen (son of Joy), a furniture maker who sources his wood from the estate of the Prince of Wales and lives in London, said he would be honoured to make a coffin for his ancestral uncle, King Richard III.

On 6 August 2012, at the pre-dig meeting, Richard Buckley confirmed the location of the first two trenches in the Social Services car park. The dig would begin on 25 August, which I told the team would be the anniversary of Richard III's interment in the Greyfriars. The media pack was ready. Annette Carson had stepped in to organize it, but LCC admitted they were short-staffed and not ideally placed to handle communications. However, Leicester University, our new partner, with much experience in the media, asked to take it on.

Three and a half years after the first meeting in the Cramond Inn, Edinburgh, my search in Leicester for the grave and mortal remains of King Richard III was on!

2

The Great Debate

A LINE OF horsemen is drawing up in the mid-morning sun. There is a wind blowing – enough to ruffle banners and surcoats, the loose silk fittings worn by knights over their armour. In the vicinity of this small cavalry force – several hundred strong – all is relatively quiet. But further away the sounds of battle can clearly be heard. There are shouts of command, delivered by call or trumpet blast, the guttural cries of men fighting at close quarters, the din of weapons striking against plate armour, the shrieks of the dying and the wounded. In the gently rolling fields of Leicestershire crops have been ripening for harvest. Now they lie kicked and trampled as bands of warriors surge towards each other, colliding with brutal impact. The date is 22 August 1485. The clash of arms – soon to be commemorated through the name of its nearest market town – is Bosworth Field.

The horsemen have drawn up in formation around a banner bearing the royal arms of England. Its colours are unfurling in the breeze. The leader of this force is the anointed ruler of the realm – King Richard III. His plan is to launch a bold cavalry charge, skirting around the fighting to attack the vulnerable rearguard of his opponent Henry Tudor. Richard wishes to seek out his challenger, engage him in personal combat, and slay him. The stakes are high. If his mounted charge is successful the battle will be brought to a close with a resounding victory. If it fails, it will end in humiliating defeat. And every mounted man grouped around the king knows this.

Richard III has ruled the kingdom of England for a little over two years. He is thirty-two years old. His reign has been marred by rebellion, and doubts about the legitimacy of his rule. He seeks to end all plotting through a decisive vindication of his regal authority on the battlefield. His men watch him intently. His face is drawn yet determined. He has slept badly and complained of nightmares where he was assailed by demons. But now those nightmares are put aside. He has drawn up his forces with steely resolve to block the line of advance of his opponent across the Roman road to Leicester and bring him to battle. And battle has now commenced.

Still the line of horsemen waits. The king dons his surcoat, with its richly coloured arms of England, lifts his battle helmet – with a crown welded to it – and places it upon his head. He pauses for a moment, and then urges his horse forward. His men immediately respond. The whole line moves in close formation, first at a walk, then a trot, and finally – as it gathers speed – surging past the lines of battling soldiers at a gallop. As the horses and their armoured riders gather momentum the earth shudders – and all feel its impact. The Battle of Bosworth is nearing its climax, and for a moment every soldier on that field of combat stands transfixed by this mighty charge.

In the opposing camp there is pandemonium. Richard's challenger, Henry Tudor, has positioned himself in the rearguard, well back from the main area of the fighting. He has never fought in a battle and hopes to avoid any action. But now a huge dust cloud spumes above the mounted force charging straight for him. A tornado is about to hurl itself into his line of soldiers. Tudor's men are also on horseback – and they will have to brace themselves against the impact of this terrible assault. Orders are desperately called out, but the thunderous approach of Richard's

riders makes it almost impossible to hear them. But in the growing din Tudor jumps off his horse and is surrounded by a small
scrum of followers, wielding pikes and whatever other weapons
are at hand. This is the last cavalry charge to be led by a King of
England. And his challenger is to meet it cowering on the
ground.

If Richard III had won this battle, killed his opponent and
through this victory laid the foundations for a long period of rule,
there is no doubt that his charge would have been given an
enthusiastic write-up in the sources of the day. But Bosworth
was a Tudor victory, and Richard's death in battle brought their
own dynasty on to the pages of our history books. It is hard to
imagine our island story without the Tudors featuring prominently within it. Yet history is written by the winners. The Tudors
– in public at least – had their own take on the battle story, and
it would do no favours to Richard in the telling.

By the end of the reign of Queen Elizabeth I, William
Shakespeare, in one of his most famous history plays, gives us an
altogether different ending to this headlong dash. In it, we find
that Richard is now alone. He is still hunting out his opponent,
but has lost the horse that carried him to his foe. He cries out: 'A
horse, a horse, my kingdom for a horse!' One of his followers
briefly appears, urging him to flee. But the king's reply is grimly
resolute:

> *I have set my life upon a cast,*
> *And I will stand the hazard of the die . . .*

And then once more the terrible refrain: 'A horse, a horse, my
kingdom for a horse!'

Shakespeare was of course unable to enact the full sequence of
these events within the confines of a late sixteenth-century
theatre. But there was a real poignancy to Richard's cry. For an
Elizabethan audience a cavalry charge – even one obliquely

referred to rather than enacted on stage – would have seemed a relic from a bygone age. Even in the late Middle Ages, full-scale mounted charges were unusual in English warfare. The English custom was to dismount and fight on foot, while cavalry actions took place in the opening preliminaries to battle, or in the rout that would signify their end. Yet to deliver a *coup de grâce* with a massed onslaught of horsemen was regarded – in the chivalric literature and practice of the time – as the finest way to win a battle.

By Shakespeare's day the grandeur of such an intention had become lost under a mound of hostile propaganda. In the version of Henry VII's court historian Polydore Vergil, Richard's charge was portrayed as an impulsive and desperate act, prompted by rage and the betrayal of those around him, who showed little stomach for the fight. Shakespeare hints at this in a series of powerful vignettes. But from a military point of view, Richard's plan required considered foresight, both in the logistics of his planning and his actual battle preparation.

His charge was unlikely to have been the product of pure impulse, for his line of horsemen had to be readied in advance. A man in the plate and mail armour frequently used in the Wars of the Roses – the civil war that by August 1485 had already raged for thirty years – needed time to position himself and get into formation. In 1485 knights in full plate armour – the most advanced military technology of its time, when warriors were garbed in closely interlocking pieces of plate, providing the best possible protection against missile and weapon attack – would also need time to gather themselves. Such measures would not be undertaken whimsically, or on the spur of the moment. It is far more likely that Richard had carefully prepared for their use. He wanted to strike at his challenger with the power and velocity of a hammer blow.

Recent battle archaeology is now telling us much more about

the site and course of Bosworth, in particular that Richard also invested in a substantial artillery train, and used it in the opening stages of the battle. These pieces would need to be carried up from England's principal armoury, the Tower of London, and then drawn up on the battlefield to block Tudor's advance. Again, preparing and transporting these guns was a considered plan, not the desperate response of a demoralized ruler. Richard wished to shock the army of his challenger. He hoped that his artillery would dominate the opening stages of the battle; he envisioned his cavalry charge would end it.

In William Shakespeare's play, the hammer strike has been replaced by the stab in the back; the battle has become an awful judgement on Richard's life and brief rule as king. And this is because – in Shakespeare's eyes, as well as the Tudor histories that he drew upon – the king deserved such a fate. They believed that Richard had betrayed many in his ruthless ascent to the throne, and it seemed to them fitting that he had now been betrayed on the battlefield. Henry Tudor's victory would be the judgement of God upon his crimes. And yet we do not see the king's last few moments of life. He exits from the stage. Then his rival appears, surrounded by his captains, and tersely announces: 'The bloody dog is dead.'

It is a death Shakespeare does not allow us to witness. The first reason why the search for Richard's mortal remains is so fascinating is that we are still seeking an answer to this question. What were his last few moments really like – what happened to the king?

For Shakespeare, more than any other, has shaped our reactions to this deeply controversial monarch. From the moment Richard appears on the stage, and delivers his first soliloquy, we are both entranced and repulsed. We are caught in the stare of a bejewelled but venomous snake, and these eyes will not release us from their gaze.

Now is the winter of our discontent
Made glorious summer by this sun of York;
And all the clouds that lowered upon our house
In the deep bosom of the ocean buried.

We are reminded of the historical events that led to this fateful moment, already recounted in Shakespeare's previous play, *Henry VI*, in its final part. The ruling dynasty Richard belongs to – the House of York – has survived the buffeting of civil war. During one period of unrest Richard's brother, King Edward IV, is briefly forced off the throne by his opponents, the Lancastrians, and goes into exile. Then Edward returns triumphantly and routs his enemies. Twelve years of peace ensue. The 'winter of discontent', the loss of the throne and exile, is replaced by stable and prosperous rule. Richard's play on words, 'Made glorious summer by this sun of York' is both historically and visually accurate, for Edward's heraldic badge is the sun in splendour, and introduces us to his consummate skill with language. Already it carries incipient menace, for Richard carries his own 'winter of discontent' within his heart. It lies deeply buried, but will soon burst forth upon an unsuspecting court with terrifying power.

Our bruised arms hung up for monuments;
Our stern alarums changed to merry meetings,
Our dreadful marches to delightful measures.

It all seems superficially pleasing – discord has been replaced by harmony, dissension is now a thing of the past. But as soon as Richard sets up this new order he begins to subvert it, with deft and sardonic humour.

Grim-visaged war hath smoothed his wrinkled front;
And now, instead of mounting barbed steeds
To fright the souls of fearful adversaries,
He capers nimbly in a lady's chamber
To the lascivious pleasing of a lute.

We learn that his warrior brother Edward, and the court around him, have gone soft and are lost in the sway of sensual pleasure. Richard mocks this, but underneath his mockery lies a far deeper disenchantment that will now be powerfully – and disturbingly – shown to us:

> But I, that am not shaped for sportive tricks,
> Nor made to court an amorous looking-glass;
> I, that am rudely stamped . . .

We begin to see that beneath the finery of his courtly attire Richard is physically misshapen, and the contortion of his mind and body is more and more fully revealed:

> . . . curtailed of this fair proportion,
> Cheated of feature by dissembling Nature,
> Deformed, unfinished, sent before my time
> Into this breathing world, scarce half made up . . .

We are carried on this torrent of images into the world of an outsider, deeply alienated from others, an alienation that is mirrored in and perhaps ultimately stems from Richard's physical appearance. Unable to be a lover, both of women and, in a far broader sense, of humanity, he roundly declares:

> I am determined to prove a villain
> And hate the idle pleasures of these days.

This is a compelling portrait, remorseless in its judgement of the man. Already it is clear that Richard is a cold-blooded killer. It is a chilling manifesto – but only if we believe the play, and the histories it was based upon.

In Shakespeare's drama, the first intended victim of his villainy is soon disclosed. Richard has another brother, George, Duke of Clarence, and he confides that he will engineer his downfall, poisoning the mind of Edward, the king, against him. And if Edward – through weakness – relents, Richard himself will ensure that Clarence is dispatched. It will be the first of a series of chilling murders that will propel Richard – on a tide of pitiless ambition – to the throne of England itself.

Richard's murder of Clarence is a pivotal moment within the play. And as this ghastly event unfolds, Richard's physical appearance is more and more disturbingly emphasized. In one instance, as he moves across the stage, a heap of insults is poured upon him: he is 'a bottled spider', 'a poisonous, bunch-backed toad'. His outer deformity is meant to mirror his corrupt inner nature. The Shakespearean Richard is hunchbacked, with a limping gait, and has a withered arm. So much invective gives us another reason why the search for Richard's remains is so important: we need to know what he actually looked like.

For in Shakespeare's drama, and the Tudor histories that underpinned it, the relentless focus is on Richard's appearance, and the dark pathology they believed grew around it. One of its most striking antecedents is a description given by Sir Thomas More in his *History of Richard III*, a source composed some eighty years earlier than Shakespeare's play, but one that would be profoundly influential on the playwright. In it we find Richard: 'little of stature, ill featured of limbs, crook-backed, his left shoulder much higher than his right, hard-favoured in appearance . . . malicious, wrathful envious . . .' We discover that Richard's birth had been difficult, that his mother 'could not be delivered of him uncut' – a breech birth – 'and he came into the world with feet forward, and also not untoothed . . .'

Having shared these details with us, More moves to what he believes are their dreadful consequences, concluding with the damning judgement: 'He was close and secret, a deep dissembler, lowly of countenance, arrogant of heart, outwardly friendly where he inwardly hated, not omitting to kiss when he thought to kill, pitiless and cruel . . . Friend and foe was much the same;

where his advantage grew, he spared no man death whose life withstood his purpose.'

For More, as for Shakespeare, the realm that Richard inhabits is a perpetual winter kingdom. Everything is frozen, and expansive sentiments of generosity, trust, love and faith are replaced by cold calculation, ruthless ambition, cruelty and an utter ambivalence to worldly values. The figure of Richard carries near demonic power and if, initially, he almost charms the audience, this only foreshadows how he will beguile the sleeping court of his brother Edward IV.

Here we encounter the three 'Ms' of the Ricardian realm the Tudors have painted for us: misshapen, Machiavellian and murderous. Richard is bent, he does not walk, but scuttles – although his gait carries a restless energy and disturbing power. Richard is Machiavellian – and this is what makes his character so compelling. He is a master of dissimulation, of hiding his true feelings, of putting on a persuasive performance that always masks his true intentions. He beguiles and cajoles, and only occasionally does that mask slip. It is this dissimulation – and its chilling consequences – that makes his character so darkly fascinating. And from this dissimulation the murderous Richard emerges, to kill and kill again.

All rivals are removed without a shred of compunction or remorse. His sights are set on the throne of England, and none will stand in his way, even the young nephews – the sons of Edward IV – whom he has promised to protect. Shakespeare presents us with a villain so alienated from the world around him that he will be cursed by his own mother. Yet his story carries a merciless momentum that leaves us near spellbound in its wake.

It is only when we pull away from this work of theatrical genius that we are left wondering what the real man – rather than the later legend – was like in fact. Was the actual Richard III so terrifying – or was his character progressively blackened by the

Tudor dynasty that supplanted him? We still seek answers to some of the controversies that surround Richard's reign, but at last have an event – both real and symbolic – that can counterpoint the power of Shakespeare's extraordinary creation. The search for the king's lost grave, and the remains that lie within it, finally gives us the chance to connect with the reality behind the Tudor myth.

In the grave's absence – and it was long believed broken up and discarded at the time of the Dissolution of the Monasteries – there was a great debate over Richard's reputation. One of Richard's earliest detractors was the Warwickshire priest and antiquarian John Rous. Rous had almost certainly seen Richard on his progress as king in the summer of 1483, and may well have met him. A few years later, with Henry Tudor victorious at Bosworth and crowned as King Henry VII, Rous wrote a history of the English kings that heaped insult after insult upon Henry's predecessor.

Rous began with Richard's birth, around which his claims were nothing less than staggering: 'Richard was born at Fotheringhay in Northamptonshire,' he commenced, accurately enough, before adding, 'and retained within his mother's womb for two years, with teeth and hair to his shoulders.' Here is the origin of the monstrous birth that Shakespeare made so much of. But Rous had only just begun: 'At his nativity Scorpio was in the ascendant . . . and like a scorpion he combined a smooth front with a stinging tail.' To make his astrological point Rous – well aware of when the king was actually born (on 2 October, under the sign of Libra) – deliberately moved Richard's date of birth forward by three weeks. He then accused him of murdering his nephews, his own wife and the saintly Henry VI, before finishing: 'This King Richard, who was excessively cruel in his days, reigned for three years and a little more, in the way that the Antichrist is to reign. And like the Antichrist to come, he was confounded at his moment of greatest pride.'

The moment of pride – a veiled reference to Bosworth being the judgement of God on Richard's rule – would become a staple theme in Tudor histories of the king. Richard III in fact ruled for slightly less than two years and two months. In adding a year to the reign, so that it would correspond to the rule of the Antichrist prophesied in the Book of Revelations, Rous played fast and loose with historical accuracy. His main concern was to win the patronage of the new Tudor king, Henry VII. Unfortunately, he had written an earlier work – a history of the Earls of Warwick, in both English and Latin – in which he praised Richard's kingship, and although he was able to recall the Latin copy and erase this unfortunate reference, the English version escaped his clutches. In it, Rous was as fulsome in his praise for Richard as he was later to be damning in his criticism: 'The most mighty Richard,' he began, 'all avarice set aside, ruled his subjects in his realm full commendably, punishing offenders of his laws, especially extortioners and oppressors of his commons, and cherishing those that were virtuous, by which discreet guiding he got great thanks of God and love of all his subjects, rich and poor, and great praise of the people of all other lands about him.'

It is hard to imagine a more dramatic about-turn, or two more different views of a crucial period in English history. Rous's principal objective seemed to be a desire to flatter the reigning king – first Richard, by praising his rule, and then Henry, by denigrating his predecessor. And if there is an element of truth in both accounts, the one almost the polar opposite of the other, this begins to show us why Richard III – the man and the monarch – is in turn both so fascinating and so controversial.

Rous's earlier praise of Richard's kingship is well-known and frequently quoted. But his preamble to it has received far less attention. Yet it is equally important. In it, Rous not only commended Richard's kingship, he also supported his right to rule.

The Tudors – and many who followed them – believed Richard was a usurper, seizing a throne not rightfully his from his nephews, the Princes in the Tower, the sons of Edward IV. But Rous implied that the king's taking of the throne was legitimate, stating that his claim was based on a lineage issuing from 'very matrimony, without any discontinuance of any defiling in the law, by heir[s] male lineally descending from King Henry the Second'.

In general terms, Rous was praising Richard's distinguished lineage, which could be traced back to the kings of the twelfth century. But he was also making a specific point. By 'very [true] matrimony', Rous meant a marriage ceremony properly observed and legally validated. And here he was comparing the validity of the marriage of Richard's parents, Richard, Duke of York and Cecily Neville, with that of Richard's brother Edward IV and his queen, Elizabeth Woodville, the latter being a deeply controversial marriage that took place in secret, with few witnesses and not even in a church, one not announced to court and country until four months after it had taken place.

When he took the throne in 1483 Richard had argued that this marriage was invalid – because Edward IV had in fact been contracted to marry someone else – and thus its offspring (including Edward's two sons, the Princes in the Tower) were illegitimate. Rous, in his reference to 'discontinuance' [invalidation] through 'defiling in the law' [legal objection], was accepting and supporting the king's claim. This claim was actually enrolled in the records of Richard's first parliament in 1484, though subsequently suppressed by the Tudors.

As a clergyman, Rous may have sympathized with Richard's moral stance on this issue. Edward IV's court had, particularly in its last years, been notoriously hedonistic. And his approval also took a swipe at Henry Tudor's claim to the throne, which had been publicized in 1484, the year before Tudor became king. For the future Henry VII was almost certainly of bastard descent on both sides of his family tree – from his Valois and Beaufort origins – and so unfit to rule, as Richard had made clear in a general proclamation to the realm. Rous may well have agreed with it. If this was so, it gave an added urgency to his wish to please the new regime once Henry had come to the throne.

Rous left us two portraits of Richard. The positive one, composed during the king's lifetime, was also accompanied by a pen drawing, in which Richard – in full martial regalia – showed no obvious sign of deformity. After his death Rous was more specific about his appearance, remarking that Richard was small in stature, and his right shoulder higher than his left. Rous's comment, although part of a hostile reworking, cannot simply be disregarded. But even if Richard suffered from such a condition, it did not seem to have hampered his courage on the battlefield, for despite the comparison with the Antichrist, Rous then chose to pay tribute to Richard for the way in which he fought in his last few moments at Bosworth. The compliment is all the more striking for being so reluctant. When on the battlefield, 'he bore himself like a gallant knight, and honourably defended himself to his last breath.'

Other commentators also chose to jump ship once Henry VII's regime was firmly established. The Italian humanist Pietro Carmeliano praised Richard in 1484 as an outstandingly pious, munificent and just ruler; two years later, after he had entered Henry's service, Carmeliano condemned Richard no less vigorously as the villainous murderer of Henry VI and the Princes in the Tower. But a coherent Tudor view of Richard III only began to emerge later, with two highly influential works composed early in the reign of Henry VIII: an English history compiled by the Italian court historian Polydore Vergil, and Thomas More's dramatic account of the reign of Richard III. Both had profound sway on the Shakespearean portrait.

Polydore Vergil's treatment of Richard III is comprehensive and well-researched. He evidently consulted with many men who could remember well back into the Yorkist period, including some who had played an important part in the government of the time. He had access to a considerable body of written material, including one or more of the London chronicles brought together early in the Tudor period, but drawing on contemporary memories of the events of Richard's rule. And because Henry VII had given his blessing to Vergil's project, he had unrivalled access to the noblemen and bishops of the Tudor court, including those who had joined Henry in exile before his invasion of England in 1485. This gives his account of the Bosworth campaign particular value. But an underlying bias is all too apparent in his work, a clear desire to interpret events in favour of the ruling Tudor dynasty.

Under the guise of historical reasoning, Polydore Vergil in fact speculated on Richard's psychology, explaining the occurrences of his reign through one consistent idea: that beneath outwardly correct and well-intentioned public behaviour, the king was privately motivated by deceit and dishonesty. As soon as he heard of his brother Edward IV's death, Vergil related that Richard 'began to be kindled with an ardent desire of sovereignty', and straight away resolved to seize the throne. He determined to accomplish this 'by subtlety and sleight', and came to power 'without the assent of the commonality' – in other words, he was a usurper. Vergil concluded: Richard 'thought of nothing but tyranny and cruelty' and at the finish, it was God who gave victory to Henry VII.

Polydore Vergil would almost certainly have been aware that Richard did in fact have a right to the throne, the *Titulus Regius*, which was formally set out in the parliament of 1484, but as Henry VII had ordered that all copies of it be destroyed, Vergil deemed it more prudent to ignore its existence rather than discuss its merits. His approach was sophisticated, invoking the deceit he believed brought Richard to the throne and kept him there as an explanation for the good government Rous and Carmeliano had first praised during the king's lifetime. For Polydore Vergil, Richard's actions were not prompted by any genuine concern for his subjects' well-being, but rather by guilt and fear: 'He began to give the countenance and show of a good man,' Vergil remarked, 'whereby he might be seen [to be] more righteous, and to procure himself support, he began many good works, as well public as private.'

An insinuation of inner turmoil was then employed in a discussion of Richard's appearance. Polydore Vergil first cited some mannerisms, probably remembered by those who had been about the king: 'While he was thinking of any matter, he did continually bite his nether lip . . . also he was wont to be ever with his right hand pulling out of the sheath to the midst, and putting in again, the dagger which he always did wear.' He repeated the description made by Rous, that 'he was short of stature, the one shoulder being higher than the other', before interlacing his own judgement, 'deformed of body . . . a short and sour countenance, which seemed to savour of mischief, and utter craft and deceit . . . as though that cruel nature of his did so rage against itself in that little carcass'. Vergil then damned Richard with faint praise: 'Truly he had a sharp wit, provident and subtle,' he conceded, before adding, 'apt both to counterfeit and deceive.' And yet he also felt compelled to praise Richard's final moments at Bosworth: 'His courage was high and fierce, which failed him not in the very death, which he rather yielded to take with the sword than by foul flight to prolong his life.'

Richard's courage was fleetingly referred to in Sir Thomas More's *History of King Richard III*, though his unfinished account did not include Richard's last battle: 'No mean captain was he in war,' More remarked, 'to which his disposition was better suited than peace. Sundry victories he had, and sometimes overthrows, but never for any lack in his own person, either of hardiness or generalship.' But this praise was a short interlude in an otherwise unremittingly hostile account.

Sir Thomas More may have been motivated to write his study of Richard as a treatise against tyranny. It was deliberately dramatic, sometimes inaccurate in its historical detail, and always ready to embellish its narrative, sometimes with speeches that were clearly invented. Although More may have consulted some written histories, including a manuscript version of Polydore Vergil's account, and had access to informants who had witnessed the key events he described, including Archbishop John Morton, in whose household More grew up, Richard's role was cast from the very beginning as that of grand villain. In pursuit of this, More gave the first full account of how the king might actually have dispatched his nephews, the Princes in the Tower, including the detail that they were smothered in their beds by pillows. New themes were introduced too, hammered into historical orthodoxy by the chroniclers who followed him. Richard was now plotting to take the throne even before his brother's death, with More being the first authority to suggest that Richard was behind the death of his brother George, Duke of Clarence.

In his history, More refashioned the mannerism in which Richard absent-mindedly toyed with his dagger into something altogether more menacing: 'His eyes whirled about, his body secretly armoured, his hand ever on his dagger, his countenance and manner was like one always ready to strike back.' He provided a compelling portrait, with Richard now the embodiment of evil, by cleverly heightening dramatic effect. This is seen in his embellishment of Polydore Vergil's account of the council meeting of 13 June 1483, a key moment in Richard's seizure of the throne.

The solemn gathering of the English council might seem a

staid affair, but More gave us a roller-coaster ride. In his version of events, Richard arrived late for this important meeting in apparent good humour, innocently asking Bishop Morton for a dish of strawberries from his garden, and then briefly left the room. But he returned with a change of mood that astonished those assembled there, suddenly rolling up his sleeve to display a withered arm, accusing the unlikely partnership of Edward IV's widowed queen and former mistress of being witches, responsible for this affliction, and then charging the chamberlain, William, Lord Hastings, of plotting against him. More related that Richard ordered Hastings's immediate execution, swearing that he would not dine until his head had been struck off.

More had abandoned his account by 1518, only partway through Richard's reign, and it is not clear whether he ever intended it to be published. But when it was finally printed in the mid-sixteenth century, it was quickly incorporated into the chronicles of Edward Hall and Raphael Holinshed, and these in turn became the principal sources for William Shakespeare's play. Hall and Holinshed consolidated the hostile Tudor view of the king. Richard was now guilty of a whole series of murders and his mind and body were progressively distorted to match them.

During the seventeenth and eighteenth centuries many saw no need to depart from the evil character so powerfully brought to fruition here. The court poet Michael Drayton, writing in 1613, saw him as 'the most vile devourer of his kind'; the following year Sir Walter Raleigh dismissed him as 'the greatest monster in mischief'. Over a century and a half later, in 1762, the Scottish philosopher David Hume saw no reason to question either the 'singular probity and judgement' of Sir Thomas More, or the even more hostile accounts of Hall and Holinshed, concluding that Richard was 'hump-backed, and had a very disagreeable visage, his body being, in fact, no less deformed than his mind'.

But there were also significant stirrings of doubt. At the time of Shakespeare's play, William Camden, in his survey of Britain, while believing that Richard almost certainly murdered his nephews and usurped the throne, was prepared to pay tribute to his qualities as a ruler and law-maker, saying: 'in the opinion of the wise he is reckoned in the number of bad men but good princes'. At the beginning of the seventeenth century the antiquarian John Stow went further, unearthing a copy of the *Titulus Regius*, Richard's right to rule, and commenting that the king's responsibility for the murder of his nephews had never been categorically proven. Stow was particularly uneasy about the way Richard was physically represented as a monster. He recalled that in his youth he had spoken to old men who had seen the king, and had told him that although short of stature he was in no way deformed. Shortly afterwards, King James I's Master of Revels, Sir George Buck, in his *History of King Richard III*, presented the first comprehensive assault on the Tudor tradition. Buck believed that one of his ancestors had fought and died by Richard III's side at Bosworth, and – consulting a range of manuscripts – now championed the king's cause, praising his courage, piety and concern for justice, and claiming that Richard's 'good name and memory' had been most foully traduced.

The best known and most influential of Richard III's defenders was Whig politician and man of letters Sir Horace Walpole, who in 1768 brought out his *Historic Doubts on the Life and Reign of Richard III*. Walpole concluded that a number of crimes attributed to the king were either improbable or contrary to his character. Walpole was undecided about the fate of Edward IV's oldest son, stating that 'I can neither entirely acquit Richard nor condemn him', though he believed the younger boy may have somehow escaped. He was also sceptical of Tudor accounts of Richard's appearance, telling of an anecdote in the Desmond family that Richard cut an attractive figure at court.

Walpole's book provoked much interest, and significantly saw the rediscovery – in private archives – of John Rous's first, sympathetic portrait of the king. On 26 February 1768 the poet Thomas Gray wrote to Walpole: 'Let me tell you,' he confided, 'that Lord Sandwich, who was lately dining at Cambridge, spoke appreciatively of your book, and said it was a pity you did not know that his cousin, [the Duke of] Manchester, had a genealogy that went down to Richard III and his son, in which the king appeared to be a handsome man.' This was Rous's illustrated history, and Walpole was subsequently able to inspect it, noting with pleasure of the etching of King Richard, next to the favourable commentary on his reign: 'The figure is traced with a pen – well-drawn.'

The great debate continued. In 1819 Roman Catholic historian John Lingard, in a vindication of Sir Thomas More, condemned Richard III 'as that monster in human shape, a prince of insatiable ambition, who could conceal the most bloody of projects under a mask of affection and loyalty'. But four years later another historian, Sharon Turner, while believing Richard probably murdered the Princes in the Tower, saw him very much as a product of his age, judging that he 'proceeded to the usurpation of the crown with the approbation of most of the great men, both of church and state, then in London'.

By the end of the nineteenth century battle lines between the king's detractors and supporters had been firmly drawn. James Gairdner, a prolific scholar and editor of chronicles and records, published in 1878 a history of Richard III utterly convinced of 'the general fidelity of the portrait [of Richard] with which we have been made familiar by Shakespeare and Sir Thomas More', declaring firmly that Richard 'was indeed cruel and unnatural beyond the ordinary measure, even of those violent and ferocious times'. A vigorous debate in the pages of the *English Historical Review* ensued, where Gairdner was opposed by the notable geographer Sir Clements Markham (who went on to write his own vindication of Richard III), who cited Richard's proven abilities as a warrior and administrator, both before he became king and afterwards, his concern for legal reform and his popularity in the north – particularly Yorkshire – and closed with the rebuttal: 'such a monster [as presented by Gairdner] is impossible in real life. Even Dr Jekyll and Mr Hyde are nothing to it.'

Interest in Richard has continued unabated. In 1924 the Richard III Society was founded, and continues to flourish, with the aim 'to promote in every possible way research into the life and times of Richard III and to secure a re-assessment of the material relating to this period, and of the role in English history of this monarch'. In 1936 historian John Armstrong discovered the only strictly contemporary account of the beginning of Richard's reign, that of an Italian visitor to London, Dominic Mancini. In 1951 Josephine Tey brought out a bestselling novel, *The Daughter of Time*, in which her detective hero, Inspector Grant, inspired by an early sixteenth-century portrait of Richard III, puts his investigative talents to unorthodox use, eventually acquitting Richard of all the charges made against him by More and Shakespeare.

Yet for the general public, the dark power of Shakespeare's villain is never far from the scene, even if few would fully agree with the historical accuracy of his portrayal. The accepted view of Richard's early career is now more positive, paying tribute to his courage, loyalty to his brother Edward IV, and his genuine piety and chivalric aspirations. Yet with all the wealth of new material that is being unearthed, we still struggle to make a connection with the real man, and to understand why he took the throne. As Paul Murray Kendall wrote in 1955, in a more sympathetic biography of this much maligned king, a succession of hostile Tudor paintings had distorted his physical appearance in the same way as they had twisted his character: 'If we cannot see his portrait clearly, we can at least choose its painter.' In a major study of Richard III in 1981, Charles Ross saw him in many ways as a strikingly conventional medieval prince, and also very much a product of a brutal and ruthless era. But his taking of the throne, and the violence that accompanied it, was still depicted as 'an unashamed bid for personal power'.

We do not come to terms with the reality of the man either by blackening his reputation or whitewashing him. Tudor sources that progressively twisted his appearance and motivation have to be treated with caution, but cannot simply be disregarded. They built on hostility that was already present during his reign, as our earliest sources, those of Dominic Mancini and the *Croyland Chronicle* – written by an official well-placed within the Yorkist government – make clear. And yet Richard's reign was all too short, and his death at Bosworth left him unable to give us his own version of his life and account for the motivation that drove him. It is indeed telling that even the most critical Tudor commentators were moved to praise his exemplary courage at the end of the battle. It is sometimes said that we end our life in the manner we have hoped to have lived it.

Retrieving the remains of this king, whose body was stripped naked and violated after his death, put on public display and then hurriedly buried at Leicester, as the victorious army of his challenger, Henry Tudor, moved south to London to claim the throne, would give vital tangibility to his life – a tangibility that could at last counterpoint the power of Shakespeare's play. Shakespeare, and the hostile Tudor tradition that he drew upon, tell us only one half of Richard's story.

The great debate we have charted really began in 1484, in the last year of Richard III's reign. His rival, Henry Tudor, an exile in France, was now claiming to be king in his own right, and sending out letters to his supporters in England explaining this on the basis of the character of his opponent, 'an unnatural tyrant and homicide'. Henry was employing character assassination to justify his right to rule, a character assassination that subsequently reached its apogee – or nadir – with Shakespeare's play. Whether we agree or disagree with these sentiments, we have been replaying this side of the debate ever since.

But Richard responded to his opponent's letters with a proclamation of his own. In it, he derided Henry Tudor's claim because through his pedigree, his family descent, he had no legitimate right to claim the crown at all. Henry was, he asserted, of bastard stock from both his maternal and paternal lineages – an observation that was fundamentally correct. This was the issue that John Rous was strongly hinting at in his earlier version of Richard III's reign. Richard, by contrast, was born from a true marriage, and this not only validated his own right to rule, but fatally undermined the right of his opponent. Richard's side of the argument revolved around legitimacy, a belief in his own legitimate right to be king and a conviction that his challenger possessed no right at all.

This was the argument the Tudors feared most deeply. We often employ the phrase 'Tudor propaganda' when discussing Richard. Yet although that propaganda grew apace over time, it was notably hesitant, even reticent, in the reign of the first Tudor king. Henry was content to be the avenging angel, sent by God to chastise an unnatural tyrant. Any departure from this script would mean revealing information about Tudor's own difficult life, the political compromises that he made in exile and the confusion over his claim to the throne, which persisted long after he had won it. And that was something Henry was most reluctant to do.

If we introduce legitimacy back into the heart of the debate we can break away from the endless sessions of a Kafkaesque court of justice, reconvening year after year, and century after century, to discuss the real and imagined crimes of this long dead king. Instead, we can give Richard III a cause to fight and die for, a cause that he could be loyal to – and loyalty was the guiding personal motto of his life. In doing so we also return to the heart of the family – the House of York – from which Shakespeare and the Tudors had plucked him. We see the power of the reverence for his dead father, whose achievements Richard admired so much, and whose rightful heir he increasingly felt himself to be. Departing from the hostile versions of More and Shakespeare, and following the contemporary account of Dominic Mancini, we encounter the force of his grief over the death of his brother, the Duke of Clarence, along with fear that he also was at risk, and an all-consuming desire to avenge his brother's fate. This interpretation, which will turn Shakespeare on its head, forms a cornerstone from which much else will fall into place.

Richard might have fought his way to the throne for no other reason than merciless personal ambition; he may also have killed for a cause – the legitimacy of his right to be king. Once we allow for that possibility, the fateful and heroic cavalry charge on the morning of 22 August 1485 begins to make more and more sense. The Battle of Bosworth saw the fall of the last King of England to die in battle and the succession of a dynasty determined to denigrate his name. To bring him back to life we do not need to try to replace a villain with a saint; rather, we need to understand better the bravery and self-belief of the line of horsemen who charged across the battlefield to meet their foe, and the astonishing courage of the king who led that charge. If we are able to allow history to be written by the losers as well as the winners, perhaps we can at last lay Richard III to rest with real dignity.

3

So It Begins

Thursday, 23 August 2012

THE ALARM GOES off at 5 a.m., but I had woken at two and
slept unevenly, questions racing through my mind. What
could go right and what wrong? What hadn't I planned for?
Would I be ridiculed for this quixotic search? The cab arrives
promptly and the journey to Edinburgh's Waverley Station is
quiet, the familiar tree-lined suburbs slipping by. Would I see
them differently on my return? Would my quest for the grave of
King Richard III change everything for me? As I board the train
for Leicester the sick feeling in my stomach finally subsides. This
is what I've been fighting for. The dig is finally happening.

As the train pulls out of Waverley Station, I'm actually following in Richard's footsteps. When I was researching Richard's life
it had come as a revelation to learn that he had once walked the
streets of Edinburgh, having been sent north by his brother,
Edward IV, in 1482 (see p. 88).

At the next stop, Berwick, it was strange to think that the train
stood on the remnants of what had once been the Great Hall of
Berwick Castle, where Richard had also stayed. The train heads
out over Northumberland, and Percy country, towards Durham,
a city that held a special place in his heart. St Cuthbert, patron
saint of Durham Cathedral, was much venerated by Richard
who had dedicated a stall to him in his church at Middleham.

Not far from Durham was Barnard Castle, one of Richard's favourite residences where you can still see his personal emblem of a boar carved into a surviving window tracery. And nearby was Saleby, the home of the Brackenbury family, his most loyal supporters and adherents. Robert is the most famous Brackenbury, the man Richard would make Constable of the Tower of London, and who would be immortalized by Shakespeare as 'Gentle Brackenbury'.

If Durham and its cathedral and Barnard Castle captivated him, it was the next stop that surely held his heart completely. York was always Richard's 'fair city', the Archbishop's Palace chosen by him as the place where he would invest his young son as Prince of Wales, and whose people had known Richard man and boy.

We're delayed at Doncaster so I miss the connection at Sheffield but, with thirty minutes to spare built into my journey, I should still make the on-site midday meeting at the Social Services car park with Richard Buckley, co-director of University of Leicester Archaeological Services (ULAS), Dr Christine Fiddler, interim Heritage Manager for Leicester City Council, and Mick Bowers, Head of Greyfriars Property Services. I check my phone. No calls or texts from the media. The press release for the launch event in the car park tomorrow went out yesterday, embargoed until midnight tonight. Perhaps in the 527 years since Richard's death at Bosworth and interment in Greyfriars Church, the world has turned too many times and there's no interest in the search for his grave. A part of me is relieved that I'll then be able to perform my role quietly, away from the media spotlight. But my relief is tinged with frustration. If no one cares about the quest for Richard III's grave then the chance finally to air the dichotomy between evil Shakespearean villain and man of good reputation – to challenge the status quo – will have been missed.

The train trundles on to Leicester. It's nearly eleven o'clock and my phone rings. It's Fiona Phythian, education correspondent for the *Leicester Mercury*, who wants to do an article on the dig for tomorrow's edition. I give her as much of the story as I can, and explain that the full story will be available tomorrow at the car park. I hear her frustration but if I say too much now this will ruin any chance we have of attracting other media to the launch. As the train pulls into Leicester Station the phone rings again. This time it's Nick Britten, Midlands correspondent for the *Daily Telegraph*, who tells me the editor wants to run a piece. Thrilled that a national is interested, I give him as much information as I can.

In Leicester, I walk the short distance between the train station and the Greyfriars Building in Grey Friars Street, which allows me fifteen minutes of fresh air to clear my head and prepare myself for what's to come. En route strangers smile as they pass – what is it about this friendly city that makes me feel so much at home? Situated in the heart of England, Leicester has always welcomed outsiders, from Saxons and Vikings, to Romans and Jews, Asians and Africans.

At Leicester City Council's Greyfriars Building reception desk I have to explain why I am here, but then Mick Bowers arrives and I'm finally let in. It's good that security is tight, but I am surprised that news of the dig hasn't filtered through. Perhaps there's no interest here either. On the way to the office on the first floor that I can use Bowers shows me the Richard III display boards, full of pictures, history, genealogy and a timeline, making a wonderful introduction for Social Services employees. Centre stage on the display is a voting sheet: 'Good Richard' (orange stickers), 'Bad Richard' (green stickers) or 'Annoyed That Their Car Park is Out of Use for the Dig' (blue stickers). There are some votes for good, some for bad but the blue section is already half full. It's a lovely moment: I think we may be about to change history; they just want their car park back.

Mike Mistry is the attendant who ensures all runs smoothly in the organized chaos that is the Leicester Social Services car park. Of particular concern are the children who are brought here into care, who typically arrive with care workers at the northern end. Our dig is not going to make his job any easier but he's affable. I spot Richard Buckley, who is already in the car park with Christine Fiddler. As Mick and I approach them, they're discussing the bike shed and Trench Two whose size and planned location may just block it. It looks as if the trench might have to be shortened to allow cyclists through, but after another look at the site plans, it's agreed there's no need to do so; the cyclists will have ample room to get round it and into their shed. I'm relieved. In the days to come every inch that we dig may count. Archaeologically, the car park is virgin ground and I only have funding to dig 1 per cent of the 17 per cent remaining open area of the Greyfriars precinct. We're about to play a very expensive and advanced game of Battleships. We will need to find the Greyfriars Church in that 1 per cent, never mind any gravesites. Not for the first time, I glance over to the northern end and the white letter 'R' painted on the tarmac.

Richard Buckley confirms that high fencing has been ordered for the site for Health and Safety reasons. I ask if we can put covers over the fencing for privacy (I'm already thinking of the potential human remains we may uncover) and he assures me that they have tarpaulin. Everything will be under control. Apparently the BBC has been in touch which is great news. If the BBC is showing interest it bodes well for tomorrow's launch and a frisson of excitement runs through our small group. As we leave the earlier tensions fade away in laughter and banter about what the next day will bring. Richard Buckley has told his team that if we find Richard he will eat his hat. It's now well after 3 p.m. and I get a text from historian and genealogist Dr John Ashdown-Hill telling me that he's arrived in Leicester. We agree to meet up later at the apartments into which we've all been booked. Annette Carson, author of *Richard III: The Maligned King*, has confirmed she'll be in Leicester at 6 p.m. and will come straight to us.

The apartments are a five-minute walk from the Social Services car park, located by the River Soar. On the way you pass the fine statue of Richard in Castle Gardens. Unlike the statue at Middleham Castle in Yorkshire, where a serpent is curled over his back to denote slanders against him, this depicts Richard III as a warrior king, a courageous fifteenth-century soldier. As I pass the River Soar my thoughts turn to the tale that Richard's remains were thrown into its depths, a story that remains powerful, no more so than in Leicester. Will the next two weeks consign it to the dustbin of history? Maybe the discoveries of the next fortnight will challenge and change English history, or maybe our theories will be proved wrong.

Back at the apartment the doorbell rings and I open the door to Annette Carson. We hug and she comes in to discuss the plan for tomorrow. I'm telling her about the BBC attending the launch when a text arrives from Richard Buckley to say that ITV Central News is also coming. It's not long before John Ashdown-Hill arrives and we discuss our respective areas of expertise for the media launch as we don't want to repeat information. John's sphere is the Greyfriars Church and genealogy, with his discovery of Richard's mtDNA sequence, and he is also well practised at repudiating the River Soar story. From her understanding of contemporary sources, Annette's competence is in defending Richard III's reputation, while knowledge of his character and the genesis of the dig project is my speciality. With our strategy for tomorrow sorted out, we bid one another goodnight.

I'm ready to collapse into bed when I get a text from Dominic Sewell, the historical equitation specialist, who has just arrived in Leicester; we agree to catch up early tomorrow morning in the car park. The phone then never stops and I spend the next two hours sorting out tomorrow's filming at the car park launch with various news crews, film crews, radio stations and newspapers. What have I kicked off?

The Media Launch

Friday, 24 August 2012

I'm up at 5 a.m., nervous about what today will bring but thankful that the weather is reasonable – overcast but not raining. John, Annette and I walk to the Social Services car park and arrive at six o'clock to find the large green gates open and a white satellite news van already in place. I notice it is parked over the letter 'R', hiding it from view. Richard Buckley and Mick Bowers are already there.

Dominic Sewell pulls up in a car jam-packed with the clothing and armour of a medieval knight. We have a quick discussion and I explain that it's his job to bring the car park to medieval life with combat display. His 'foot soldier', Henry Sherry, a re-enactor from the Wars of the Roses group, puts on his 'murrey', a dark reddish purple and blue tunic, the colours of the House of York, while Dominic climbs into his hose and padded undergarments aided by Josh, his 'squire', who then straps on his armour. They are soon joined by Dr Tobias Capwell, Curator of Arms and Armour at the Wallace Collection in London. It's a great honour to have a leading expert in this field with us. Toby will talk about Richard, his armour and Bosworth. Claire Graham, the Ground Penetrating Radar (GPR) specialist from Stratascan, is setting up her equipment and running a final analysis of the Social Services car park area. We joke about how far the project has come since we last met in this car park for the original GPR survey a year ago. I see Carl Vivian starting to film for the University of Leicester and meet Colin Brooks, their photographer, who explains that they will be recording all events at the dig for the partners.

The presence of Assistant City Mayor, Piara Singh Clair is a welcome boost and gives the Looking for Richard project its official launch. Michael Ibsen, the genetic descendant of Richard III and his seventeenth-generation nephew, is due from London today and Dr Turi King, the DNA expert from Leicester University, will obtain his DNA sample. Everyone working in the car park will have to give their own DNA sample too, just in case there's cross-contamination.

I spot Alex Rowson, associate producer at Darlow Smithson Productions (DSP), setting up his equipment. Dr Julian Boon from Leicester University, the inventor of Personality Profiling, is here. As part of the Looking for Richard project I had commissioned him and Professor Mark Lansdale to do the first-ever Personality Analysis of the king. I ask Dr Boon what he will talk about to camera and he confirms his overriding view that Richard III was essentially a well-meaning man living in difficult times. If one of the UK's leading psychologists, who has spent the past eighteen months profiling Richard, has come to this conclusion, it needs to be heard. Michael Ibsen arrives and is engulfed by news teams. He takes it all in his stride. It's an added bonus to have a genetic descendant with us on launch day, bringing Richard's world directly into ours. Turi King and Ibsen make an extraordinary team and collecting his DNA by mouth swab is filmed live; it's quite surreal to see a living relative of a king having his DNA taken in a car park. The whole place is crammed with news crews and media.

Richard Buckley is pleased that the gazebo has sides so there will be somewhere to shelter if the weather turns. He wants to start spray-painting the car park today to mark out the areas of Trench One and Trench Two so that the buzz saw can cut them ready for tomorrow's machining work. He's keen to get on and

I agree. We don't know how much time we may need. Every moment counts. He gives the go-ahead for marking up the trenches with yellow paint and archaeologist Leon Hunt, who put the Archaeological Desk-Based Assessment together for the project back in the spring of 2011, begins the task. He too is quickly surrounded by cameras.

By late afternoon, everyone has left. I look back at the deserted car park. The long, rectangular layouts of the two thirty-metre trenches shine brightly in yellow spray paint. Beside them, and sometimes crossing them, is the faintest of cuts carved into the once pristine tarmac, like a perfect precision puncture wound. The letter 'R' is now encased within the cuts of Trench One.

The Dig: Day One

Saturday, 25 August 2012

The long-awaited moment has arrived: 25 August and the day King Richard III was interred here in the Greyfriars Church, 527 years ago. Annette and I arrive at the car park just as the 360-degree excavator is ripping into Trench One, and the first piece of tarmac is removed. John Ashdown-Hill is already here, as are Carl Vivian and Colin Brooks, recording the moment for the partners. The DSP team, following everything for Channel 4, are keen to tell the story of the real, historical Richard III and Annette Carson suggests we have a meeting to discuss primary sources soon. She and Ashdown-Hill can't stay indefinitely as their costs are mounting daily, so we agree to meet in the gazebo at 1 p.m. when everyone will be taking a break.

Excavation is now under way at the northern end of Trench One and the noise is terrific. Ashdown-Hill, Carson and I think this was the site of the church. The machine will very shortly be going right over the painted letter 'R', close to where my instinct told me Richard's remains lay when I first came here. I still believe it. Nothing has changed my mind. If Greyfriars Church isn't where we expect, all our research, Ashdown-Hill's template of the Greyfriars layout, my intuition – everything will have been for nothing. As the machine delicately prises off the top layer of tarmac the letter 'R' crumbles away. I can't take my eyes off the excavator and have to pinch myself as I watch. Over three and a half years of non-stop cajoling, bringing partners on board, getting everyone on-side, and raising considerable funds, has brought us to this moment.

I'm introduced to Mathew Morris, Richard Buckley's lead archaeologist at the dig and site director. We chat briefly before he goes back to the machining. The weather is good, part sun, part cloud and the DSP team check their phones for an update: some time later in the day a large and prolonged shower is forecast. Then the machining suddenly stops. Richard Buckley and Mathew Morris are looking into the trench, which isn't that deep, or long, pointing to what might be a small medieval wall at the most northerly end. It's a couple of feet down, clearly running north–south. None of us can quite believe it as we've been machining for less than ten minutes. Richard points out the old stone, yellowy-white in the rich, clay soil. It's a straight wall. This early on a potentially medieval structure is a good sign and it's quite high up, signifying that the medieval layer may not be too far down. He explains how this could relate to the 2007 dig they performed at Grey Friars Street when he and his team uncovered the medieval layer two feet down, which could indicate the level here. If so it's also very good news for costs and timing. That dig was the closest excavation to this car park, and made me think that the Social Services site could be the potential location of the church.

Half an hour later the small medieval wall to the northern end of Trench One is gone, replaced by earth and red-brick rubble and what looks to be solid, red-brick walls poking through at a lower level. 'False alarm, I'm afraid,' Buckley says wearily. It looks as if the Victorians used the medieval stone for one of their own walls, possibly foundations for an outhouse building we know was here from the maps Buckley had investigated. The archaeologist can see my disappointment but tells me to take heart: 'We've found medieval stone and that's a good sign.' As the machining continues Turi King arrives and we tell her about the 'medieval wall'. I take the opportunity to have a chat with her about the potential finding of human remains and protecting DNA. She assures me that they have the protective suits, masks and gloves ready to go. I quiz her about possible contamination and she gives me a lot of information. But one thing sticks in my mind: it's never good to get water on remains.

The machining of Trench One is going well, the archaeologists eagle-eyed as each layer of earth emerges. The excavator goes down and down but it looks like there's only Victorian rubble and red-brick walls poking through, all to the northern end. I'm really disappointed – gutted actually. There appears to be no medieval archaeology where I believed the church and Richard's final resting place would be. Nothing. My instinct has never let me down before. I tell myself it's only day one and that we have a great team of professionals on this project with two weeks of digging to go. Whatever we find will enhance Richard III's story and our knowledge of the period.

After a short break for breakfast, I walk back to the car park to find Richard Buckley gone and the excavator standing idle. Mathew Morris explains that the machine has thrown a track. I'm thinking time and money: I only have a small contingency for overtime. Buckley arrives back on site with Stevie Stell the excavator driver who, utilizing the pulling power of the excavator, is going to use a massive chain to re-engage the track. We've got to get it back on today. Buckley asks how much I have left in the kitty from the international appeal. About £800, I say. 'We can do a lot with that,' he replies. 'Don't worry, we'll make up the time.' The excavator roars back into life. I watch the driver gently pulling the chain that is tied to the track and wrapped around its powerful scoop. The DSP team fly past me to film the repair. It's slow, careful work and inch by inch the massive track slides smoothly back into place. Richard Buckley gives the thumbs up as the driver trundles the excavator back over the northern end of Trench One. The scoop arm drops down and begins to lift out giant clods of earth, debris and rubble, swinging them on to the spoil heaps. I check my watch. It's 2.15 p.m. We're going to be okay.

Buckley has left to see his family, when suddenly Mathew Morris's hand shoots into the air. The excavator stops and Morris jumps into the trench. He looks up at me.

There's a bone.

He's pointing to a long, but clearly smashed, bone lying in an east–west direction, about five feet down in the trench. I ask if it's human. We've found so many animal bones already that I don't trust what I'm seeing. Morris nods. He says it looks like a leg bone and bends to perform gentle trowel work around it. It may just be an odd bone, so he's looking to see if there are any others with it.

I realize that Morris's head, poking out at me from the trench, is only a few feet from where the letter 'R' once existed and right where I had my intuition. My heart is pounding. I feel odd, as if I'm somehow here but not here. My legs are moving, taking me to the edge of the trench. I'm jumping in, getting to Morris as fast as I can. I see the leg bone. It's brown and dirty, covered in earth and mashed up a little, scraped by the scoop of the excavator which has taken some of its side away. 'It happens,' Morris says quickly. 'We try our best but it can happen, especially when we're not expecting things to be where they are.' The bone is clearly human. Morris scrapes carefully at the soil around it and a second bone begins to show through. He clears the earth around it a little. This other leg bone is lying beside the first, directly adjacent to it. It looks as if we might have a burial, maybe a whole skeleton. The odd sensation I'm experiencing won't go away. All I can think is that it's Richard. I hear myself telling Morris that we're right beside the 'R' that marked the spot. I want him to believe me – to believe it – to believe what he's seeing. He's smiling, telling me not to get my hopes up, because the two bones may be the only remains here. 'We don't even know if there is a skeleton,' he says. 'We have to remember that we've found no medieval archaeology in this part of the trench. It could be anyone and from any age, not even medieval. The level they're at may be far enough down to indicate they are fifteenth century but it's only an indication at the moment.'

I just want to be alone here but the cameras are all pointing, and everyone is staring down at the first real find. Morris tells the driver to move the excavator further down the trench to scoop out the earth and rubble there and the crowd follows the machine. I'm left at the northern end and for a moment the absurdity of what I am doing hits me. I'm in a trench in a municipal car park in Leicester looking at a couple of lower leg bones and thinking they are those of a king. I tell myself I have to go with what feels right, what my instinct is telling me. That has been the story of this project from the start and I'm not going to stop now.

I climb out of the trench and glance over at the spire of the cathedral rising over the car park to the north. Looming above it is the darkest storm cloud. I suddenly remember the weather forecast and know we only have moments before it arrives. I'm thinking about the exposed bones and how to protect them from rain when a tempest hits. Everyone is rushing for cover. I yell at Morris to get something to cover the bones with, the fear of losing the DNA coursing through me. Annette Carson shouts that she's got bubble-wrap, her voice as panicked as mine. The rain's coming down in sheets. I sprint while pulling on a luminous protective coat, jumping into the trench just as Morris hurls down some large plastic finds bags. The DSP team are in the gazebo, hurriedly donning their coats and fixing a plastic cover on the camera, then they rush out again to film in a downpour fast becoming a deluge. Everyone's under cover but I can't leave the trench. The remains must be protected.

Knowing that we shed DNA continually, from a distance I hurriedly place the plastic bags over the bones as best I can so as not to contaminate them, grabbing clods of the heavy earth to cover the plastic sheeting – anything to stop the rain getting in. I pick up some rocks and place them around the covering, away from the bones, but close enough to hold the plastic bags in place as a wind whips up from nowhere and thunder rumbles overhead. I'm covered in mud, soaked to the skin but the bones are now protected. I'm strangely exhilarated as I race for the nearest cover. Morris is sheltering in the covered walkway and I witter on about how Shakespeare would have loved this scene; he looks at me as if I'm barking mad.

The storm passes and sunlight shafts down on to the car park. It is abruptly quiet and a profound feeling of complete peace washes over me. And I know then in the deepest part of me that if this is Richard he wanted to be found – was ready to be found. All at once I remember what day it is: 25 August, the anniversary of Richard's burial in the Greyfriars, the day he was laid to rest. In the days, months and years to come it might also become known as the day he was found again.

Day Two

Sunday, 26 August 2012

I awake feeling strangely disconnected. Did yesterday's find really happen or was it all just a dream? Am I merely making something out of nothing because I need it to be something? Jumping to conclusions – ridiculous conclusions – by sheer force of will?

Annette Carson was astonished at the discovery but far more sanguine than me, happy to accept everything with an open mind. She understands my conviction that this is Richard. Neither of us can rationally explain the discovery of remains where my instinct told me they would be; that they really may be what we have been searching for. John Ashdown-Hill returned to the car park late yesterday afternoon. He was excited about finding human remains in the area where his research concluded the choir of the Greyfriars Church should lie. He'd been dismayed by the lack of medieval archaeology in the vicinity but agreed we would soon know if the bones were important – or just old bones.

Carson and I arrive in the car park just as the machining of Trench One is finishing. The trench is deep, exposing what could be the medieval layer at 1.5 metres beneath the modern car park. Richard Buckley tells us that there could be a robbed-out wall (an area showing the course of an ancient wall but no longer with any stone) at the southern end of Trench One – possibly medieval – with a smaller one next to it, which also looks to be very old, but doesn't appear to have deep foundations. He explained that it's odd to have a medieval wall without foundations, and that the gap between these two (possibly) ancient artefacts does not relate to any medieval structure he's come across before. I peer into the trench. It looks like plain earth and rubble until Buckley tells me what to look for; a robbed-out wall will merely leave its shadow in the earth. He also points out where the smaller wall and its stone now seem to be poking through. I ask him what he thinks it is. He says it's difficult to tell at the moment and that we need to get the team in this week to clean it up properly, thus giving us a better idea. I can't contain myself any longer and ask if he's heard about yesterday's find. Buckley smiles. 'You mean the human remains, the bones?' I nod, adding, despite myself, 'You do know where they were found?' He reminds me that we have to go with the evidence, and that they probably aren't anything significant. I ask him what we should do about the remains and he says, 'We don't know enough about the site – even if we're actually in the Greyfriars precinct – so we can't go digging up human remains every time we find them. And we may find more.' I know that he's right and impatience is getting the better of me.

I'm concerned about security. We have human remains confirmed on site and are overlooked by windows on every side. If this news leaks out there are people around who might be interested in stealing a bone or two of a king. Richard Buckley says his team will be discreet, and anyway, he reckons that because the bones have been found without context, nobody will be interested. Stevie moves the excavator over to the yellow marker lines of Trench Two and, under Mathew Morris's direction, starts ripping up more of the car park. I ask Morris about the high Heras fencing and the tarpaulin that will cover it. My mind keeps going back to the fact that the northern end of Trench One is so close to the entrance of the Social Services building and a busy thoroughfare, but I'm reassured that it will be well shielded from the public gaze. This is to protect the sensibilities of the public too, since many people find the sight of bones and human remains upsetting. And of course the remains could be those of a named individual with living relatives.

I find myself less interested in Trench Two, probably because

I've convinced myself that the northern end of the site is all that matters. In Trench Two Morris is guiding the excavator over what could be an existing medieval wall and asks Stevie to skim an inch of soil off the top at one point which he does with great skill. No sooner have they done this than Turi King arrives and we take her to the site of the human remains. Morris gives her the full rundown of what has been found, then, wearing protective gloves, he gently lifts off the rocks, earth and plastic covering. As King looks down at the lower leg bones and sees how smashed up one of them is, I nervously enquire about the storm water. She explains that it's actually tap water that's the big problem because of the chlorine and potential DNA it contains. So I got soaked to the skin and rushed about like an idiot when I didn't have to? She laughs, but points out that it was good to protect them anyway. Once she's finished, Morris covers the bones with the plastic sheeting, rocks and earth again and this time he covers the good leg bone, the one that the excavator missed, with lots of earth to protect it further. King agrees that it's best to leave the remains where they are until we know more about them, most importantly whether they are in the Greyfriars precinct because if they are not then they could belong to anyone, from anywhere. I'm surprisingly comfortable with this. I know that the bones are protected and that Turi King is happy with everything.

And as I keep reminding myself, I don't really know if these are the remains of King Richard III. I have to be logical and go with the evidence.

Social Services car park: looking east towards the former Grammar School car park over the wall. Letter 'R' is directly ahead, just before the wall in first parking bay to the left. Philippa had her intuitive feeling in second parking bay to right of letter 'R' where remains were discovered

'R' marks the spot with Richard III banner and portrait. Photograph taken during Ground Penetrating Radar Survey, Social Services car park, 28 August 2011

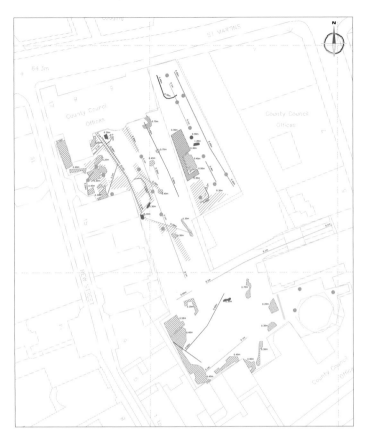

Ground
Penetrating
Radar Survey
results for the
three car parks

Annette Carson and Dr John Ashdown-Hill at Trench One, Social
Services car park at the start of the dig, 25 August 2012

Trench One, Social Services car park. Leg bones discovered immediately before first concrete structure crossing trench in foreground

Richard Buckley and Philippa Langley at Trench Three in the former Grammar School car park. With them are Pete Woods (film director at the dig) and Alex Rowson (associate producer) from Darlow Smithson Productions

Philippa Langley at exhumation with Dr Turi King and Dr Jo Appleby
in Trench One, Social Services car park

Skeletal remains discovered in Trench One in the Social Services car park.
Remains showing hands off to the right and possibly still tied

Philippa Langley and Michael Jones at the grave site

Removing the remains. Philippa Langley and Dr John Ashdown-Hill with Richard III banner over remains box

The 'Time Tomb Team'. (*From left to right*) Archaeologists Jon Coward, Mathew Morris, Leon Hunt and Tom Hoyle

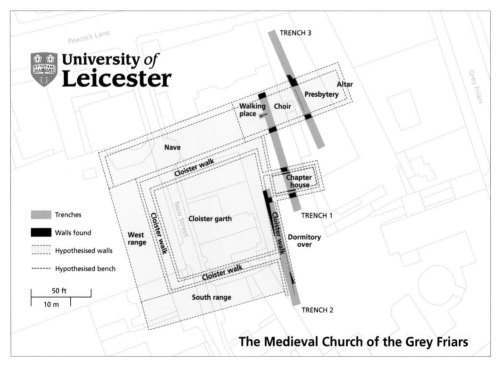

Site map of the Medieval Church of the Grey Friars post dig. Grave location in Trench One shown by marker at walking place. Circle denotes head positioned in the west

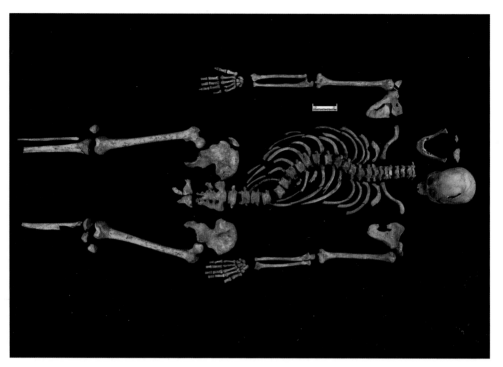

Skeleton of Richard III

(*From left to right*) Philippa Langley, Dr Stuart J Hamilton,
Robert Woosnam-Savage, Dr Jo Appleby

(*From left to right*) Sir Peter Soulsby, Sarah Levitt and Dr Phil Stone
with facial reconstruction of Richard III

Facial reconstruction
of Richard III with
sixteenth-century
portrait in background

The original modest
tomb design in
Yorkshire stone: 7' long
x 3'6 wide x 2'3 high

4

Yearning for a Noble Cause:
Richard's Early Career

RESPONDING TO the flurry of interest in Richard III as the search for his remains got under way, Christie's put up for auction a document of his written before he became king. It was drawn up at the Yorkshire castle of Pontefract on 22 April, and although no year was given, internal evidence suggested it was probably around 1476. It concerned a legal dispute between some tenants of another magnate, Ralph Neville, Earl of Westmorland. Although it was a relatively minor dispute, Richard had been petitioned to provide redress.

It was one of the few surviving letters drawn up under his signet, and signed by Richard himself and his secretary John Kendall. The estimated price was set between £8,000 and £12,000, but in the event it went for around double the original estimate, selling at £21,250. This was a remarkable price for one medieval manuscript, and showed the strength of interest in Richard that had been aroused.

Richard's concern for justice and law-giving was a notable feature of his brief reign as king. Tudor histories – unable to deny this – put a different spin on it, suggesting that although Richard brought in measures to further these aims, they were a sham, the semblance of being a good ruler, to distract people from the terrible way in which he had seized the throne. Yet Richard's belief in effective justice, and a willingness to champion the rights of the poor, had begun far earlier and can be clearly seen during the rule of his brother, Edward IV. To understand Richard as monarch, and the way he took the throne, it is vital to focus first on his early career, and, from this, get a sense of both the man and his motivation.

Richard was born at Fotheringhay Castle in Northamptonshire on 2 October 1452. He was the youngest son of Richard, Duke of York and Cecily Neville, and the youngest surviving of twelve children. His birth may have been difficult, but there is no evidence that he was physically ill, or his life was in danger. His mother Cecily would later write of the painful after-effects of this birth, lamenting in a letter to Margaret of Anjou in the spring of 1453 of the infirmity of her 'wretched body', and the results of 'sloth and discontinuance', which in the last few months 'hath grown and grown'. It appears that Cecily was still recovering from Richard's birth several months later. It may well have been a traumatic and dangerous breech birth, where the mother could not be delivered 'uncut', as Thomas More suggested; perhaps the germ of this formed the basis of the hostile Tudor tradition.

At the time of Richard's birth his father, Richard, Duke of York, was in open conflict with the crown. Earlier that year, he had challenged the weak monarchy of Henry VI directly, in February 1452 marching to Dartford at the head of an armed force with a petition of grievances. This strategy backfired: York was forced to relinquish his demands, and at St Paul's Cathedral swore a solemn oath that he would never take up arms against the king, an oath that York subsequently felt he had no choice but to break.

As a baby and small child Richard would not have been aware of these concerns, although he may have felt the tension that affected his mother Cecily, who keenly followed her husband's political fortunes. Cecily complained to Margaret of Anjou in 1453 that her husband's fall from favour had caused her to be 'replete with such immeasurable sorrow and heaviness as I doubt not will of the continuance thereof diminish and abridge my days, as it does my worldly joy and comfort'. Cecily dreaded this period of political exile, entreating Margaret that York should no longer be 'estranged from the grace and benevolent favour . . . of the king our sovereign lord'. These were heartfelt sentiments, and as Richard grew up he certainly would have heard much more about this exile from court, and reflected upon it.

When Richard was born, Richard, Duke of York was the wealthiest magnate in the realm. He had a distinguished record of service to England's ruling dynasty, the House of Lancaster, which he had represented as king's lieutenant, first in France and then in Ireland. He had a keen commitment to good government, and the provision of justice, and was also strongly influenced, as a warrior, by the code of chivalry, in which he took a scrupulous interest. Many of these traits would be passed on to his youngest son, who also bore his name, and consciously adopted by him as a way of commemorating his father and his legacy.

However, in the 1450s Richard, Duke of York had moved from being a loyal servant of the Lancastrian King Henry VI to a political opponent. At first he had insisted that his grievances were not with the king himself, but with the ministers around him, particularly Edmund Beaufort, Duke of Somerset. There is no reason to doubt this statement. York resented Somerset's dominance over the king, and had good reason for doing so. Somerset had presided over the disastrous loss of Normandy in 1449–50, the duchy that had been triumphantly conquered by Henry V in the years following Agincourt, and regained by the French some thirty years later in a swift campaign that met only token opposition from the English forces stationed there. York believed Somerset's regime was corrupt and found his conduct cowardly. The military collapse in Normandy was a shameful episode, and York's indictment of it fully justified.

York was outraged at the hold Somerset retained over Henry VI, even in the aftermath of this debacle. He deeply distrusted his rival, believing Somerset sought to undermine his position within the realm. York was acutely conscious of the nobility of his lineage, and his descent from the royal blood of Edward III, which in the absence of any offspring of Henry VI gave him the right to be heir presumptive to the crown, a right he believed that Somerset was denying him. York was also aware that if descent through the female line was given precedence, his claim to the throne was superior to that of Henry VI himself.

Manuscripts circulating within York's family circle emphasized the duke's distinguished pedigree, and likened him to the Roman general Stilicho, a courageous and worthy warrior undermined by an effete and corrupt court party. These were themes that left a deep impression on his youngest son. York's vendetta against Somerset was virulent; it culminated in the First Battle of St Albans in 1455, when Somerset, accompanying the royal army of Henry VI, was sought out and killed, thereby ending the battle.

York had by now allied himself with a branch of the powerful Neville family, led by the Earl of Salisbury and his son, the Earl of Warwick. Tension with the government of Henry VI and his strong-willed queen, Margaret of Anjou, had become more and more pronounced in the latter part of the decade, and in October 1459 York, Salisbury and Warwick had once more taken up arms – this time against the king directly. But on 12 October at Ludford Bridge, near York's castle of Ludlow on the Welsh Marches, the Yorkist army dispersed in chaos. That night York and his confederates held a desperate council of war. Fearing the vengeance of the Lancastrians, it was agreed that part of the family should go into exile. The decision was made in terrible haste. York and his second son Edmund, Earl of Rutland would go to Ireland; his oldest son, Edward, Earl of March, would join the Earls of Salisbury and Warwick and attempt to reach Calais. York's youngest sons, George and Richard, were left behind with their mother Cecily.

This was a dangerous and quite terrifying moment. Cecily, her daughter Margaret and her sons George and Richard were now at the mercy of the Lancastrian army. And those troops were rapidly approaching. As one chronicler put it: 'King Harry rode into Ludlow, and spoiled [pillaged] the town and castle, where he found the duchess of York and her two young sons, then children.' Richard, who had just turned seven, was now to see the family home wrecked by marauding soldiers. But another account suggested the situation was more desperate than this: 'The town of Ludlow,' the chronicler related, 'then belonging to the duke of York, was robbed to the bare walls and the noble duchess of York unmanly and cruelly was entreted [dealt with] and spoiled [robbed or raped].'

This was a most startling allegation. The source, known as *A Short English Chronicle*, was favourable to the Yorkists, but also well-informed and reliable. The charge was quite specific, and was likely to have been accurate. If so, Cecily certainly suffered physical violence and probably sexual violence as well. The young Richard, witnessing this appalling attack on his mother, and only too aware that his father and elder brothers had left him, must have feared for his life.

In fact, Cecily and her young children were made prisoners of war. They were taken to the Lancastrian parliament that met at Coventry, where York was charged with high treason and his lands confiscated. Cecily pleaded for mercy from Henry VI, and received a royal pardon, and she and her children were now placed in the custody of Cecily's sister Anne, Duchess of Buckingham in Tonbridge Castle in Kent. The fortunes of the House of York had reached a nadir. But in the summer of 1460 the Earls of Salisbury, Warwick and March returned from Calais at the head of an army, defeated the Lancastrians at the Battle of Northampton, and captured Henry VI. Margaret of Anjou fled with her son Edward, eventually reaching the safety of Harlech, and taking ship to Scotland.

Cecily and her young children now moved to London, where they stayed in a fine Southwark house that had belonged to the old warrior Sir John Fastolf. And it was here that they heard the news that York had returned from Ireland and landed at Chester. Cecily immediately hastened to meet him, leaving the children in London, and a letter of 12 October 1460 provided an appealing vignette: 'And she [Cecily] has left here both her sons, and her daughter, and the Lord of March [Edward] cometh every day to see them.' It is touching that Edward – ten years older than Richard, who had just celebrated his eighth birthday – had made time, with all the pressing political and military concerns, to visit his younger siblings so regularly. Perhaps, after what they had been through, he wanted to reassure them about the future.

When York returned from Ireland the dynastic stakes had been raised, for he now championed the superiority of his own lineage over that of the ruling Lancastrian dynasty. York emphasized that his pedigree ran from Lionel, Duke of Clarence, the second surviving son of Edward III, whereas the Lancastrians were descended from John of Gaunt, Edward's third son. These facts were already well known, and had been when York remained a loyal subject to Henry VI. Political circumstances were now forcing his hand.

The issue of inheritance to the crown was complex. Lionel had only left a daughter, Philippa, who had married Edmund Mortimer, and it was the granddaughter of this union, Anne Mortimer, York's mother, who brought the claim into his family. For it to be effective, inheritance through the female line would have to be given precedence, and this was something the judges and lords of the realm were most reluctant to do. Also, as they and many others were well aware, York and his family had for a long time accepted Henry VI as rightful king, and given their oaths of allegiance to him.

In the event, a compromise was reached. York was able to secure an agreement from parliament at the end of October 1460 known as the Act of Accord, which now nominated him as Henry VI's heir, at the expense of Henry's own son, Edward, Prince of Wales (born in 1453). The king was a Yorkist captive and may well have been coerced into agreeing to this. From a Lancastrian point of view, York was unprincipled and ruthless; by attempting to claim the throne for himself he had reneged on his earlier oaths of allegiance to Henry VI. But this was not a course of action York had embarked upon lightly.

York was a principled man and he was only too conscious of oaths of loyalty and valued them highly. His belief in his own rightful claim had been forged in an atmosphere of escalating threat and menace, and seemed to have been a genuine response to his continued ostracism from court and government. York had been conspicuously loyal to Henry VI as the king's lieutenant in France and Ireland. He now feared for his political future and indeed his own life.

When the terms of the arrangement were publicized throughout the realm they led to a full-scale resumption of war. Queen Margaret refused to accept the Act of Accord, and championing the rights of her son, Edward, raised a massive northern army in defiance of the agreement. York marched to meet it in atrocious winter weather. He had stumbled into a trap. At the Battle of Wakefield on 30 December he was overwhelmed by the far larger army of his opponents. York and his second son Edmund died in the fighting.

Within the House of York Wakefield was remembered as 'the horrible battle'. Chilling details about the fighting had begun to leak out, that Edmund, Earl of Rutland – now seventeen – had actually been killed in cold blood, fleeing the battle, and that York's body had been desecrated, his dismembered head mockingly adorned with a paper crown and then nailed to York's Micklegate Bar. One account – the Register of the Abbot Whethamstede, a source close to the House of York, and one Richard would certainly have known about – provided an even more harrowing version. For in Whethamstede's account York was captured still alive: 'They stood him on a little anthill,' the abbot related, 'and placed on his head, as if a crown, a vile garland made of reeds, just as the Jews did to the Lord, and bent the knee to him, saying in jest "Hail King, without rule. Hail King, without ancestry. Hail leader and prince, with no subjects or possessions." And having said this, and various other shameful and dishonourable things to him, at last they cut off his head.'

These images of martyrdom and desecration appalled the whole of York's family, and had a particularly strong impact upon his youngest son, Richard, who years later led the formal reburial of his father in the family resting-place at Fotheringhay. York's eldest son, Edward, Earl of March was now the Yorkist successor to the throne, and he fought bravely to uphold that claim, winning a stirring victory at Mortimer's Cross on 2 February 1461. But on 17 February his ally Warwick's army was defeated at the Second Battle of St Albans, allowing large numbers of Lancastrian soldiers to approach the capital. Still mourning the loss of her husband and son, Cecily decided that her youngest sons were no longer safe if the Lancastrians entered London. Even though they were aged only eleven and eight, Cecily now believed they represented a dynastic threat to the House of Lancaster – and if Lancastrian troops reached the capital the boys might well be killed. So she speedily sent them to the safety of the Burgundian Netherlands until the danger had receded.

But the Lancastrians never entered London. They halted, and

then returned to the north of England. Edward and Warwick were able to join forces, and arrived in the capital together. On 4 March 1461 the Earl of March was acclaimed King Edward IV in London. Later that month, on 29 March, he won a decisive victory over the Lancastrians at Towton, cementing his hold over the country. A new Yorkist dynasty had been born.

Richard and his brother George returned to England that summer. George was created Duke of Clarence. And in October 1461 Richard was granted a suitable title of his own, the dukedom of Gloucester. After the high drama of the last few years Richard's life once again became quieter. Documents reveal little of his whereabouts over the next few years. Cecily, whose piety was matched by her political acumen, now held a commanding position at the Yorkist court. He probably spent time with his mother at Fotheringhay and at her London residence of Baynard's Castle. There were also lodgings for both boys in royal palaces such as Greenwich.

In May 1464 Edward IV secretly married Elizabeth Woodville, although the match was only announced to an astonished political community some four months later. The *Croyland Chronicler* wrote: 'King Edward, prompted by the ardour of youth, and relying entirely on his own choice, without consulting the nobles of the kingdom, privately married the widow of a certain knight, Elizabeth by name . . . This the nobility and chief men of the kingdom took amiss, seeing that he had with such immoderate haste promoted a person sprung from comparatively humble lineage, to share the throne with him.' Dominic Mancini added bluntly: 'On that account, not only did he [Edward] alienate the nobles . . . he also offended most bitterly the members of his own house.' Mancini related that neither Edward's mother nor his two brothers ever really came to terms with this disastrous match.

In the autumn of 1465, now aged twelve, Richard made a highly important move to the household of Richard Neville,

Earl of Warwick, known to posterity as 'the Kingmaker', the most powerful aristocrat in the kingdom. In 1461 Warwick's support for the Yorkist cause had been an important contributor to Edward IV's victory, and the king now chose him to be Richard's tutor. This experience would leave a lasting impression on Richard, as he accompanied Warwick to his northern fortresses of Middleham, Sheriff Hutton, Penrith and Barnard Castle. It was in Warwick's household that Richard met his life-long friend Francis, Lord Lovell, and his future wife – one of the Kingmaker's daughters – Anne Neville.

Although Warwick had been the pillar of the Yorkist cause, Richard had joined his establishment at a time of a souring in his relationship with the king. The cause of this was the Woodville marriage. This secret and unsuitable match had taken place when Warwick was abroad negotiating a foreign marriage alliance for the king. Warwick felt humiliated by the bizarre turn of events and never forgave Edward for it. Edward's generous patronage of the new queen's impoverished and acquisitive family, and dis-agreements over foreign policy, only served to drive Warwick and the king further apart.

Richard had remained with Warwick until Edward IV brought him back to court early in 1469, just after his sixteenth birthday. The earliest surviving letter composed by Richard, Duke of Gloucester can be dated to 24 June 1469. It was written at Castle Rising in Norfolk, where Richard was on pilgrimage to Walsingham with his brother Edward IV. Richard, having left the tutelage of the Earl of Warwick, was now coming of age, emotionally and in his political judgement. He related that he had been given a position by the king in the north, and needed to travel there in some haste. He was short of money, and asked for a loan of £100, to be repaid next Easter. The main body of the letter had been dictated to a chancery clerk. But the post-script was in Richard's own hand, and in it, he spoke directly and commandingly to the recipient. 'Sir John Say,' he declared, 'I pray you that you fail me not at this time of my great need, as you will that I show you my good lordship in the matter that you labour me for.'

Putting it simply, Richard was making clear that if Say helped him, Richard would provide a favour in return, in a matter that Say had already petitioned him about. This was the principle of 'good lordship', a fact of aristocratic life in the fifteenth century. The authority of a nobleman depended upon his ability to protect his servants' interests, and be confident that these servants would help him in return. Support could take the form of a loan, or the performance of specific duties, alongside a more general desire to uphold the lord's interests. The letter showed that Richard already fully understood and had mastered these techniques. Over the next few years, he would put them to good effect, building up a powerful network of personal loyalty.

Soon afterwards shocking news arrived: Richard's former mentor, the Earl of Warwick, was now in open revolt against the king. Warwick's grievances against the Woodvilles could no longer be contained. According to the *Croyland Chronicler*, the reason for his rebellion was 'the fact that the king, being too greatly influenced by the urgent suggestions of the queen, as well as those who were in any way connected with her by blood, had enriched them with boundless presents and by always promoting them to the most dignified offices about his person.' Richard's older brother Clarence joined Warwick's cause, but Richard stayed loyal to Edward. On 26 July Warwick's followers defeated one of the king's leading Welsh supporters, William, Lord Herbert, at Edgecote, and shortly thereafter the king was captured. Yet Warwick was not able to dominate Edward in the way that Richard, Duke of York had manipulated Henry VI in 1460. Edward was released from Middleham in early September 1469, possibly after Richard's intervention.

Richard was rewarded for his loyalty with the important military office of Constable of England in October 1469. But the compromise brokered between the king and Warwick was an uneasy one, and by February 1470 both Warwick and Clarence were plotting again. In a remarkable sequence of events Edward first drove Warwick and Clarence out of the country, only to be faced – some six months later – by the most unlikely alliance of Warwick and the Lancastrian Queen Margaret of Anjou, arranged by the wily French king Louis XI. Edward IV underestimated the seriousness of this threat, and in October 1470 he and Richard were forced to flee, to Holland.

Warwick restored the Lancastrian king Henry VI, held prisoner in the Tower of London; Edward negotiated for enough military support from his brother-in-law Charles, Duke of Burgundy to regain the crown. In March 1471 his small fleet landed in Yorkshire, profiting from the neutrality of Henry Percy, whom Edward had restored to the earldom of Northumberland the previous year. Edward managed to move south unmolested and join forces with William, Lord Hastings in the Midlands. As Edward's support gathered momentum Clarence, sensing the tide was turning against Warwick, abandoned the earl and submitted to his brother.

On 14 April 1471 the armies of Edward and Warwick met at Barnet, a chaotic battle fought in a swirling mist, and Richard displayed great courage in the mêlée. He was slightly wounded in the combat; a number of his retainers were killed around him. Edward won the victory and Warwick was found slain on the battlefield. The king now turned his attention to the invading Lancastrian army of Margaret of Anjou, which had landed in the West Country. Showing great energy, the king pursued the Lancastrian forces and brought them to battle at Tewkesbury on 4 May. Richard was given the honour of commanding the vanguard, and he did so with distinction, repulsing an impetuous attack by Edmund, Duke of Somerset and throwing the whole Lancastrian line into chaos. The result was a decisive Yorkist victory, with Henry VI's son and heir, Edward, Prince of Wales, killed in the fighting.

Civil war was a harsh schooling ground, and Richard had acquitted himself well. As constable he now presided over the swift trial and execution of the Duke of Somerset – hauled out of sanctuary in Tewkesbury Abbey on Edward IV's orders on 6 May – and more controversially for his reputation was likely to have been in the Tower of London on the night of 21 May, when the victorious Yorkist army returned to the capital and when Henry VI was most probably murdered. Tudor sources made much of this, but there is no contemporary evidence that Richard was actually present when Henry VI died, and Edward IV was almost certainly responsible for ordering it.

As a child, Richard had witnessed terrible violence against his own mother; as a young adult, his character and personality had been forged during a shocking period of civil conflict. In the midst of it, Clarence had betrayed Edward IV's trust but Richard, to his great credit, had remained steadfastly loyal. The potent atmosphere of quarrels and intrigue, murders and executions, would have left a lasting impression on the adolescent duke. This was the environment in which Richard was introduced to political life.

Edward IV now chose to reward his most trusted supporters with positions of regional power within the realm. Richard's upbringing with the Earl of Warwick in the 1460s made him an obvious candidate to take over the earl's role as royal lieutenant in the north. In the months following Tewkesbury Richard acquired Warwick's office of chief steward of the northern parts of the Duchy of Lancaster and occupied forfeited Neville estates in Yorkshire and Cumbria. And to underline his position as Warwick's successor, Richard married one of the earl's daughters,

Anne Neville, shortly after Easter 1472. He was determined to secure his rightful share of Warwick's landed estate.

Clarence had already married Warwick's other daughter, Isabel Neville and the two brothers fought bitterly over the lucrative Neville inheritance. The *Croyland Chronicler* gave a vivid window on the opening of the dispute: 'A quarrel began during Michaelmas term 1472 between the king's two brothers that proved very difficult to settle . . . So much dissension arose between the brothers, and so many acute arguments were put forward, on either side, in the presence of the king, sitting in the council chamber, that all present, even lawyers, marvelled . . . Indeed, these three brothers, the king and the two dukes, possessed such outstanding talents that if they had been able to avoid discord, such a triple bond could only have been broken with the utmost difficulty.' Finally, in 1474, Edward IV brokered a settlement – one that denied the rightful claim of Warwick's nephew and nearest male heir, George Neville, Duke of Bedford, and also the rights of Warwick's widow, Anne Beauchamp, who was now treated by Edward's decree as if she were legally dead. Her rights now passed to her daughters, and thus to their husbands, Richard and Clarence.

However, there was a flaw in the Neville inheritance. Edward IV had inserted a clause in the act of settlement that allowed his brothers to enjoy the lands and pass them on to their male heirs only as long as Warwick's nephew, George Neville, Duke of Bedford or his successors were still alive. This stipulation did not pose a problem during the remainder of Edward's reign, but was dramatically thrust to the fore at the start of Richard's Protectorate in May 1483. In the meantime, Richard began to cultivate former Neville servants and create a powerful northern affinity.

Richard's actions were entirely typical of any great magnate of the fifteenth century. A lord of the realm would bind men to his cause, often retaining their loyalty through a carefully drawn up

contract, where an annual fee would be paid in return for speci-
fied acts of service. Richard built up a following in an area riven
with feuds and disorder, and showed considerable skill in doing
so. In a letter of his, written at Middleham on 19 October 1474,
he requested one follower, William FitzWilliam, to ride with
him to the king: 'Trusty and well beloved,' Richard began, 'we
greet you. And for as much as the king's grace, by his most hon-
ourable letters [drawn up] under his privy seal, has commanded
us in all goodly haste to come to his highness at London, we
therefore desire and pray you – all excuses laid apart [aside] – that
you ready yourself with eight horses to accompany us thither,
and that you meet us at Doncaster on the 25th day of this present
month. And that you fail us not thereof, as our faithful trust is in
you.'

Such a letter, with its commanding tone, followed the form
used by any great lord building up his influence. Richard had by
this time also secured the East Anglian estates of the Lancastrian
renegade John de Vere, Earl of Oxford and showed no qualms in
pressurizing the earl's elderly and infirm mother to hand over her
own lands as well. When the countess seemed reluctant to
comply, Richard threatened to take her on a winter journey
from London to his Yorkshire residence at Middleham, with
potentially lethal consequences. These charges against Richard's
conduct were made in a hostile Tudor parliament, and they
neglected to say that the duke eventually settled the issue through
legal process rather than physical force. But Richard could be
aggressive and intimidating in pursuit of what he regarded as his
rightful inheritance, and as he built up his power in the north
between 1473 and 1474 he clashed with other magnates, particularly the Earl of Northumberland and Lord Stanley, who resented
his intrusion into their own areas of interest.

However, these actions have to be placed in an overall context. These were turbulent and dangerous times, and many

aristocrats were utterly ruthless in building up power within the localities. The Stanley family stopped at nothing to further their hegemony in northern Lancashire, using their influence at court to gain possession of the heiresses to the Harrington estate, subsequently imprisoning them and marrying them against their will.

Richard was still only twenty-one at the time settlement was reached over the Neville estates. He could be impulsive and headstrong; but he was learning other skills, forging loyalty in an area of divided interests, sharing a deeply felt piety with his wife, Anne Neville, together becoming patrons of Queens' College, Cambridge, and setting up religious foundations at Middleham and Barnard Castle. His devotion to the memory of his father found concrete expression in July 1476, when he acted as principal mourner at the reburial of Richard, Duke of York whose remains were reverently carried from Pontefract to Fotheringhay.

As Richard and his fellow mourners processed towards Fotheringhay, York's martial prowess was remembered and honoured. York's epitaph, composed by the heralds, was given due prominence; it celebrated all his achievements and paid particular attention to one stirring feat of arms. At Pontoise, in 1441, the duke had come close to capturing the French monarch Charles VII in an audacious night-time raid. York was at this stage King Henry VI's representative in France and his royal lieutenant. In Charles, he had faced a rival to Henry's claim to rule over the country and he decided to confront his challenger personally. On 20 July 1441 York's forces, showing great daring, crossed the River Oise at night, surprised and routed the French troops guarding the crossing and closed in on the French king's residence. They were poised to capture Charles VII, who only escaped from their clutches by fleeing his dwelling with moments to spare, leaving a bed still warm when the English soldiers arrived. It was the exceptional bravery of one of the French king's followers, Guillaume du Chastel – who sacrificed his life to buy precious time for Charles's escape – that prevented York from achieving an astonishing success.

This was an action Richard sought to emulate. His book collection showed a very real piety, and also a fascination with the cult of chivalry. In one book, a collection of romances, Richard had written one of his mottoes, 'tant le desieree' ('I have longed for it so much'), at the bottom of the manuscript page of the story of Ipomedon, the 'best knight in the world'. There was a yearning here, a yearning for a noble cause, seen in Richard's opposition to the peace treaty with Louis XI at Picquigny in 1475, and his wish – alongside his brother Clarence – to support his sister Margaret, Dowager Duchess of Burgundy, with an army when her lands were threatened by the French king. But such aspirations came to nothing.

In the summer of 1477 Richard's brother Clarence was arrested and put on trial. According to Dominic Mancini, Richard believed the Woodvilles to be behind this, and feared he was also at risk. No contemporary source implicated him in his brother's arrest, and even Polydore Vergil (who claimed to have got his information from questioning Edward's surviving councillors) put the blame firmly on the king and did not mention Richard at all. It was only in Thomas More's account that Richard became involved. More reported the opinions of 'some wise men', that Richard was not dissatisfied with the arrest and subsequent execution of his difficult older brother, and may have welcomed it as removing one barrier between himself and the throne he was already planning to usurp. However, More did remain noticeably cautious, adding, 'of all this point there is no certainty, and whosoever divineth upon conjectures, may as well shoot too far as too short.' Later Tudor histories overrode such caution and by Shakespeare's time Richard was portrayed as the undoubted architect of Clarence's misfortune.

Mancini's contemporary account was very different, portraying Richard overcome with grief at his brother's death. It is true that Richard had benefited from a share of Clarence's lands, but this did not make him responsible for his overthrow. It is also said that the trial of Clarence could not have proceeded if Richard had stood by his brother and resolutely opposed it. Yet when both brothers had wanted to lead an army to the aid of their sister Margaret, Dowager Duchess of Burgundy in February 1477, the king, strongly influenced by the Woodvilles, had thwarted their demands.

Mancini clearly stated that the queen and her Woodville relatives were behind the fall of Clarence and Richard also felt he was in danger. This account is confirmed by important new evidence of Richard retaining a mass of supporters in the north, as if he were under threat of attack. In July 1477, within weeks of Clarence's arrest, Richard demanded that all the tenants of the bishopric of Durham – lands where he held a strong influence – swear an oath of loyalty to him and be prepared to fight on his behalf. It was a dramatic measure, one usually only undertaken at a time of war.

The archival discovery begins: 'At the court held in the month of July 1477 all the tenants subscribed to an oath – the tenor of which follows.' The oath is then given, to be sworn in English, with each man's hand placed upon the Bible as he repeats it: 'I become true servant to my lord of Gloucester and faithfully promise to be ready to do him service as well in time of war as in peace [as] next mine allegiance . . . at all times when I shall be required by the officers of the said duke . . . and with none other ride, nor go, nor do service. And truly behave me in all other things as a true servant ought to do to his lord, so help me God and holy doom and this book.'

The new Bishop of Durham, William Dudley, had already allowed Richard to tap the resources of the bishopric, appointing his men to important administrative posts within it, but this was a remarkable declaration of intent. Such force was not, in the event, needed, but when Clarence was executed on 18 February 1478 Richard swore that he would be avenged. And within three days of that execution he spoke in the preamble of his religious foundation at Middleham about the mutability of human fortunes, the unworthiness of the individual and the trials and tribulations that a man faced in the world. The phrases he used were more than conventional. 'Knoweth it have pleased Almighty God,' Richard wrote, 'to enable, enhance and exalt me.' Although only a younger son, he had been raised to great heights and honoured with great riches, and above all, at this time of peril, through God's favour 'had been delivered from all evil and hurt'.

In the last years of Edward IV's reign Richard came more rarely to court. He busied himself in the north. He had now achieved a good working relationship with the Earl of Northumberland, and the two respected each other's areas of influence. Richard had brought men from both the Neville and Percy affinities into his own service, healing the divisions between the two families that had plagued northern society for a generation. His councillors were fully employed as arbitrators in local disputes, and in one case, successfully resolved in April 1478, Richard expressed his desire to see 'good concord, rest and friendly unity' between the two parties, 'for the peace and weal [well-being] of the country in which they lived'.

Richard's concern for justice was now firmly established. In 1480 a humble peasant, John Randson of Burntoft in County Durham, appealed to him in a dispute with Sir Robert Claxton, one of the leading gentry of the region. Randson complained that he was being prevented from working his land. Claxton was the father of one of Richard's retainers and the father-in-law of another. Yet after investigating the dispute, Richard did not hesitate to intervene on behalf of the lesser man, warning Claxton 'so to demean you that we have no cause to provide his lawful remedy in this behalf'. Most lords would have supported the interests of their retainers; Richard's impartiality and sense of fairness won him the respect of northern society.

That respect was cemented by his military leadership. 'Such was his renown in war,' Mancini said, 'that all difficult tasks were entrusted to him.' Richard's greatest martial opportunity lay not in a war with France but with border warfare against Scotland. He took the initiative against the Scots, leading vigorous raids into their territory in 1480 and 1481. And here, in the summer of 1482, he achieved his greatest success, leading an army into Edinburgh and also restoring the town of Berwick to English rule.

The recapture of Berwick was a triumph that won fulsome praise from Edward IV. On 25 August 1482 Edward wrote happily to Pope Sixtus IV: 'Thank God, the giver of all good gifts, for the support received from our most loving brother, whose success is so proven that he alone would suffice to chastise the whole kingdom of Scotland.' The *Croyland Chronicler*, perhaps reflecting the views of the Woodville faction at court, commented disapprovingly that the campaign had used up much money and achieved little, but few agreed with such sentiments. William, Lord Hastings and the Calais garrison fired their guns in celebration on hearing that Richard had reached Edinburgh. London merchant George Cely wrote appreciatively of the many Scottish towns and villages taken. And the recapture of Berwick delighted the country. 'I was a captain ere Berwick was won' became a popular saying – even finding its way into an Eton school book. Richard conducted the campaign with skill, co-operating well with the Earl of Northumberland and showing good political judgement as well as military ability.

There was a telling moment towards its end. The Scottish

Duke of Albany, whom the English had supported as a challenger to the Scottish king, James III, came to terms with James's regime, and began organizing an army for the relief of Berwick, whose castle was still holding out against an English besieging force. Richard challenged him and Albany dissimulated, saying it was only a ploy to satisfy the Scottish council. Richard was unconvinced, and his response was as direct as Albany's was duplicitous. He declared forcefully that if Albany opposed him at Berwick, 'he would defend the besiegers or die in the attempt.' Albany backed down.

Victory in the war against Scotland sealed Richard's reputation in the north. He was given the wardenship of the West March for life. His achievement was further rewarded by the creation for him in February 1483 of a county palatine, an area that Richard would have governed with special authority and autonomy from the rest of the country. This comprised Cumberland and a large stretch of south-west Scotland, which it was his declared intention to conquer. By such means, Mancini related, Richard put as large a distance as possible between himself and the queen and her family.

But beneath the joy Edward IV was presiding over a dangerously fractured realm. When the king was no longer there to hold its pieces together, it would split asunder.

5

The Discovery of the Church
and the Location of the Nave

Day Three

Monday, 27 August 2012

I LEAVE MY apartment and cross town to get settled into the Belmont Hotel, the base booked by the production company and where I'll be staying for the rest of the dig with the DSP film crew. By the time I arrive at the Social Services car park, it's mid-morning. The excavator is quiet and there's no driver. Mathew Morris and the team got Trench Two dug out yesterday so Stevie's not needed. We're right on schedule.

The northern end of Trench One, where the remains were uncovered, has no medieval archaeology whatsoever. Richard Buckley, who has arrived to investigate, believes there could be any number of reasons for this; it's all guesswork at this stage. Most likely, there is simply no medieval archaeology in this part of the site. Or, when the Victorians built their outhouse, as shown by the goad maps, they destroyed the medieval archaeology and just threw it all away. Or, the Church of the Greyfriars is on the south side of the car park.

My heart lurches. If the church is on the south side it's game over. With so much development there, Richard's grave would be under one of the buildings, lost for ever. Richard Buckley, seeing my concern, gives me a shoulder hug. 'It's only day three,

Philippa – and only day one of the real archaeology. There's a long way to go yet.'

We discuss the coming two-week project and agree that on Friday, 31 August, at the end of the first week, we'll have an on-site meeting to assess progress and consider the siting of Trench Three for the final week's investigation. Trench Three is to be dug either at the northern end of the site, in the former grammar school car park, or at the southern end, across the main parking area in the Social Services car park.

The weather is fine again with no rain. Trench Two is show-ing what looks like an existing medieval wall and a medieval robbed-out wall, running north–south. There also appears to be a mortared floor in the centre. It's encouraging, Buckley explains, to have medieval deposits poking through already and he is par-ticularly pleased with progress in Trench Two. He shows me how the team are cleaning the site and removing the debris to reveal what is beneath. This is all fine, but I can't stop wandering over to the northern end of Trench One. Staring at the gouged-out earth, I'm willing something to appear. I feel that if I gaze at it long enough it will give up its secrets and make the Victorian installation disappear. 'Ruddy Victorians,' I mutter. Clearly, I would never have made an archaeologist. As I watch the team at work I'm in awe of their professionalism; how each scrap of earth is important; how each tiny piece of whatever they find may lead them to uncover the facts about an entire site and understand its purpose.

In Trench Two archaeologist Pauline Carroll is on her hands and knees, cleaning the central area with her trowel. In a few short hours, with much of the loose debris removed, her work reveals a good deal of the mortared floor as well as some interest-ing anomalies within the trench. A smiling Richard Buckley, happy with progress, leaves to enjoy what is left of the bank holi-day. His team, under the careful guidance of Mathew Morris, continue with the uncovering work. Tomorrow the Social Services offices will be open again, meaning the site will be busy, children in care will be brought in, and the public might wander in through the open gates. I look at the tarpaulin on the Heras fencing. It covers some of the main parts of the site, but not others. I ask Morris if this can be improved upon and we decide to put up some more. Knowing that we've already uncovered remains, it's best to be cautious.

In Trench One, archaeologists Tony Gnanaratnam and Tom Hoyle are clearing out the southern side. This trench still has more debris to give up, rocks and boulders which will involve heavy labour, but they are now on their hands and knees doing some trowel work. Then I notice archaeologist Jon Coward at the northern end of Trench One, rubbing his chin and staring at one particular spot. I'm with him in a heartbeat. He points to a great mound of what looks like medieval stone and rubble, which he reckons has been in-filled at a later date and could be a well or just a 'ruddy great hole', but thinks it should be checked out. Something is nagging at him. It's the voids: the spaces between the rocks. I jump in to get a closer look and see the deep, dark gaps between the yellowy rocks. He explains that he needs to see what's below. It looks like a really big job, because some of the boulders are huge. I say that it would be really useful if we could find out more about the northern end because of what the Victorians have done to obliterate it. Coward's outer shirt is off as he begins heaving the great boulders out of the way. I can't help but smile, and thank him. Someone is investigating the northern end of Trench One!

Day Four

Tuesday, 28 August 2012

After breakfast at the Belmont Hotel with the DSP team we're on site by 7.45 a.m. This will become our daily routine for the dig, which is feeling more and more like *Groundhog Day*, the film in which the same day is constantly repeated and which became a running joke among us. I didn't help by always eating the same breakfast. The social workers are heading to work, threading their way through the car park and asking if we've found him yet. Ricardians Dr John Ashdown-Hill and Annette Carson have completed their filmed interviews at the dig for the documentary and have headed back home. They'll return at the end of the two-week project. It's odd not having them here and I feel strangely isolated.

Archaeologist Martyn Henson is working in Trench Two. Here smaller debris is still being removed in many areas but it looks like there is a clear robbed-out wall running north–south at the northern end and an existing wall running north–south at the southern end. Between the walls, the exposed mortar flooring is showing signs of diagonally laid square tiles. Their imprint has formed a diamond pattern, almost Jacquard in nature, and quite stunning. Pieces of broken local medieval stone tiling and common green ware pottery have been found in the spoil heaps so it seems we are at the medieval level across the site. A shout goes up. In the rubble layer of Trench Two, Senior Supervisor Leon Hunt has found the most beautiful half tile, in almost pristine condition. He and Morris believe the exquisite outline, which shows the feet of a bird, might be the eagle design from the Wessex style of tile, a well-known medieval pattern, probably made locally. Also, poking through in the central area of Trench Two, and within the mortared flooring, is a strange anomaly. It looks to me like the top of a medieval tomb as its top is rounded, smooth like alabaster. Morris doesn't think this is likely but as it is cleaned its smoothness becomes more apparent, as does its depth.

In Trench One, Tony Gnanaratnam is uncovering more of the strange low stone wall without any foundations that was found on day two and is perplexing Richard Buckley. It seems to have a flat top with a curving lip structure over one side. Buckley thinks it could be a bench and wonders what this may tell us about the site, and where we are. He appears to be convinced we're in the Greyfriars precinct. Gnanaratnam has also uncovered what looks to be a robbed-out wall running east–west that might connect with the northernmost end of Trench Two.

At 4 p.m. we pack up and head back to the hotel. It's been a good day. We've discovered medieval walls and tiles, and it seems that we are indeed somewhere in the Greyfriars precinct.

Day Five

Wednesday, 29 August 2012

It's raining, pouring down. We do what little we can but by 11 a.m. with the forecast showing no sign of any let-up, it's confirmed: rain has stopped play. I'm concerned about the time (and money) we're losing but site director Mathew Morris is reassuring. He reckons we'll be able to make it up in the coming days when the weather is expected to be much drier, and he can always draft in extra help to get us back on track if need be.

Happy with that, I meet up for lunch at Piero's with Sue Wells, joint secretary of the Richard III Society, and Sally Henshaw, secretary of the local Leicestershire Branch. We discuss King Richard's banner and standard currently being designed by the College of Arms in London, which will be presented to Leicester Cathedral by the Richard III Society to mark the search for King Richard. If Richard is found, it is hoped the flags will hang above his tomb.

Day Six

Thursday, 30 August 2012

It's 8 a.m. and Ricardian Karen Ladniuk, a lawyer from Brazil who donated to the International Appeal that saved the dig, has flown in. Under the supervision of archaeologists Heidi Addison and Pauline Houghton, she'll help clean Trench Two. Ladniuk is thrilled and within half an hour her keen eyes spot a tiny silver Roman coin.

By the end of the morning, Trench Two is cleaned and revealing much more information. By chance, the trench has been dug along what could be a long north–south corridor. After measuring the small (two-metre) space between its outer edges, Buckley thinks it may be one of the friary's cloister walks. If so, he's not sure whether it's on the western or eastern side of the square courtyard or 'cloister garth' it would have bordered. Moreover, it's still unclear where the Greyfriars Church might be located in relation to it as, lacking any uniform pattern, medieval churches could be sited to the south or north of the cloister.

The smooth anomaly in the central area of Trench Two, which I hoped could be a tomb top, appears to be a stone step, its roundness, the archaeologists are hypothesizing, intended to prevent the barefooted friars from stubbing their toes. It makes a lovely story. It's strangely compelling to touch something that may have been trodden on in Richard's day. None of the team has ever come across a step like this before, so we decide to christen it the Leicester Step.

At the southern end of Trench Two the medieval wall has

survived there partially intact above floor level, another rare discovery in Leicester, I'm told. I ask Buckley about it but he's at a
loss to explain why this wall hasn't been robbed. He then shows
me what looks like the remains of a doorway that leads through
it from west to east. Slowly but surely Greyfriars is coming to life.

In Trench One it looks as if our strange wall without a foundation is a bench built up against a (robbed) wall, which could
have been inside a room. By lunchtime careful key-hole investigation of the robbed wall has found a second, similar bench, with
evidence of floor tiling between them. These parallel benches are
a major breakthrough, giving Richard Buckley and his team an
important clue as to which part of the friary has been found. The
benches suggest a place where people could have sat and talked,
which Morris explains in a medieval friary would have been
the chapter house. As the chapter house is normally built off the
eastern side of a square cloister, this would make the corridor
joining it, over in the northern end of Trench Two, the eastern
cloister walk. To confirm this, the team will need to expose
more of the southern end of Trench One to see if it reveals
another east–west robbed-out wall, running parallel to the more
northern one. They will also have to extend the northern end of
Trench Two slightly to see if this more northern wall does travel
east–west and intersect the trench at this point.

To the north of the chapter house, the ground in the northern
end of Trench One is too disturbed for any guesswork as to
which side the church might be on, with this area, potentially,
outside the friary buildings. I wander back to see Jon Coward in
the northern end of Trench One for the millionth time. It's hot,
thirsty work and he's got some way to go to clear the large quantities of heavy rubble. Having looked again at the maps of the
area, Richard Buckley has confirmed that the coal cellars built
here by the Victorians for their outhouse are making it nigh on
impossible to interpret the archaeology. It also doesn't help that

a later garage, with a possible inspection pit, had been built here in the 1930s, its massive concrete walls still visible, and immovable.

Stopping for a moment to take a drink, Jon Coward tells me that he's found something, and points to a small area in Trench One directly behind where he is working. I can see a short red-bricked Victorian wall, forming a small square area. 'Smell it,' he says. I jump down into the trench and take a good sniff. It's a bit pungent. 'A Victorian lavatory,' he says, and shows me where its doorway would have been. I'm shocked that we can still smell it. He laughs and says if we dig down we'll probably find what's causing it! I make a face and try to make light of it but, climbing out of the trench, it cuts me to the core. As I watch Coward back at work, I look at the Victorian lavatory. It's directly over a wall, and only inches from the human remains, the lower leg bones, discovered on the first day of the dig. A final resting-place next to a leaking Victorian lavatory is not fit for anybody, never mind a king.

Tony Gnanaratnam is continuing his trowel work in the southern end of Trench One and shows me his latest find, a beautiful piece of stained-glass window. I ask if we can be sure it's medieval. It will have to be properly cleaned but Gnanaratnam, one of the most experienced archaeologists on site, thinks it looks like it. In no time the find has drawn a crowd of archaeologists. Stained glass means a high-status building, which could be the Greyfriars Church. Jon Coward also has a new find. In the rubble he's been clearing he has uncovered a carved masonry mullion, with a slot. Richard Buckley and Mathew Morris explain that the slot would have held the lead, which would have held the window, perhaps of stained glass. There's a tangible feeling of excitement as the team heads back to work and I wonder what else Trench One might reveal. I don't have long to wait.

In the afternoon Jon Coward's work on the massive rubble

heap with voids is just about done. Beneath the rubble is a massive robbed-out wall, its shadow an enormous dark stain in the ground. It seems about 1.5 metres thick. I look at Mathew Morris. 'It's big enough,' he says. 'It could be the southern wall of the church.' Jon Coward is smiling, the sweat dripping off him, and I hug him. Richard Buckley checks the area and instructs Coward to clean it up as much as possible. He too is smiling.

'It might be the church,' he says. 'Let's see what tomorrow brings.'

At 4 p.m. we down tools, and I tell the DSP team that I'll walk back today instead of taking a lift in their vehicle. I want time to think. As I head to the hotel through the New Walk, a beautiful tree-lined Georgian avenue that bisects Leicester's city centre streets, for the first time I'm happy in the knowledge that the search for Richard was the right thing to do. And I know that whether it is him, or someone else, we can't leave the remains where they are.

Day Seven

Friday, 31 August 2012

I arrive to see a truck at the northern end of the car park preparing to remove some of the modern infill to give us more room and help safety on site. I check the area where the bones are, as I do every morning. And I'm shocked. The ground has been disturbed, someone's been poking about. Security personnel Ken John and Luke Thompson check the CCTV. The only way in is over the high Victorian red-brick wall of the former grammar school, which is currently empty. The Social Services car park is locked each night. It doesn't look like anything has been taken as the plastic sheeting covering the bones is still in place, but someone's been looking. Has word got out?

It turns out there's nothing on the CCTV except pigeons, but two or three of the big blocks of brick near the bones have been dislodged. A pigeon couldn't do that. As we try to figure it out, one of the truck drivers comes over to say that earlier, he'd jumped into the trench and accidentally dislodged some of the stones there. I hope he hasn't damaged anything. Although a relief, it's a stern reminder to bring in the night security I'd budgeted for. Thompson tells me that rumours about bones being discovered are already doing the rounds of the social workers. The last thing we need is this news getting out.

Jon Coward is in the northern end of Trench One continuing his cleaning work. Tony Gnanaratnam is mapping out the southern end, recording all measurements and dimensions. He'll then move into Trench Two and do the same there. These measurements will give Richard Buckley and his team a much better understanding of the buildings and spaces we're looking at. I'm about to wander over to Trench Two when Gnanaratnam shows me what's been found in the southern end of Trench One. When he was clearing the last of the rubble to try to locate a possible southern east–west robbed wall, he uncovered further pieces of window tracery. They're stunning, almost intact. Mathew Morris confirms they're medieval, and could be from the church. But there's more: archaeologist Pauline Houghton has also found a medieval roof tile with a ridge crest. It's damaged but still glazed, further denoting a high-status building, and its close proximity.

Richard Buckley is due for our on-site meeting, and I'm pacing up and down. We might have found a church wall, stained glass, window tracery and a glazed roof tile, which means the remains uncovered on the first day might be situated in the church itself. Buckley arrives, checks the finds, and we agree to dig Trench Three in the north of the site, in the former grammar school car park, directly adjacent to and east of Trench One. In a confined space, this trench will be twenty-five metres long. If Jon Coward's wall is the only indication we have of the Greyfriars Church, then Trench Three will test if the massive robbed-out wall from Trench One can be picked up at the new position. Buckley tells me to keep my fingers crossed and hope for a positive result. We have one week left to dig.

He asks what I want to do with the human remains found on the first day of the dig as, without any archaeological evidence to give them some context, they are of no interest to him. He doesn't know if they are a burial, but thinks their position could be in the nave and could belong to a friar. Buckley knows what my response will be and smiles, and as expected I say that I want the remains in Trench One exhumed. They're beside my letter 'R'. Buckley wants to wait and carry out some possible exhumations, should we find any more remains, in the former grammar school area to the east so asks if I have the funds to cover this one. I have nearly £800 left from the International Appeal, and ask if that will be enough. 'More than enough,' he says, and it's agreed. Buckley will apply for the Exhumation Licence as soon as he's back at his office. It's a weekend so it won't come through until Monday, 3 September. The excavator will then dig out a western slot over the remains both to see whether they are a complete burial and to aid the exhumation.

I ask about Harriet Jacklyn, the osteologist, who has been ill and is unavailable for the project. A replacement has been appointed and, although not quite as experienced as Jacklyn, is certainly up to the job. I suggest calling in a metal detector expert and Buckley agrees to contact Ken Wallace, a reliable and experienced professional.

We head over to Leicester's Guildhall, a magnificent fourteenth-century timber-framed building where Richard Taylor from the university has called a press conference at 11 a.m. to update the media on the dig's progress. Assistant City

Mayor Piara Singh Clair will speak on behalf of LCC, and is delighted to hear the positive results from the dig so far.

In the afternoon, Richard Buckley calls from his office to say he needs to amend our agreement to allow DSP to film the human remains. The original agreement allowed for specific photography but not filming. They, and Carl Vivian, have already filmed the lower leg bones, but I'm aware that a potential full set of human remains is a different matter to individual bones. Filming will be needed for the historic record. Reminding myself of the conditions in place to protect the remains from general circulation if they are those of Richard III – an identifiable individual – I agree to the change and ask Buckley to confirm that nothing else in my agreement is to be altered, which he does. The change allows the filming of human remains on dedicated memory cards that will be kept securely by ULAS.

Later that day, Trench Three in the former grammar school car park is outlined with yellow spray paint by Leon Hunt and Mathew Morris. It is then buzz-sawed ready for machining first thing next morning, when Stevie, the excavator driver, will be back.

Day Eight

Saturday, 1 September 2012

It's 8 a.m. and I meet archaeologist Steve Baker, our site supervisor for the weekend work. Baker guides the excavator and Stevie, its driver, out on to a quiet St Martins and into the former grammar school car park. The final twenty-five-metre-long Trench Three is machined in the north of the site, immediately adjacent to, and east of, the Social Services car park – and Trench One. At the medieval level in the centre of the trench, large areas of mortared flooring are appearing, along with possible grave cuts. These are excavations made in the earth to bury a body or coffin and generally have straight edges. There is also an area of paving with medieval floor tiles in the south of the trench.

Excitingly, it looks as though there is a continuation of the massive east–west robbed-out wall from Trench One together with an equally large northern one, running parallel. Could this really be the Church of the Greyfriars?

Day Nine

Sunday, 2 September 2012

The cleaning of Trench Three reveals two grave cuts in the large central mortared floor area. It also looks as if the large robbed-out wall to the north had a buttress on its northern edge, facing on to St Martins. The estimated width between the two great parallel robbed-out walls is 7.5 metres which is, Richard Buckley informs me, consistent with priory churches (the exact width turned out to be 7.4 metres).

Everyone is getting really excited about Trench Three. Buckley and Morris believe we're in the east end of the Greyfriars Church, but are not exactly sure where yet, although the grave cuts are highly suggestive. We might be near the altar or choir, which means that the human remains found on the first day would be in the nave of the church.

Day Ten

Monday, 3 September 2012

Richard Buckley wants to find out more about what they are uncovering in Trench Three. It looks like the mortared floor in the central area is much higher than the surround. At this stage, however, he won't be drawn on what it might be, but he's very keyed up. The others are much happier to speculate though. Could it be the choir of the church and the location of the burial of Richard III? Quantities of inlaid medieval floor tile have also come from the new trench. To the south, and outwith the church building, there is now a definite area of random paving using medieval floor tiles of different sizes that may have been robbed from the friary buildings and re-laid at a later date. Buckley speculates that this might be paving from Robert Herrick's garden.

With the grave cuts and robbed-out walls being on the right orientation (east–west), and with associated building materials consistent with a medieval religious house, Buckley is as sure as he can be that we have found the Church of the Greyfriars. At an on-site meeting with Sarah Levitt from LCC, he says he wants to dig an additional (fourth) trench in the Social Services car park to pick up the west end of the church (or at least confirm whether it carries on into New Street), and expand Trench Three in the hope of revealing more of the interior of the church and the burials it contains.

With more difficulties, and costs, arising from a fourth trench in the Social Services car park, it's decided instead to expand Trench Three using the contingency fund available within the original budget. Two central slots – east and west – will be cut into Trench Three starting tomorrow. Both slots will be large enough to reveal a significant portion of the archaeology without hitting services or undermining the nearby dividing wall between the car parks, or the former grammar school building.

News of the discovery of the Greyfriars Church is passed to Leicester's mayor, Sir Peter Soulsby, who immediately authorizes a third week for the dig. The extra week will be paid for by LCC with help from the university. The Exhumation Licence has now come through from the Ministry of Justice, made out to ULAS as the archaeological contractor. Jo Appleby, lecturer in bio-archaeology at the university and our osteologist, is unavailable today so it's agreed that the exhumation in Trench One will start tomorrow morning when she's back. Turi King, also a trained archaeologist, will assist.

I can't quite believe that we may have found Herrick's garden. I feel the need to get involved and help with some of the cleaning work under the guidance of archaeologist Neil Jefferson. At the southernmost end of Trench Three it looks like the pattern of the tiling is heading in a circular direction. Could this be the central area that held Herrick's 'handsome stone pillar', the last known marker of King Richard's grave? If so, what does it tell us about the remains in Trench One? They could be too far away from here to be those of King Richard. Or, as Herrick's central area is situated outside the church, did he get the location of Richard's grave wrong? Tomorrow's exhumation might hold some clues.

6

Seizing the Throne

ON 9 APRIL 1483 King Edward IV passed away. This monarch, who had begun his reign in the spring of 1461 with so much heady optimism, had died unnaturally early, at the age of forty. He left a court dangerously divided and the king's personal charm – which had kept many of these tensions at bay – could now no longer be exercised. And he had left no clear provision for the government of the country until his oldest son and heir Edward V, twelve at the time of his death, came of age. This uncertainty, and the hatred or deep suspicion that still existed among the aristocracy of the realm about the family of his queen, Elizabeth Woodville, was a ticking time bomb that would blow up with terrible force, leaving carnage in its wake.

The sequence of events that followed has normally been told with Richard, Duke of Gloucester as the villain, usurping power not rightfully his by a series of strikes against an unsuspecting political community. The reality was rather more complex. When Edward IV died there were three power bases in the country. The first lay in London, where the king's court had assembled, government was carried out, and the council was now ruling the country on behalf of the twelve-year-old Edward V. The second was in Ludlow, on the Welsh Marches, where Edward V was actually staying, nominally head of the king's council for Wales, although affairs were in fact directed by the queen's brother, Anthony, Earl Rivers. And the third was in the north, at York, where Richard, Duke of Gloucester was to travel from his residence at Middleham to receive oaths of loyalty from the northern community to the new king.

The queen and those members of her family in London held the advantage. They were at the centre of government, and they were first to be informed of the king's death, although rumours of his serious illness had been spreading earlier, and they took immediate action to enable their own faction to gain control as rapidly as possible. Their measures were principally directed against the young king's uncle, Richard, Duke of Gloucester.

On 11 April, two days after the king's death, the council met. From the testimony provided by Dominic Mancini, who was in London at the time of these events, we learn that shortly before his death Edward IV had added a codicil to his will naming his brother Richard Protector of the Realm, and giving him control of the kingdom until the coronation of Edward V took place. The Woodvilles now concentrated all their efforts on overturning this provision.

Their immediate intention soon became clear: to disregard the late king's wishes, ignore Richard's appointment as Protector and instead take political control themselves. Their plan was simple: to bring the young king to London at the head of a large army, rush forward the coronation to the beginning of May, and then, with the king crowned, and holding all offices of government and with an army at their back, rule the country as they pleased with the young king as their figurehead. This scenario could not have been more threatening to Richard.

A series of stormy meetings took place, against the backdrop of the continuing arrangements for Edward IV's funeral. The Woodvilles took prompt steps to strengthen their position. Another of the queen's brothers, Sir Edward Woodville, was put in charge of the fleet. The late king's treasure was quickly divided between the queen, Sir Edward, and her eldest son by her first marriage, Thomas, Marquis of Dorset. Dominic Mancini's account – our most important contemporary source – is clear that the council, dominated by the Woodvilles, embarked upon this course because they did not want political power to pass to Richard. Their raid on the late king's treasure – and for Mancini this was tantamount to theft – was confirmed by an extant financial memorandum dating from this time, which showed the remaining financial reserve dispersed among the queen's kin. Its consequence was a sudden and dangerous shift in the balance of power in the kingdom. 'We are so important,' said the Marquis of Dorset, 'that even without the king's uncle [Richard] we can make and enforce our own decisions.'

News of Edward IV's death reached Ludlow on 14 April. Anthony, Earl Rivers, the guardian of the young king, had already put in hand dispositions to recruit a substantial force to accompany Edward V to London. In March, he had sent instructions to his business agent in London, Andrew Dymmock, who was to send him copies of the royal letters patent that enlarged his political powers in Wales and gave him authority to muster troops. The Woodvilles intended to raise a large army, and only the determined resistance of the late king's chamberlain, William, Lord Hastings, who opposed their plan in council, briefly restrained their ambitions. Hastings took the extraordinary step of threatening to retire to Calais and mobilize the garrison there on his own behalf, if his wishes were not met. As a result this force was limited to 2,000 men. It was still a considerable body and Hastings was powerless to prevent the coronation being moved forward to 4 May. The Woodvilles intended to crown Edward V as soon as he reached London, and seemed on the verge of achieving a coup, one that would leave them in command of the country.

Richard heard of Edward's death a day later, on 15 April. At the same time, or shortly afterwards, he received a letter from

William, Lord Hastings informing him of what was taking place in London. It is likely that Hastings warned him of the unbridled ambition of the Woodvilles, and he may even have suggested that Richard try to seize control of Edward V before the young king reached London. However, with the Woodvilles already mobilizing armed support for their cause, this was not an easy course to pursue.

Faced with this dangerous situation, and careful not to be wrong-footed by these rapidly moving events, Richard acted correctly. He informed the queen of his support for the regime and that he would come to London to offer his loyalty to the new king.

On 19 April Edward IV was solemnly buried at Windsor. On that day, with remarkable prescience, John Gigur, the warden of Tattershall College in Lincolnshire, wrote to William Waynflete, Bishop of Winchester: 'Now our sovereign lord king is dead – whose soul Jesus take in his great mercy – we do not know who shall be our lord and who shall rule over us.' The Woodvilles were doing their best to resolve Gigur's uncertainty. The following day a council meeting was held where, according to the *Croyland Chronicler*, 'the most urgent desire of all present was that the Prince should succeed his father in all his glory.' In fact, the council was dangerously divided, with a small but important group, clustered around the figure of William, Lord Hastings, strongly opposed to what the queen's family was doing.

On 21 April Richard held a remembrance service for his brother at York and had all the nobility of the region swear an oath of loyalty to the young king. Richard wrote to Anthony, Earl Rivers, suggesting that they rendezvous on the journey south. This proposed meeting carried an undercurrent of menace. Richard was all too aware that two previous Dukes of Gloucester who had aspired to the Protectorate, Thomas of Woodstock in the fourteenth century and Humphrey, Duke of Gloucester, uncle of Henry VI, in the mid-fifteenth, had died violently or suddenly. Woodstock was murdered – probably on the orders of Richard II – in 1397; Humphrey had died in suspicious circumstances in 1447. The Woodvilles held the political and military initiative, and their forces would considerably outnumber Richard's own personal retinue.

This was a threatening scenario, but Richard's reaction to it was restrained. He had limited his retinue to 300 men, although he could certainly have recruited more. In September 1450 his father, Richard, Duke of York, had also restricted his retinue to around 300 men on his return from Ireland to demonstrate his continued loyalty to the Lancastrian King Henry VI. And Richard and his entourage were still in mourning for his brother, Edward IV.

If events were to change, Richard had a vital factor working in his favour: his courage and proven experience in war. In contrast, it was rumoured that the outwardly affable and cultivated Rivers, who enjoyed the panoply of the joust and tournament, was – in a moment of crisis – in fact a coward. In 1471 Edward IV had responded to Rivers's request to go abroad on pilgrimage with the dismissive remark that it was entirely typical of him, with the country in a state of turmoil, to try to absent himself as quickly as possible. Five years later, in 1476, it was Charles the Bold, Duke of Burgundy, who was to make a similar observation. Rivers had arrived at Duke Charles's court full of grand gestures. He first offered his services to the duke for his forthcoming campaign, but when told that the enemy army was rapidly approaching had a sudden change of heart, and abruptly made his excuses and rode off at speed. Duke Charles bluntly told the Milanese ambassador that Rivers had left 'because he is afraid'.

Richard knew that he was outnumbered by the Woodville forces, but would have trusted in the excellence of the 300 or so men in his personal retinue. His northern followers were tough, experienced in war and resolutely loyal. Richard had fought with these men on the Scottish border and knew their quality. And it was quality not quantity that would count in any confrontation with Earl Rivers. As one astute contemporary writer – known as Gregory's Chronicler – had observed, the outcome of a clash of arms was not determined by the number of troops in the engagement, but the prowess of the 'fee'd men', those men retained by fee to follow their lord. Richard had retained a strong following among the men of the north and he was confident of the mettle of his supporters.

On 24 April Rivers and Edward V left Ludlow for the Midlands and then for London, and Richard departed from York for Nottingham. Richard desperately needed allies and he had now made contact with another leading magnate isolated from the court and suspicious of the Woodvilles, Henry, Duke of Buckingham. Buckingham had been staying on his Welsh estates at Brecon when news reached him of Edward IV's death and he was now also heading towards the Midlands. Rivers had suggested that they should all meet at Northampton on 29 April, allowing them the chance to progress to London together. It was – outwardly at least – a well-intentioned and conciliatory gesture. But whether his real motives were as accommodating remained to be seen.

On 29 April the Woodville fleet suddenly and hurriedly put to sea, with the 2,000 men retained by Sir Edward Woodville now reinforced by a further 1,000 troops gathered by the Marquis of Dorset. The remains of the royal treasure was loaded on board and taken with them. Later that same day, the royal party accompanying Edward V moved through Northampton and on to Stony Stratford, a further thirteen miles away. Rivers then returned to Northampton to meet Richard and Buckingham, taking his retainers with him, but leaving the king and his entourage at a safe distance.

What now transpired can be interpreted in two very different ways. The commonly held view, elaborated on in later Tudor sources but also found in the contemporary account of Mancini, saw Rivers as an innocent victim.

In this version of events, Edward V asked Rivers to go and greet Richard, and pay his respects. The earl may have wanted to convince Richard that the council's plans were in the best interests of the country. But Rivers was adopting a conciliatory approach, although he ordered the young king to continue his journey to London the next morning, with or without him. Rivers then travelled back to Northampton, explaining to Richard, who had lodged in an inn there, that the reason for Edward V's unexpected departure was a lack of suitable accommodation. Rivers's own retainers were nevertheless posted in Northampton and all the villages around it.

Richard apparently accepted this situation with equanimity, inviting Rivers to dine with him that evening. Richard and Rivers began dinner, and the Duke of Buckingham arrived later. According to Sir Thomas More, 'there was made that night much friendly cheer between the two dukes [Richard and Buckingham] and Earl Rivers.' Seeing nothing amiss, Rivers was lulled into a false sense of security, and retired for the night at a neighbouring inn in good spirits. The following morning he found himself under arrest. Richard and Buckingham then hastened to Stony Stratford, seized other Woodville supporters of the young king – Rivers's nephew Sir Thomas Grey and the king's chamberlain Sir Thomas Vaughan – dismissed the majority of Edward V's followers and replaced his entourage with their own supporters. The young king's protests were roundly dismissed, and he was escorted to London under Richard's watchful guard.

Edward V's brave complaint against the arrest of members of the Woodville family he had grown up with, and clearly trusted, was recorded by Mancini, and was almost certainly based on eyewitness testimony. Richard, while showing all due deference to the king in person, was brusque in his response: Rivers had made an attempt against himself and Buckingham, and was now paying the consequences for it. The king should properly be surrounded by those of the old blood of the realm, not by new and dangerous upstarts, a slighting reference to the Woodville family's pretensions.

Knowing the course of historical events over the next two months, it is easy to see this as an excuse or a pretext to take control of the king's person, a control that Richard would never subsequently relinquish.

But Richard's justification may have been based on the true course of events. If Rivers was unsuspecting and well-meaning, and had blundered into a trap, it is hard to see why he had been vigorously recruiting a substantial army to escort Edward V to London. It is entirely plausible that this armed force had in fact been deployed to confront Richard and Buckingham, possibly with the intention of arresting the two dukes or even ambushing them, and this was the real motive for first moving Edward V a safe distance away, to Stony Stratford. If this was indeed Rivers's intention, Richard may have learned of it, and struck first.

This was certainly what Richard claimed when reporting his action to Edward V, saying that he had heard about the ambush from an informer in Rivers's camp. An echo of such a scenario can be found in events some twenty-three years earlier, at the beginning of the Wars of the Roses. In January 1460 the Lancastrian regime of Henry VI had ordered Rivers (then more modestly titled as Sir Anthony Woodville) and his father to Calais to arrest and imprison those Yorkist lords sheltering there, the Earls of Warwick and Salisbury, and Richard's oldest brother Edward, Earl of March (the future Edward IV). Learning of this, the Yorkists had struck first, launching a daring attack on the

Woodville forces still assembling at Sandwich, and dispersing them before they were able to put this plan into effect. Both the Woodvilles were seized and taken back to Calais, where they were berated in front of the garrison soldiers for their upstart pretensions in attempting to arrest those of far greater aristocratic lineage and nobility of blood than themselves.

A contemporary chronicler vividly described the scene, in the great hall of Calais Castle, as the Woodville father and son were hauled in under the cover of darkness:

> My lord Rivers was brought to Calais, and before the lords with eight score torches, and there my lord of Salisbury rated [insulted] him, calling him a knave's son that he should be so rude as to call him and these other lords traitors, for they shall be found the King's true liegemen when he should be found a traitor. And my lord of Warwick rated him and said that his father was but a squire . . . and was only by marriage made himself a lord, and it was not his part to have such language of lord's being of the King's blood. And my lord of March rated him in likewise.

Social standing, nobility of blood and the true aristocracy of the realm were invoked again in Thomas More's rendition of the quarrel that broke out, in the presence of Edward V, at Stony Stratford on 30 April 1483. Richard and Buckingham had already arrested Earl Rivers, and explained to the young king that they had done so because of the ambush Rivers had set up, and out of fear for their own safety. Now they turned on Rivers's nephew Sir Richard Grey. More related: 'They picked a quarrel with Sir Richard Grey, the king's half-brother, saying that he, and the Marquis [of Dorset] his brother and the Lord Rivers his uncle, had planned to rule the king and the realm, and to set variance [quarrels] amongst the lords and to subdue and destroy the noble blood of the realm.'

There is an uncanny similarity between the dramatic about-turn at Sandwich and Calais in 1460 and that of Northampton and Stony Stratford in 1483. However, in the first, we are inclined to believe the complaint of the Yorkist lords, because their grievances were subsequently written up positively by chroniclers supportive of the new dynasty of Edward IV. In the second, we are disinclined to believe the complaint of Richard and Buckingham for much the same reason, as it was then reported negatively by sources sympathetic to the Tudors. But were they in fact so very different? In Richard's case, it was a complaint he upheld scrupulously, in a letter to the Mayor and common council of London before he arrived in the capital, explaining the course of events and in a parade of captured Woodville weaponry once he reached it.

As news of what had happened was brought to London, the queen's initial reaction was to raise another army and free Edward V from Richard's clutches. Sir Edward Woodville's fleet was now at sea, and the Marquis of Dorset attempted to enlist fresh men for this new cause. But there was little enthusiasm for such a scheme among the magnates arriving in the capital for the expected coronation. As Mancini observed: 'When they had exhorted certain nobles, who had come to the city, and others to take up arms, they perceived that men's minds were not only irresolute, but altogether hostile to themselves. Some even said openly that it was more just and profitable that the youthful sovereign should be with his paternal uncle . . .' This was a sign that Richard's letter to the Mayor of London, in which he explained that his actions were not directed against the king but his Woodville following, was at the time both believed and accepted by much of the political community.

The Woodville coup had failed, and faced with this collapse of support the queen took her younger son Richard and her daughters – together with her son by her first marriage, the Marquis of Dorset, and her brother Lionel, Bishop of Salisbury – and retreated into sanctuary at Westminster Abbey. Richard entered the capital on 4 May, and the royal council, with Woodville influence now largely removed, confirmed his position of Protector. Lord Hastings vouched for Richard's good intentions towards the new monarch. And for the next five weeks, Richard was to govern the country in Edward V's name. The young king was first lodged in the Bishop of London's palace, and shortly after moved to the Tower of London, but at this stage he was installed in the royal quarters there, not imprisoned, and this was a course of action sanctioned by the entire council. His coronation was postponed until 22 June, but in the meantime all necessary preparations for the event were put in hand. It seemed that Edward V would soon be crowned King of England.

According to the Tudors, all this was mere pretence. The court historian Polydore Vergil believed that when Richard seized Earl Rivers at Northampton he had already decided to take the throne himself. Thomas More suspected that he was planning this even before the death of his brother, Edward IV. Governing in the name of Edward's young son and successor was thus a sinister sham, allowing Richard time to make good his own plans to usurp the throne. If this was true, it was far from obvious at the time. All acts of government in this period were carried out in Edward V's name, Edward acting 'by the advice and assent of our most entirely beloved uncle, the duke of Gloucester, protector and defender of our realm', or 'by the advice of our council'. If it was a deception, it was an elaborate one; there was little sign of anything untoward. As the *Croyland Chronicler* put it, Richard 'exercised this authority with the consent and the good will of all the lords'.

If Richard was indeed masking his true intentions, and playing a double game, it is surprising that one of his first actions on reaching London was to ask the council to authorize the trial of Earl Rivers and his confederates Sir Richard Grey and Sir Thomas Vaughan for treason. These men were now securely

held in Richard's keeping in the north, and as an additional precaution had been separated, with Rivers held at Sheriff Hutton,
Grey at Middleham and Vaughan at Pontefract. If Richard was
already planning to usurp the throne, he would be able to eliminate them whenever he wished. Richard's request to the council
– which was refused, on the technical grounds that when the
ambush attempt was made he was not yet Protector – comes
across as motivated more by genuine anger than duplicity.

The records of Edward V's fledgling government ran for a
little over a month. With the royal treasury emptied, money was
scarce, but Richard's concerns as Protector seemed genuine
enough. Maintaining the English outpost at Berwick, won so
importantly the previous year, was a high priority. Henry, Earl of
Northumberland – Richard's most senior commander in the
Scottish campaign of 1482 – was installed as captain there and a
vigorous building programme was ordered, to bring the fortress
up to scratch. A naval force was also gathered to deal with the
Woodville fleet, now lying off the Downs, but no fighting was
necessary since Richard's tactic of promising pardons to those
who deserted achieved the desired result peacefully.

On 15 May 1483 Richard made a major grant to his principal
ally the Duke of Buckingham, who was given unrivalled power
in Wales to replace the influence of Earl Rivers, who had led
the prince's council there. Buckingham was allowed a wide
mandate, to assemble troops wherever he saw fit, 'for the keeping and defence of the peace in these parts' and the financial
backing to put this policy into immediate effect. Ludlow Castle,
the centre of Rivers's regime on the Marches of Wales, was to
be handed over to Buckingham straight away. The urgency of
these measures showed continued concern over the army that
Rivers had recruited from this region the month before, which
although dispersed might still be a source of unrest. Their thor-
oughness suggested that military action may indeed have been

attempted against Richard and Buckingham on 29 April at Northampton.

And so things continued. On 9 June a newsletter was written by Simon Stallworth, the London business agent of Sir William Stonor, a leading member of the Oxfordshire gentry. Stallworth gave his master a detailed account of events in the capital. The letter reflected a sense of calm, that despite the changes that had taken place all was under control. He reported on recent political activity, and his information was quite specific, that 'my lord protector, my lord Buckingham, and all the other lords were in the council chamber from 10.00 [a.m.] to 2.00 [p.m.] . . . there is great business against [around] the coronation, which shall be a fortnight from today', and Stallworth then had time to consult with Richard personally over a practical matter, and to relay his response to Stonor. Although the queen and her son Richard, Duke of York, Edward V's younger brother, were still in sanctuary in Westminster Abbey, Richard and Buckingham were maintaining the routine of government, Edward V was visibly receiving visitors in his Tower apartments and plans for the coronation were well under way.

Stallworth's letter gives us a window on the political landscape of the time. Richard's administrative diligence was clear. It may have been a masquerade; it may also have been genuine. The Tudors believed Richard had by this time prepared a coup that would enable him to usurp the throne; yet he may also have been overtaken by events beyond his control. For things were now to change rapidly.

On 10 June Richard sent a dramatic letter to York. Further letters were dispatched to his principal northern followers the next day. In them, he made a powerful appeal for help, asking for men to be sent to his aid in London: 'to assist us against the Queen, her blood adherents and affinity, which have intended, and daily doth intend, to murder and utterly destroy us and our cousin, the duke of Buckingham, and the old royal blood of the realm, as it is openly known, and by their subtle damnable ways forecasted the same, the final destruction and disinheritance of you and all other inheritors and men of honour, as well of the north parties as other countries [regions] that belongen us.'

We are reminded of the oppressive menace Richard felt after the arrest and execution of his brother George, Duke of Clarence, powerfully described by Mancini, and the call for assistance Richard put out to his northern followers in the weeks following Clarence's arrest. The mass retaining of supporters among the tenants of the bishopric of Durham in July 1477, and the oath of loyalty Richard demanded from them, was proof that he felt in real danger. Here Mancini was forthright: Richard believed that the Woodvilles were behind the arrest of his brother, and were looking for an opportunity to engineer his own downfall.

Now that threat was once more in the ascendancy. Beneath the day-to-day activities of the Protectorate Richard's position remained alarmingly insecure. With the coronation planned for 22 June, his tenure of power would last only a matter of weeks. For once Edward V had been crowned, precedent dictated that a Protectorate be replaced by a ruling council. And this council – within which the king would exercise a greater say – could authorize the release of the Woodvilles Richard held in captivity and a restoration of their influence. If Richard believed he had been in deadly peril at Northampton on 29 April, he would soon be in deadly peril again.

If Richard's political future was insecure, so too were his northern landed estates – and the income and support he drew from them – which he had built up with such care in the reign of his brother, Edward IV. These estates – and the affinity he had created around them – formed Richard's heartland and the source of his power. Yet Richard's right to pass down his Neville lands to his son and heir, Edward of Middleham, was dependent on the survival of a nephew of Warwick the Kingmaker, George Neville, Duke of Bedford. But on 4 May 1483, the day of Richard's entry into the capital, Neville had suddenly died without marriage or children. To secure his Neville legacy, and avoid the 'disinheritance . . . of the north parties', the eventual dispersal of his northern estates that he evoked in his letter, new legislation would have to be pushed through parliament to protect his title to his lands. And were the Woodvilles to regain their influence, they would strongly oppose this.

These concerns must have weighed heavily on Richard's mind. There is evidence that he sought a solution through a break with precedent, and an extension of the term of his Protectorate beyond Edward V's coronation. But such an extension would have to be ratified by parliament and the royal council. The council was ready to support Richard in the days leading up to the coronation; it was unclear whether it would continue to back his mandate in the weeks and months after it. This matter may have been raised – perhaps unsuccessfully – in the unusually long, four-hour council meeting that Stallworth referred to in his letter on 9 June.

However, the power of Richard's language on 10 June – its sheer emotional force – is striking. The sense of threat is tangible, with fear of the Woodvilles paramount, who 'intended, and daily doth intend, to murder us'. Once more the events of 29 April 1483 were rehearsed, showing again Richard's belief that on this occasion the Woodvilles intended to ambush, arrest or even kill him. But the phrase 'daily doth intend' is more puzzling. What was this present danger? Rivers, Grey and Vaughan had been arrested, the queen had fled to sanctuary and Woodville power, for the time being at least, had been dispersed. The lack of immediate threat makes the letter seem suspicious, a ploy or false justification for bringing an army of supporters down to London. And news of a northern army bearing down on the capital would be enough to intimidate any opposition, if Richard was now considering whether to seize the throne.

The crucial phrase in the letter was 'forecasted the same', which had a very particular meaning in the fifteenth century, that of conspiring to bring about someone's death through astrological divination or prediction, seen as a form of witchcraft. In the late Middle Ages it was a treasonable offence to draw up, without authorization, the horoscopes or birth charts of a member of the English royal family. Such sensitivity may seem quite extraordinary to a modern audience, yet belief in the power of such acts was very real to a medieval one, and had already featured prominently in a number of high-profile trials, the most notorious being that of Eleanor Cobham, Duchess of Gloucester, who was convicted in 1441 of using astrological forecasting to bring about the death of King Henry VI, and condemned to imprisonment as a witch. Richard was now accusing the Woodvilles, and particularly the queen, of using witchcraft in an attempt to bring about his own death.

Fear of the Woodvilles and witchcraft was not a sudden invention of Richard's; rather it stemmed from the mysterious circumstances of Edward IV's marriage and Elizabeth Woodville's maternal lineage. For her mother, Jacquetta of Luxembourg, could trace an ancestry back to the first Count of Luxembourg, who – as legend had it – had married a magical being, the water goddess Melusina. Jacquetta knew of this legend, which was stated in her own family tree, and she owned a copy of a rare manuscript of the history of Melusina. Melusina may have been a theme at her daughter Elizabeth's marriage and at royal jousts. The legend took on a more sinister meaning in July 1469, when the Earl of Warwick, allied with George, Duke of Clarence, went into rebellion against Edward IV, executed Jacquetta's husband and one of her sons, and then put Jacquetta herself on trial for witchcraft. Witnesses were called, claiming that Jacquetta had brought about the marriage of Edward IV and Elizabeth Woodville, five years earlier, through sorcery, though the trial was never brought to a conclusion. Its memory lingered on, and Richard was later to make a similar claim about the marriage in the *Titulus Regius* that justified his own claim to the throne: that it was enacted by witchcraft. His fear of the Woodvilles practising witchcraft against him – however implausible it may seem to a modern audience – could have been quite real.

A near-contemporary London chronicle also claimed that Richard's opponents were using 'divination' against him. Even if Richard's fear of witchcraft was genuine, he could still have circulated this information in June 1483 to disguise his real intentions. But another reference is tellingly found among a personal archive rather than being intended for public consumption. Lewis Caerleon had been employed as an astrologer for Elizabeth Woodville and was subsequently arrested by Richard, and imprisoned in the Tower. In 1485, in the margins of astronomical material in his possession, Caerleon noted: 'after the composition of these tables [of eclipses], *which I lost through the plundering of King Richard* [my italics], I, being imprisoned in the Tower of London, composed other tables.' Richard had taken this issue seriously enough to confiscate and search through Caerleon's private papers.

Matters came to a head in the remarkable and quite terrifying council meeting of 13 June. According to both Polydore Vergil and Thomas More, Richard charged the queen and Edward IV's mistress Elizabeth [Jane] Shore with witchcraft, and then involved Lord Hastings in this accusation. Polydore Vergil said that the sorcery had produced in Richard 'a deep bodily feebleness', preventing him from resting, eating or drinking over the last few days, in other words from the time he wrote his letter to York, which first mentioned his fear of witchcraft. More, by contrast, used dramatic embellishment, such as appealed to Shakespeare, with his baring of a newly withered arm. Both writers made it clear that they thought Richard's belief in a conspiracy against him was no more than his own invention.

More vividly portrayed the councillors' amazement at such a charge, particularly as it linked both the queen and the king's mistress in the plot. As More put it, with all his lawyer's reasonableness, 'she [Elizabeth Woodville], of all people would least make Shore's wife of her counsel, whom of all women she most hated, as that concubine the king her husband had most loved.' For More and Vergil believed that Richard and Buckingham planned the arrest of Hastings with the same ruthless opportunism that had been employed against Rivers at Northampton.

The immediate execution of Hastings, without trial, was a shocking act, whatever the reason for it. And it was most convenient for Richard, if he had already decided to take the throne himself, to have the leading moderate in the council out of the way, a man who had strongly supported him as Protector but was unflinchingly loyal to the sons of Edward IV. Hastings's death removed the focal point for any opposition to Richard – and would have intimidated or cowed the doubters into submission. And yet there was a terrible spontaneity to this event, as if some highly charged emotional secret had startlingly been revealed. For if Richard had planned and calculated it in advance, giving Jane Shore a starring role in the conspiracy – the point made much of by More – the supposed master of dissimulation was adopting a quite bizarre strategy. It was almost as if Richard were inviting disbelief. The charge against Shore was so odd it might actually have been genuine.

After Edward IV's death there was a quarrel over Elizabeth [Jane] Shore – the king's favourite mistress – between the Marquis of Dorset and Lord Hastings, with both men competing for her favour. Richard's distaste for the sexual immorality of his brother's courtiers would only have been heightened when he learned of this; and if Hastings, perhaps fearing Richard might delay Edward V's coronation, had begun a desperate effort to make contact with the queen in sanctuary, it is not impossible that Shore could have been used as an intermediary. We will never know. But whatever the reason for it, Hastings's execution was a dreadful moment. He was a popular and well-liked figure, and his death universally regretted. As the *Great Chronicle of London* remarked: 'and thus was this noble man murdered for the truth and fidelity he bore unto his master [Edward V].' Richard may have planned to dispose of Hastings, and – once this obstacle to his ambition was removed – deliberately sought out the throne. Alternatively, he may have ordered the execution on the spur of the moment, and then realized, after undertaking it, that only the power and prestige of kingship would now protect his position. Or finally, he may indeed have uncovered evidence that Hastings was now plotting against him, as both Richard and Buckingham were subsequently to claim.

On 16 June a deputation was sent to the queen, still in sanctuary at Westminster Abbey, led by the ageing Archbishop of Canterbury, and she was now persuaded to release her younger son Richard, Duke of York into Richard's keeping. After the escape of Thomas, Marquis of Dorset from sanctuary, Richard had surrounded the abbey with troops. Edward V and his brother were now moved to the inner apartments of the Tower. They were occasionally seen playing in the Tower gardens, but more usually glimpsed behind barred windows. Preparations for the coronation of the young king were abandoned, and the writs that were to summon the first parliament of his reign cancelled. Orders were sent north for the execution of Rivers, Grey and Vaughan. Events were developing a terrible momentum.

On 21 June 1483 Simon Stallworth wrote a second letter to his master Sir William Stonor. His tone had now changed completely. There was no mention of private business matters;

Stallworth was entirely focused on what was happening in the capital and how things might unfold there. He began by saying Stonor was lucky to be away from it all: 'with us there is much trouble and every man doubts another.' He described the sudden execution of Hastings, 'beheaded soon upon noon', and how, in its aftermath, two other councillors, Thomas Rotherham, Archbishop of York, and John Morton, Bishop of Ely, had been imprisoned. He related details of the surrender of young Richard, Duke of York from sanctuary, the abbey being surrounded by 'harnessed men' [soldiers in body armour]. Richard and Buckingham had received the prince with 'many loving words'; he was then sent to the Tower to join his brother there. Stallworth hoped he would be 'merry' at this reunion without fully believing what he was saying; 'blessed be Jesus', he added uneasily. News was spreading in London of the approach of Richard's army of northern supporters; some – in the grip of panic – imagined it might be 20,000 strong. Stallworth recorded that Eliabeth [Jane] Shore was also in prison: 'what shall happen to her I know not.' And then, whether as a result of illness or sheer distress, Stallworth was unable to carry on. 'I pray you pardon me of more writing,' he concluded, 'I am so sick that I may not well hold my pen.'

Stallworth did not say it outright, but he clearly suspected that Richard was now aiming for the throne. Revelations abounded. One repeated the slur that Edward IV had in fact been illegitimate, a rumour first spread by Warwick and Clarence in 1469, but now – according to Dominic Mancini – sensationally confirmed by Richard's own mother, Cecily, Duchess of York, who had flown into a 'frenzy' [a bout of hysteria], claiming that Edward was conceived out of an adulterous affair, and that Richard, Duke of York was not his real father. And then there was the disclosure that Edward IV's marriage to Elizabeth Woodville was invalid, because Edward had been pre-contracted to marry someone else, Lady Eleanor Talbot, the daughter of

John, Earl of Shrewsbury. This startling information meant that under Church law the children of Edward and Elizabeth were illegitimate, and could not inherit the throne.

On 22 June Richard's own claim to the throne was publicly proclaimed in a sermon by Ralph Shaw at St Paul's Cross. Shaw stressed that Richard – far smaller in stature than his brother Edward – most clearly resembled his father, Richard, Duke of York and was his only true heir. The bastardy of Edward IV was then alluded to; according to Mancini, Shaw said: 'Edward was conceived in adultery, and in every way was unlike the late duke of York, whose son he was falsely said to be, but Richard, who altogether resembled his father, was to come to the throne as legitimate successor.'

Mancini believed that the disclosure of Cecily's adultery was the real justification for Richard taking the throne. If so, it would mean putting the elderly duchess before an ecclesiastical examination, and although one later source confirmed that Cecily was willing to make such a deposition, this was something that Richard – who had stayed at his mother's London residence of Baynard's Castle during much of his Protectorate – was most reluctant to do. So the pre-contract issue was favoured instead. On 25 June Buckingham read out a petition to assembled lords and commoners at Westminster. It was later enrolled in the records of Richard's parliament as the *Titulus Regius*. It began by attacking the corrupt influence exercised by the Woodvilles over Edward IVs government: 'such as had the rule and governance of this land, delighting in adulation and flattery, and led by sensuality and greed, followed the counsel of persons insolent, vicious and of inordinate avarice.' Richard had remained loyal to his brother, but the sense of alienation from Edward's court, and the revulsion against his hedonistic lifestyle is here all too painfully apparent. The laws of the Church had been broken, the petition declaimed, and all justice set aside.

The petition then impugned the validity of Edward IV's marriage. It had been done without the assent of the lords of the land, and through the practice of sorcery and witchcraft, both by Elizabeth and her mother Jacquetta. It had taken place in a private chamber, 'a profane place', rather than publicly in a church. And then the pre-contract issue was introduced. Because of this, Edward and Elizabeth had in fact been living in adultery, and their children were therefore bastards, and could not inherit the crown. Edward IV's own bastardy was alluded to without being made explicit, Richard's birth within the realm of England being praised, and finally the petition noted that because an act of attainder had been passed on Richard's brother, George, Duke of Clarence, this also debarred Clarence's offspring from inheriting. Clarence's son and heir, Edward, Earl of Warwick, had been kept in the wardship of Thomas, Marquis of Dorset. Dorset had fled into sanctuary, and Richard now brought the boy up to London. But in contrast to the sons of Edward IV he was not imprisoned, instead being kept in the household of Richard's wife, Anne Neville.

This was the potent mix of accusation, allegation and self-belief that propelled Richard to the throne. The Tudors saw it as a web of fabrication, masking Richard's cruel ambition to seize a crown never rightfully his. But in the powerful crucible of events in the summer of 1483 Richard was under serious threat. He quite possibly feared for his political future, and even for his own life. In these dramatic circumstances, Richard may genuinely have come to believe not only that taking the throne was the only way out of his difficulties, but a rightful claim was being presented to him by providence.

If this was so, the way Richard brought it into effect was undoubtedly as ruthless as others during this tumultuous era, including Henry Bolingbroke's taking of the throne (as the future Henry IV) in 1399, his own father's attempt to seize it in

1460 and his brother Edward's regaining of it in 1471. It was a sign of the times. But Buckingham's petition stunned many who heard it. Mancini related that there were some who believed that Richard had been overcome by 'an insane lust for power'. And this tradition was drawn upon and amplified by the Tudor chroniclers. But others accepted the logic of realpolitik upon which it was based.

It was no longer desirable or safe to have a Woodville-dominated government. And although the *Croyland Chronicler* insinuated that the entire document had been drawn up by Richard in advance, its charges were not in fact without substance. Edward IV's illegitimacy could not be entirely dismissed; the accusation had been made in 1469, and had featured in the act of attainder passed against Clarence in 1478. Edward was defensive about it. Tudor chroniclers glossed over this by saying that Richard chose to slander his mother, and that this was further proof of his wickedness. But if we follow the testimony of Mancini, Cecily herself was behind the revival of this issue in 1483.

The pre-contract matter brought up the deeply divisive issue of the Woodville marriage, which many of the English aristocracy had never been able to accept fully. According to the French chronicler Philippe de Commynes, Robert Stillington, Bishop of Bath and Wells, was the real source for the revealing of the pre-contract, rather than it being conjured up by Richard, as the *Croyland Chronicler* imagined. When the *Titulus Regius* was overturned in the first parliament of Henry VII's reign, it was clearly stated there that 'it was Stillington's bill'; in other words, that the bishop was behind the allegation. Parliament wished to question Stillington on the matter, but strikingly Henry, who had arrested the bishop in the aftermath of Bosworth, refused their request and instead gave Stillington a free pardon. It seemed that Henry, rather than seeking a chance to discredit Richard, was uncomfortable about what might be disclosed, and chose instead to let the matter pass.

While Buckingham was delivering the petition to an assembled audience at Westminster, Rivers, Grey and Vaughan were executed at Pontefract. The next day, 26 June, after formally receiving a further petition from lords and commons, Richard symbolically chose to occupy the king's chair in the court of the King's Bench at Westminster. He was now monarch and rightful heir of the Yorkist dynasty. The reign of Richard III had begun.

7

The Discovery of the Skeletal Remains

Day Eleven

Tuesday, 4 September 2012

I T's 7.45 A.M. at the Social Services car park. A few clouds are floating around but it's going to be another warm, sunny day. I'm introduced to Simon Farnaby, presenter of the Channel 4 TV documentary who, like me, is from Darlington and we rattle on about familiar places. It's good to have this bond. Farnaby's only prior knowledge of Richard III came from Shakespeare's play so the research has been something of a revelation for him, but he's up for the challenge to try to uncover the real Richard III.

I go across to say hello to Dr Jo Appleby, the osteologist who'll be working with Dr Turi King on the exhumation. She's young but Richard Buckley assures me her knowledge is top-notch. Carl Vivian from the university is filming again, which makes three cameras in the car park, including DSP's new cameraman. I'm on edge. I don't want the cameras here, yet I know they have to be to record whatever we find, but I can't stop myself being anxious to protect these remains.

I phone Mick Bowers, Head of Greyfriars Property Services, and Luke Thompson in security because I want the blinds down at all the windows facing on to the site. While Mathew Morris and I put more tarpaulin over the fencing all the blinds are lowered; the gravesite is now protected from any visual intrusion. I walk over to the northern end of Trench One, and look down at the plastic sheeting poking through the earth that covers the remains. It's a sad and vulnerable sight.

Turi King and Jo Appleby, clad in their white masks, suits and gloves, head towards me and Trench One. Meanwhile Richard Buckley is excited about Trench Three, telling me it's full of finds and the team is enjoying excavating it. The western slot in Trench Three will be dug this morning to try to expose more of the grave cuts there, so it may get a bit noisy with the excavator. He asks me what I'll be doing. I reply that I'll be watching the exhumation; I'm not going anywhere else. He gives me his 'Are you all right?' look. I say I'm fine and I'll enjoy sitting in the sunshine watching the girls do their stuff. He gives me a shoulder hug before sauntering off to Trench Three. I watch him go, this big bear of a man with such a big heart, and thank God that he agreed to come with me on this car park adventure.

I fetch another bucket from Morris's van at Turi King's request, then pull up a chair for myself from the gazebo. It's going to be a long day. King and Appleby kneel in the earth below me and set to work. I take a deep, steadying breath; it's 10.30 a.m.

The painstaking work of scraping away at each morsel of earth proceeds slowly, not helped by last night's rain, which has made the soil dark, wet and sticky. The tiny tools they are using remind me of implements in children's plasticine kits. King laughs at my remark and says they are exactly like that, but have been thoroughly sterilized to protect any DNA and avoid contamination. Appleby explains that the foot and hand bones are tiny and can be easily overlooked, so they must feel every small bump, every minute piece of soil before it goes into the buckets. They can't afford to miss anything; the smallest piece could prove crucial in the lab analysis.

The top layer of earth has been removed. It doesn't seem to have made much of a dent in the layers over the remains, yet the buckets have produced a large spoil heap beside me. As I lift the buckets to help, they are heavy, not only because the Leicester earth is thick clay with largish stones but also because a good part of the loads is rubble from the Victorian building work.

The late morning sun is creeping over the tarpaulin, and the girls are beginning to sweat. The western side of the slot, where the skull will be if it is a fully articulated skeleton, looks a little short. King chips away at it with her mattock, similar to a pick-axe, but it's difficult in her protective gear. By lunchtime, when they down tools, she's done most of it, leaving another great mound of earth, rocks and rubble on the burial site which will need checking this afternoon. If we're looking at a complete set of remains, I can't see how they'll be ready to remove today. Neither can King and Appleby, but suggest that things may speed up in the afternoon.

There's a buzz of news from Trench Three adjacent to us. The two grave cuts in the central flooring have been exposed further and it looks as if there is more flooring and what might be an internal wall. The Church of the Greyfriars is coming to life, slowly revealing its secrets. We in Trench One are the 'also-rans' in today's news. We discuss the remains in our trench and agree that they should be taken out of this smashed-up place. The others think they're unlikely to be of interest even if they do turn out to be a fully articulated set of bones and complete burial. I nod but say nothing. For the academics and scientists evidence is paramount.

After lunch, King and Appleby get back to work. Suited up again, they look like investigators at a crime scene, which I find somehow appropriate. As the only non-scientist/academic, I always seem to be quietly apologizing for my beliefs and intuitions. It's an isolating thought. But then I look around. There is such a feeling of camaraderie and everyone is so excited by the dig that I realize we are a real team and I am part of it; in a sense it's *my* team, after all.

King and Appleby are working almost directly below where I had my intuition and only a few feet from the letter 'R' that led me here. I haven't felt that instinct since the first day when we exposed the bones. It was that sensation that began my quest for the king and has brought me to this moment. And now, after nearly four years of fighting, it's all quiet – serene even. The excavator is silent, Richard Buckley and the film crew are all in Trench Three, the blinds are down in the windows all around, and I think how perfect it is. If these bones are Richard's, his exhumation will be peaceful. And, I suddenly realize, carried out by women. I wonder what he would have thought of that.

The layers of earth are solid as the sun makes its way round the car park. The two women won't manage to uncover the remains today but will get as much soil off the area as they can. Tomorrow Turi King will be in Switzerland at a conference so Jo Appleby will do the exhumation, with Mathew Morris overseeing it. As I try to contain my disappointment that we won't exhume the remains on this perfect day and set-up, I hear clanking behind the tarpaulin. I investigate and see a ladder going up at a window; it's a pest control company come to remove a wasps' nest. I manage to persuade them to come back at the end of the week. If news of the exhumation gets out, any hope of it being peaceful will be lost.

At 4 p.m., while King and Appleby are recovering the lower leg bones to protect them and finishing up for the day, we hear about the discoveries in the new slot in Trench Three. They've found more flooring and tiles from what seems to be two levels, so a new medieval floor may have been put in at a later date. They also found what look like human bones, probably discovered by the Victorian builders and returned to a hollow dug into the ground, which the archaeologists call a charnel burial. From the street, the public could see the length of the trench but not into it so no fencing and tarpaulin were needed to shield the removal of the remains found in the charnel.

Simon Farnaby is filming as Leon Hunt works round the bones. Jo Appleby arrives, minus her *CSI* wear as Hunt has said that he thinks the remains are female so no DNA analysis will be needed to confirm if these are the remains of Richard III. After investigating the skull and pelvis, Appleby confirms that the remains are indeed female. I have only one female on the list of potential burials in the Greyfriars Church: Ellen, wife of Gilbert Luenor, a possible founder of the friary, who may have died about 1250. I look at the grave cuts. As man and wife, they would have been buried together, so is this Ellen? If not, who? There can't be many single female burials in a priory church.

Mathew Morris brings a finds box, a simple brown rectangular cardboard container, long enough to fit a femur bone. It's rather sad: mortal remains reduced to a cardboard box. Hunt asks how it's going in Trench One, and I explain that the remains won't be recovered today. Simon Farnaby asks me why I'm so fixated on them when there's so much happening here, in Trench Three. I tell him briefly about my intuitive experience in 2005 and the 'R' on the tarmac: the reasons why I began this search in the first place. 'Interesting one,' he says. 'Bonkers one,' I reply. He laughs. 'Sometimes bonkers is good. It got us here, didn't it?' I want to hug him for that.

Day Twelve

Wednesday, 5 September 2012

The day dawns like any other recently, blue skies and unbroken sunshine. It will be the day I never forget.

At 7.45 a.m. everyone is still buzzing about the grave cuts in Trench Three, and eager to get on with the new eastern slot that will be cut there this morning in the hope of revealing more of them. I'm not really interested. My mind is still on Trench One.

I'm alone again on the plastic chair in the sunshine, enjoying the solitude as Jo Appleby works below me. Appleby picks up the mattock, chipping away at the western edge of the slot. It's hot, heavy work and I try to help by grabbing some of the bucket loads of earth she passes up.

Leon Hunt comes to tell us that the eastern slot in Trench Three is already exposing more grave cuts and I really should take a look. I arrive to see enormous slabs of dark grey slate on the spoil heaps. Morris says they're probably left over from the Victorian buildings, part of their infill. They look like grave tops to me. He cleans one off but it's local slate with no markings, so . . . Victorian rubble.

Back at Trench One, before I can sit down, Appleby says I need to look at something. A smooth expanse of creamy yellow bone is poking out of the earth at the far western end, almost beneath my feet. It's the top of a skull with a large gash in it. Battle wound? No. She apologizes, and says that she was using the mattock when it crunched into something. When she brushed away the soil, she realized the mattock had driven straight into the skull, the clean white edges of the crack indicating the newness of the damage. She's mortified and explains that as the leg bones are so much lower in the earth, the skull should not have been where it is. She thinks it must belong to different remains. The real skull, if the leg bones are articulated, she says, will be beneath this. Seeing my concern, she tells me not to worry, and assures me that the damaged skull is not part of the same remains. Morris arrives and sees the crack. 'It happens,' he says.

It's not the start I was hoping for. If there is more than one burial here, it could be a lengthier process to determine if one is

Richard. Appleby exposes more of the skull, which is perfectly round with no other marks or wounds, but needs a lot of work before it can be removed from the earth. It looks like the skull of a male. The large upper leg bones, the femur bones, are now exposed, as are the arm bones. The foot bones have gone, thanks, it would seem, to the Victorian builders, and it was probably a shroud burial since the hands are still in place over the pelvic area and the legs are together.

The leg bones look strong and healthy, with no marks or battle wounds. One of the lower leg bones was mashed up a little by the excavator as the trench was being dug but the others are in good condition. The arms are normal with no marks or battle wounds, and no signs of being 'withered'. It also looks as if the skull is part of the same remains as there is no other in the ground, but Appleby can't understand why it would be so high up in relation to the rest. I ask how tall he was. She can't be certain as she doesn't have a measuring tape, but the size of the femur, the longest bone in the body, is reasonable so he wasn't small. I look down at the remains, trying to gauge his height from my own leg. I'm five foot nine and the remains look roughly that or slightly less.

I ask Appleby her opinion as to the possible identity of the remains. Since there are no wounds, normal arms, good height and a shroud burial, located in the nave of the church, she believes it could be a friar. Morris agrees. As I look down at the bones, I remember from contemporary sources that Richard was reputedly small in stature, and begin to think that this can't be him. I feel odd, as if the world were closing in on me.

Truth be told, I'm shattered by this news and want time on my own to digest it so I head off to Piero's, stopping at Trench Three on the way. Everyone there is hugely excited. Richard Buckley is filming with Simon Farnaby and the DSP team beside three grave cuts, one of which, the central one, has everyone transfixed. It's a long cut in the central flooring of the church, a place of great honour, but there are bricks poking through the top soil which they need to investigate. There's also a new wall exposed by the earlier western slot that could be the remains of the base of a choir stall. A square piece of an elaborate stone frieze, virtually intact, has been found, as well as the most beautiful window tracery in the eastern slot, which may be from the east window of the church.

No wonder the team are all in Trench Three again. If we are looking at part of the east window then this could be the choir of the Greyfriars Church and, more importantly, Richard's grave could be here. I look at the tracery which is so perfect, as though it fell into the ground yesterday, not several centuries ago. Jon Coward is smiling. 'Not bad for a morning's work,' he says. I ask about the grave cuts and we chat about the middle one that is cut into the flooring and runs much further east. Coward is not totally convinced it's a burial, as he hasn't yet removed the top layer of soil with the bricks, which he thinks are most likely Victorian, but could be Georgian and have to be checked out.

I can understand everyone's interest in this cut. We believe that Richard was interred in the choir and if you're going to bury a king it would surely be in a place of honour, in a central position with the floor cut to accommodate him. If this is Richard's grave and it has modern rubble at its surface, did the Victorians or Georgians accidentally remove him? I'm interested but strangely not concerned. I'm still reeling from the disappointment in Trench One.

In Piero's I have no appetite and sit at the back. Mohcin, who works there, brings me my drink and tries to cheer me up. I hadn't realized I looked as miserable as I feel. Why did I get the intuitive feeling for a friar? I try to reason with myself. Perhaps this friar has a story to tell, something that might throw some light on Richard and his time. Perhaps I need to focus on Trench Three. I wander the Leicester streets, then sit by the soothing fountain in Town Hall Square, and ponder what I have to do next.

Back on site, I head to Trench Three. This, I've persuaded myself, is where I should be, but I don't get there because the DSP team want to film me at Trench One. Simon Farnaby has a question he wants to put to me before we see Jo Appleby in the trench but he won't tell me what it is before the cameras roll. He looks rather on edge, so I don't push it.

'So, Philippa, do you remember that story you told me about where you felt Richard was buried and how that came about? Can you tell me about it?'

I'm thrown. Is this relevant now? But I tell him as light-heartedly as I can about my goose-bumps that day and the letter 'R', and the feeling that I was walking on Richard's grave.

At the trench, the cameras roll as Jo Appleby bends down and removes a light covering of earth from the chest cavity and upper vertebrae. The spine has the most excruciating 'S' shape. Whoever this was, she states, the spinal column has a really abnormal curvature. This skeleton has a hunchback.

The word hits me like a sucker-punch. No, I can't take it in. Are they saying this is Richard? I look again at the acute 'S' shape of the spine. If this is Richard, how can he have worn armour with a hump in his back? Appleby says she wouldn't try but confirms that the arms are normal, there was no 'withered arm'. Farnaby says he could have been a hunchback but still been the nice guy. But it doesn't add up. How could he fight with his head tilted downward? How could he see? The faces of Dr Tobias Capwell, Dominic Sewell and the other combat and weaponry experts I'd spoken to whirl before me. Personal descriptions of Richard come to mind; written by people who met him, none mentioned any acute abnormality.

There's more. Appleby explains there is a wound at the top of the skull and damage to the base inflicted at or around the time of death. She lifts the skull that she has released from the earth and turns it round. There's an indent on the inside with two small flaps of bone hanging from it. Directly above this, on the outside top of the skull, there is a small square puncture wound like that inflicted by a poleaxe. Appleby turns the skull over. At the back is a massive cleave wound, suggesting a blow that would have taken off most of the back of the head. This is not a friar dedicated to peace. This is a man who could have died in battle. I'm reeling.

Replacing the skull, she demonstrates how the remains looked in situ when she first uncovered them. I can see how high the skull is in the earth. The neck has been forced up so that the head is sticking out, jerking forward and downward onto the chest. The evidence is there, staring me in the face. I'm trying to discern the man from the bones, but can see nothing. Appleby lifts the skull again showing the massive cleave wound and the face. Suddenly there is hair, blood and humanity.

I flop down on to the spoil heap behind me. Farnaby puts his arm around me and asks if I'm all right. I feel as if I've been hit by a train. The others want me to be excited because it looks as though we may have found Richard but all I can hear is the pounding in my ears and the awful word 'hunchback' in my brain. Appleby is talking about the Paralympics, the men and women who overcome disabilities to become superhuman heroes. This was Richard, who became a warrior king in spite of everything. She's trying to help me comprehend what I'm seeing.

But that's not why I'm in turmoil. The hunchback stigma, if confirmed, will allow modern historians with their reputations tied to Tudor propaganda to claim that their chosen sources have been validated. Any hope of revealing the man behind the myths will be lost and the cardboard cut-out caricature held up as incontestable.

Filming stops. Everyone is elated. I catch their excitement and smile, but it's a mechanical smile. They think it may be Richard whereas I know it's Richard. The joviality of the Time Tomb Team helps me cope but I just want to be alone.

I head to Trench Three where Jon Coward is working by himself. He's excited about the trench, since they may be able to confirm exactly where they are in terms of the east end of the church, and therefore the burial in Trench One could be in the choir. I ask him if he has heard about the discoveries at the exhumation yet. He looks blank. When I tell him I can almost see his mind whirling. If the remains are indeed in the choir of the church then the likelihood of them being King Richard is even greater. I return to Trench One, where John Ashdown-Hill has arrived and is standing by the remains. We hug. He is white and in shock; strange that this should be our reaction. He too comprehends what this will mean for Richard's reputation.

The exhumation work resumes. Jo Appleby bags up each bone and Mathew Morris brings another brown cardboard finds box. I find myself thinking how sad it is. Appleby hands up a clear plastic finds bag containing a small piece of rusted metal, possibly iron, approximately two to three centimetres long, which looks as if it has a sharp point. It was found in the upper back between the second and third thoracic vertebrae, but not lodged in the bone. Turning it over, I ask if it could be the tip of a weapon that snapped off in the mêlée after it was thrust into his flesh – a pike maybe. Appleby doesn't know.

It's getting late and the site slowly clears. Richard Buckley is back, amazed by the news of the discovery. He doesn't normally swear, he says, but he did on this occasion. Ashdown-Hill has a modern copy of Richard's royal banner, and I'd like to place it over the finds box for its departure from the site. We won't be doing this again, and I want to mark the event, to pay him what respect we can. Richard Buckley agrees, and leaves.

Morris and Appleby bag the final remains, and I see the skull up close for the first time. The face is short with well-defined features, the skull itself almost delicate in appearance, not the heavy-browed Neanderthal type you sometimes see. Only the skull seems to have the creamy yellow appearance, whereas the bones are mostly dark with the clay soil clinging to them. The bones are being put into the bags still dirty to protect them as some are quite fragile. They'll be cleaned in the lab for analysis. I reflect on how Richard was found. We so often see human remains with the awful gaping mouth of death, but not this time; Richard's skull, with its acute angle, looks as though he had just nodded off to sleep in the grave, his head fallen forward on to his chest.

It's nearly 7 p.m. and Richard is out of the ground. I ask Jo Appleby if she would like the honour of carrying the box with the royal banner covering it to the van, but she declines. She's not comfortable as we don't know for certain that it's Richard. It doesn't feel right for me to do it, so then who? Suddenly it dawns on me: John Ashdown-Hill; without his research we wouldn't be here. I hold the cardboard box, as he places the banner over it, he takes the box and carries it as we walk to Mathew Morris's van. Ashdown-Hill places the box inside then Morris closes the door.

It's a peaceful moment and I feel enormous relief that it's all over. Then all at once Jo Appleby is angrily telling us that what we're doing isn't right, that everyone should be treated the same. On top of everything else, it's the last straw and I'm furious. She's forgotten, or doesn't know, the struggle I've had to find this man. I tell her so in no uncertain terms, but feel guilty about it. As a scientist, she is dedicated to evidence and while I agree that in death we are all equal, at that moment, at the end of my journey, with the agony of discovery, I feel emotional. Then I calm down because Jo Appleby is right: he hasn't been identified yet.

As Morris closes the site, I look at where Richard had lain. Two yellow field markers are all that remain, the western one marking the position of his head, the eastern the extent of his leg bones. Gazing at these two simple markers I should be happy, or perhaps sad, but I just feel numb.

But we weren't quite at the end of the journey. The next morning I tell Sarah Levitt at LCC the news. She blanches and informs Sir Peter Soulsby, Leicester's mayor, who utters one word: 'Bugger.' Phil Stone, chairman of the Richard III Society, gasps, as does the private secretary to the Duke of Gloucester.

I give the news to Annette Carson, back at home in Norfolk, and she drops everything to arrive the next day. By this time one of the cameramen reveals that he too suffers from curvature of the spine. That evening, after a long day's filming with a heavy camera, he's in considerable pain.

At my reunion with Annette the mood is subdued. Neither of us has any doubt that the man in the grave is someone we have sought to understand most of our adult lives. Annette shares with me an indefinable sense of the weight of history, and a potent awareness of many people's expectations.

On Saturday, 8 September, there is a public open day at the dig. LCC gives me the honour of leading the first and final tours, and Michael Ibsen, seventeenth-generation nephew of Richard III, is on my first one. It's a difficult day. Many of the public who come are emotional at the possibility of finding Richard's remains but we're not allowed to say anything about the discovery in order to give the university time to corroborate the find.

We're into the third, extra, week of the dig. The university is due to hold a news conference on Wednesday, 12 September and intend to run with the hunchback findings. I fight hard against this with Richard Taylor, their Director of Corporate Affairs, until the initial analysis comes through. This reveals that although the skeleton had a curved spine, it was not what is sometimes inappropriately termed 'hunchbacked'; it didn't have kyphosis. It looks as if Richard III had severe scoliosis, which is a condition, not a disability, and doesn't rule out an active lifestyle. He could fight, it seems, as the records said he did, but his right shoulder may have been higher than the left.

So why was there confusion at the graveside regarding the position of the skull on the chest? It seems the grave was cut too short, forcing the head upward and forward as the body was lowered in feet first. Was the burial carried out in a hurry? It is, of course, speculation at this stage, but I try to contain my joy. What we can now see fits with the contemporary descriptions we have of Richard. We may be able to uncover the real man after all.

At the 12 September press conference, the university confirms the discovery of the two sets of human remains, one female, the other male, revealing important information about the male skeleton: the remains appear to be that of an adult male located in the choir of the church where it was reported that Richard III had been buried. On initial examination, the skeleton seemed to have suffered significant peri-mortem trauma to the skull which appears consistent with, although not certainly caused by, an injury received in battle. A barbed iron arrowhead was found between vertebrae of the skeleton's upper back. It is also revealed that the skeleton had acute spinal abnormalities, confirming severe scoliosis – a form of spinal curvature. This would have made the right shoulder visibly higher than the left, consistent with contemporary accounts of Richard's appearance. Finally, the skeleton did not show signs of kyphosis – a different form of curvature. The man did not have the feature sometimes inappropriately known as a hunchback and did not have a withered arm.

By now Ken Wallace, the metal detector expert, has discovered numerous artefacts including Lombardic-style copper alloy letters in Trench Three, and a 'D' in Trench One, which could be from tomb inscriptions. Sadly, they do not spell 'Richard' and date from the late thirteenth to mid-fourteenth centuries. Wallace has also found a medieval silver halfpenny in Trench Three, and in Trench Two pointed archaeologist Kim Sidwell to another beneath the ground. Sidwell then carefully unearthed a medieval silver halfpenny bearing the head of Edward IV, which the archaeologists believe dates it to around 1468–9. In Trench Three, Leon Hunt and Jon Coward have also discovered the most beautiful inlaid medieval floor tile in almost pristine condition. Its design is similar to the half tile found by Hunt earlier, but this, they believe, is a heraldic eagle from the arms of Richard of Cornwall as King of the Romans and dates from around 1277.

Measurements from the site have enabled Richard Buckley and his team to plot the locations of the Greyfriars Priory Church and buildings as archaeologist Andy McLeish, with much experience in urban archaeology, completes the drawings. It seems that the medieval window tracery, *circa* 1400, might have been unearthed at the time the Victorian grammar school was built, since the tracery's similarity to the medieval gothic-style windows of the school's chapel is startling. It appears likely that the tracery inspired the Victorian builders to replicate it and it now represents a very visible modern connection to Leicester's medieval past. Buckley has suggested that the friary may have been built of grey sandstone, with slate roof tiling (also discovered) and decorated with glazed ridge tiles. But there was another intriguing discovery: he and his team could detect stains of red-brick dust on the fifteenth-century masonry fragments. It would need further analysis but this could suggest that the east end of the church was built, or faced in, brick and if so, Buckley confirmed, the Greyfriars Church would be one of the earliest medieval brick buildings in Leicester.

In the final week the gravesite is painstakingly examined by Tony Gnanaratnam. He finds church floors in the sides of

Trench One that match those in Trench Three and he exposes the north wall of the church at the very northern end of Trench One. Richard Buckley and his team believe that the burial in Trench One might have taken place in the south-west corner of the choir, with the grave positioned against the southern stall. We also discover that Vickie Score at ULAS has been busy baking. In the gazebo, Richard Buckley is presented with perfect miniature cake hard hats. Roaring with laughter, he munches into them.

The dig closes on Friday, 14 September and I'm finally able to go home. Trench Three has revealed several grave cuts and a large lead-lined stone sarcophagus. Leon Hunt says it might not be hermetically sealed as he can see a small gap in the top. I wonder if this could be the grave of Sheriff Moton (later known as Mutton), or one of the important provincial ministers of the Greyfriars order (William of Nottingham and Peter Swynfeld). Richard Buckley would like to investigate further and has proposed a new dig so perhaps one day we will find out. The site and graves will be protected with a geo-permeable membrane before being filled in, with the exception of the area that contained Richard's remains. This will be left open for posterity. LCC is planning a new Richard III Visitor Centre in the former grammar school where a 'Sold' sign will appear shortly. A new chapter in the story of the Greyfriars of Leicester is about to begin.

Back at the laboratories in the university, work is only just beginning.

8

Richard as King

O N 26 JUNE 1483, the first day of his reign, Richard III seated himself on the marble throne of the Court of the King's Bench in Westminster and summoned the judges from all the various courts. The king made clear his wish 'that they justly and duly administer the law without delay or favour', emphasizing that they do so, 'to any person, as well as to poor as to rich'. Richard's concern for justice had been a feature of his rule of the north in his brother's reign, and now it would become the signature of his own kingship. Richard would return to the Court of the King's Bench on a number of occasions during his reign, personally observing important trials and discussing legal issues with the judges concerned. He demonstrated an unusual interest in the law for an English sovereign, and his enquiries were informed ones, showing that he had more than a layman's legal knowledge. Richard would introduce important changes to the legal system, and his first and only parliament would pass major reforming legislation.

It remained to be seen whether these aspirations of good kingship would offset the controversial manner by which Richard had seized the throne. On 28 June 1483, two days into his reign, Richard III granted the dukedom of Norfolk to his loyal supporter John, Lord Howard. The introduction to the grant was both unusual and striking, showing – if we accept its rhetoric at face value – that Richard saw himself as being appointed by God as the man most suitable to be king: 'We, who under his providential design rule and govern his people,' the king began, 'endeavour by his grace to conform our will and acts to his will . . . to illumine [honour] those noble and distinguished men who are most worthy of public weal [esteem] . . .'

The wording, which echoed the preamble to Richard's foundation of a religious community at Middleham five years earlier, with its sense of destiny and spiritual protection, showed that Richard had moved beyond seeing his brother Edward IV's marriage pre-contract as an impediment to his nephew's claim to the throne. He now believed himself engaged on a divinely ordained mission of reform, one that would restore morality to a corrupt courtly way of life through a reinvigorated royal legislature.

Late medieval monarchy was a mixture of self-belief and pragmatism. John, Lord Howard had proven abilities, and was being promoted because he was a close ally of Richard and vital to the strength of his regime. And yet Richard was also righting an injustice. In November 1481 Howard ought to have received a half share of the lucrative inheritance of John Mowbray, Duke of Norfolk, on the death of his daughter and heiress Anne. However, Edward IV, strongly influenced by his queen, ignored both Howard's rights and his proven record of loyalty to the House of York, and instead granted the lands to his younger son, Richard. This decision alienated Howard from the Woodvilles. Thomas More commented dismissively of Richard's patronage that 'by great gifts he won himself unsteadfast friendships', but this royal grant won Howard's unswerving loyalty. Howard vigorously suppressed the Kentish section of the revolt against Richard in October 1483, and fought and died in the king's service at Bosworth.

Another victim of Edward IV's grant of the Mowbray lands to his son in 1481 was William, Lord Berkeley, and on the same day that Richard created Howard Duke of Norfolk he also elevated Berkeley to the earldom of Nottingham. The witness list to this creation suggested that an influential group of noblemen – including the Dukes of Buckingham and Suffolk, the Earls of Arundel, Lincoln and Northumberland and Lords Dudley and Stanley – had become disenchanted with the Woodville family and were, as a result, prepared to support Richard's accession as king. Richard also had the backing of Thomas Bourchier, Archbishop of Canterbury, Thomas Kempe, Bishop of London, and Robert Stillington, Bishop of Bath and Wells, who had revealed to Richard the existence of Edward IV's pre-contract of marriage earlier that month.

Even Lady Margaret Beaufort, mother of Henry Tudor, was at this stage willing to support Richard. On 5 July, on the eve of the coronation, she and her husband Lord Stanley sought an interview with the king at the Palace of Westminster at which Richard's chief justice William Hussey was also present. The possible return of her son Henry to the Yorkist court was under discussion and Margaret was also concerned about money – the substantial ransom that was owed her family by the French House of Orléans. Richard gave his full backing to her efforts to recoup this sum; Margaret, always the pragmatist, agreed in return to play a prominent part at Richard's coronation.

And at the sumptuous coronation ceremony of 6 July 1483 a substantial number of the English aristocracy were in attendance. They swore a remarkable oath of fealty to Richard III:

> I become true and faithful liegeman unto my sovereign lord King Richard III by the grace of God King of England and to his heirs, Kings of England, and to him and them my faith and truth shall bear during my natural life, and with him and his cause and quarrel at all times shall take his part and be ready to live and die against all earthly creatures and utterly endeavour me to the resistance and suppression of his enemies, rebels and traitors, if I shall know any, to the uttermost of my power, and nothing count that in any way be hurting to his noble and royal person.

The liturgy was enacted, the king was anointed, he took his own oath and afterwards feasted. Richard had made two important innovations to the ceremonies: he took the oath in English – the first time this ritual had not been conducted in courtly French; and he decided that the holy oil should in future be housed with the other regalia in Westminster Abbey. These two personal interventions were indications of Richard's own cultural interests and choices: he wished to update the ceremony in the interests of clarity and understanding, and he revered relics and religious ceremonial.

Richard, following the example of his brother Edward IV, also knew how to dress like a king and present himself in a regal setting. It took the literary ability of Sir Thomas More to stamp upon the Tudor imagination the idea that Richard was 'little of stature, ill-featured of limbs . . . hard-favoured of visage', or, as Shakespeare was to put it, 'not made to court an amorous looking-glass'. He does not seem to have been ugly in appearance. The more flattering of the two early portraits, in the Royal Collection, shows a not uncomely man, despite the lines of anxiety on the brow. He seems also to have possessed a pronounced taste for personal finery, fully in keeping with a respect for the dignity of kingship. For his coronation he wore, above a doublet of blue cloth of gold, 'wrought with nets and pineapples', a long gown of purple velvet, furred with ermine and enriched with 'powderings' of bogey-shanks, thin strips of fleece from the legs of lambs – a visually striking ensemble.

It was essential to dress to impress in late medieval society, and a failure to do so would have been greeted with scorn and derision. Later on the day of his coronation Richard changed into a long gown marked with the insignia of the Order of the Garter and with the White Roses of York. On the morning after it, the royal household supplied him with several changes of clothes (in crimson cloth checked with gold) together with a gift from his queen, a long gown of purple cloth of gold wrought with garters and roses, and lined with no less than eight yards of white damask.

Nor does the life of his court seem gloomy or restrained. Richard entertained at Middleham, in early May 1484, a German visitor, Nicolas von Poppelau, who was much taken by the king's graciousness towards him. For eight days he dined upon the royal table, and on one occasion Richard spontaneously gave him a gold chain, taken from the neck of 'a certain lord'. Poppelau was also struck by the magnificence of the music during the royal mass. Richard's interest in music as king is clear. He issued one warrant to one of the gentlemen of his chapel 'to seize for the king all the singing men as he can find in all the palaces, cathedrals, colleges, chapels and houses of religion', and some of his musicians were identifiable composers. Not all of them were concerned with sacred music; there were also the courtly dances, commented on – with clerical disapproval – by the *Croyland Chronicler*, recalling an 'unseemly stress upon dancing and festivity' during the court's celebration of Christmas in 1484.

Successful kingship was in part a matter of keeping up appearances. Jewels and plate were an equally important part of display and an indicator of the taste of the king. One sign of Richard's personal preferences was the bequest to him by Sir John Pilkington of his great emerald set in gold, for which the king had previously offered Pilkington as much as 100 marks (£66 13s 4d). Richard gave a good servant, William Mauleverer, a ring with a diamond, and George Cely a ruby with three pendant pearls. When he was short of cash, the royal jewels he pledged included a salt cellar and a helmet of Edward IV, both in gold and jewelled, and twelve images of the apostles in silver gilt. Richard arranged for his northern household to have for display a gold cup with a sapphire, and another of jasper decorated with gold, pearls and other stones.

A king or great lord needed to be surrounded with such magnificence to emphasize his place within the estate or social hierarchy of the realm. The records of the time give us further tantalizing glimpses of this: the jewels and silver vessels Richard bought in 1473 from the goldsmith Jacob Fasland and charged to the account of the receiver of Middleham; the furs and other costly clothes purchased for the duke and his 'most dearly beloved consort' on a Christmas shopping spree in London in December 1476, charged on this occasion to the account of his East Anglian receiver; and in the lavish celebrations of Christmas 1484, of which the *Croyland Chronicler* disapproved. Richard was also a builder, and this virtue won him the praise of John Rous, even in his otherwise hostile account composed in Henry VII's reign. Richard III in fact built extensively, at Middleham, Barnard Castle, Warwick and Nottingham; at Barnard Castle the carved white boars that marked his new work can still be seen today in castle and in town.

When Richard wished to win the loyalty of the Irish peer John FitzGerald, Earl of Desmond he sent him fine clothing of cloth of gold and velvet, along with a gold collar weighing twenty ounces, adorned with the Yorkist badges of roses and suns and Richard's own personal emblem, the white boar. A sense of finery was expected of medieval monarchs and was a vital part of how they communicated the majesty of their kingship. When the Lancastrian Henry VI was paraded before the people of London in April 1471, in a desperate bid to rally support around his regime, contemporaries were appalled by his shabby blue gown, which brought home to them how the ailing and unworldly king had lost all sense of the dignity of his office.

Richard's religious foundations also won Rous's praise. 'He founded a noble chantry for a hundred priests in the Cathedral of York,' Rous noted, 'and another college at Middleham. He founded another in the church of St Mary of Barking by the

Tower, and endowed Queens' College, Cambridge with 500 marks of annual rent.' This was outward show, but it was based on real religious practice, the practical piety expected of a king: knowledge of the liturgy, devotional practice and a wish to find solace in prayer.

Such outward qualities, vital for a late medieval ruler, are evident in Richard III if we look past Shakespeare and the Tudor chroniclers. As Dominic Mancini observed in 1483: 'The good reputation of his private life and public activities powerfully attracted the esteem of strangers.' And it was not just strangers. He inspired the devoted service of many men who came into contact with him, especially those such as Lovell, Ratcliffe and Brackenbury, who came early into his life and career. Men were prepared to fight for him, and if necessary to die for him. His tenant, Robert Morton of Bawdry in south Yorkshire, made his will on 20 August 1485, as he was 'going to maintain our most excellent king Richard III against the rebellion raised against him in this land'.

Above all, Richard had the virtue of fortitude. This was bound up with the practice of chivalry, and at the heart of chivalry was the profession of arms: fighting, raw courage and the quest for renown. Richard's chivalric credentials were impeccable, and it was the one virtue even his enemies were prepared to allow him. His physical courage cannot be doubted. He had fought in two battles under Edward IV when only eighteen, and it was his prowess in the first – Barnet – that won him the divisional command in the second – Tewkesbury. His campaign against the Scots in 1482 earned him high praise from his brother and plaudits throughout the realm. And in 1484 he told Nicolas von Poppelau: 'I wish that my kingdom lay upon the confines of Turkey; with my own people alone, and without the help of any other princes I should like to drive away not only the Turks but all my foes.'

Richard may have been small in stature, but physically he was remarkably strong, a point repeatedly made by Scottish ambassador Archibald Whitelaw in an address to the king on 12 September 1484: 'Never before,' Whitelaw stressed, 'has nature dared to encase in a smaller body such spirit and such strength.'

Outward display was thus all-important, but it is far harder to gauge Richard's inner motivation. The newly crowned Richard III shortly began a progress of his realm, where his qualities could be revealed to his people. The king's intention was to show himself in person around the country, to overcome any lingering doubts about the nature of his accession and thus promote his claim to the throne.

On his tour, Richard showed particular marks of favour to certain towns: at Oxford he attended learned disputations; Gloucester was given a charter. At Warwick he was joined by his queen, and he may also have met John Rous. At Nottingham, where Richard agreed on a new building programme for the castle, his secretary John Kendall happily wrote ahead to the city of York on 23 August 1483: 'The king's grace is in good health, and likewise the queen's grace, and in all their progress they have worshipfully been received with pageants, and his lords and judges sitting in every place, determining the complaints of the poor folk with due punishment of offenders against his laws.'

At the beginning of September Thomas Langton, Bishop of St David's, who was in Richard's entourage during this tour, wrote to the prior of Christ Church:

> I trust to God soon, by Michaelmas, the king shall be in London. He contents the people wherever he goes, better than ever did any prince; for many a poor man that has suffered wrong for many days has been relieved and helped by his commands in his progress. And in many great cities and towns were great sums of money given to him, which he has refused. On my faith I never liked the qualities of any prince as well as his; God has sent him to us for the welfare of us all.

This was largesse, a quality determined by greatness of heart, as both Nicolas von Poppelau and Archibald Whitelaw were to praise the king in 1484.

York was honoured as the place where Richard chose to invest his son as Prince of Wales. York's leading citizens and clergy were fully involved in the ceremony, and 13,000 white boars cut out of cloth, the king's personal badge, were distributed to spectators. The city responded by putting on a magnificent reception for him, and later staging a special performance of its Creed play.

The *Croyland Chronicler* was sceptical about Richard's real motives:

> Wishing to display his superior royal rank as diligently as possible in the north, where he [Richard] had spent most of his time previously, he left the city of London, and passing through Windsor, Oxford and Coventry, came at length to York. There, on a day appointed for the repetition of his crowning in the metropolitan church, he presented his only son, Edward, whom that same day he had created Prince of Wales, and arranged splendid and highly expensive feasts and entertainments to attract to himself the affection of many people.

Richard clearly was greeted joyfully in the north, and the Tudors were uncomfortable about this. Polydore Vergil began with a descriptive account, almost certainly drawn from eyewitness testimony. It was remarkably positive – until Vergil started twisting the knife:

> At York, Richard III was joyfully received of the citizens, who for his coming made for several days public and open triumph . . . When the day of procession was at hand, there was a great confluence of people for desire of beholding the new king. In which procession, very solemnly set forth and celebrated by the clergy, the king was present in person, adorned with a notably rich diadem, and accompanied with a great number of noblemen; the

queen followed, also with a crown upon her head, who led by her
hand her son Edward, crowned also with so great honour, joy and
congratulations of the inhabitants, as in show of rejoicing they
extolled King Richard above the skies.

And then the tone changed: 'The king began afterwards to take
on hand a certain new form of life, and to give the show and
countenance of a good man, whereby he might be accounted
more righteous, more mild, better affected to the commonality,
and more liberal, especially to the poor . . .'

While in Yorkshire, Richard personally intervened in a long-
running dispute involving the Plumpton family. The preamble to
the king's award, made on 16 September 1483, was not intended
for public consumption – and rather than being mere show,
clearly demonstrated Richard's concern for justice and his considerable understanding of the law: 'We, intending rest, peace
and quiet amongst our liege people and subjects,' Richard began,
'have taken upon us the business and labour in this behalf, and
reply by good deliberation, having heard and examined the
interest of the said parties . . . and by the advice of the lords of
our council and our judges thereunto called.'

These were noble sentiments, but Richard's progress was cut
short by a threatening rebellion against his rule that broke out in
October 1483. It involved loyalists to Edward V, die-hard
Lancastrians and, most remarkably, the Duke of Buckingham.
Buckingham's motives in rebelling after having gained so much
through Richard's accession will probably never be known to us.
Margaret Beaufort, having promised her support to Richard,
instead decided to throw in her lot with the Woodvilles. Her
motives were purely those of ambition and self-aggrandizement;
a consummate plotter – whom Polydore Vergil called 'the head
of that conspiracy' – she now saw a chance, through a marriage
alliance between her son and Elizabeth of York, of advancing
Henry Tudor to the English throne.

But Richard dealt with the risings with conviction and self-belief. Unrest in Kent was quashed by his loyal lieutenant John Howard, Duke of Norfolk, Buckingham's revolt in Wales ran out of momentum, and Richard bore down on the main area of opposition – in the West Country – in person. By the time the king had reached Exeter proceedings against him had all but collapsed. Henry Tudor, sailing from Brittany to support the revolt, saw what was afoot and promptly sailed back again. Buckingham was captured and executed at Salisbury on 2 November and the rebellion was all over.

In the aftermath of the revolt, which had been largely drawn from the southern counties, Richard stiffened his control there with trusted men of the north. The north–south divide was very real in late medieval society, and the king was taking a risk in introducing so many northerners to southern government. He showed leniency to Margaret Beaufort, confiscating her lands but allowing her to be held in the custody of her husband Thomas, Lord Stanley, whom Richard still trusted. But the king also sought to win support through a better provision of justice. Once again, his sentiments seemed sincere rather than contrived.

Richard's royal proclamation began: 'The king's highness is determined to see due administration of justice throughout his realm, and to reform, punish and subdue all extortions of the same.' It then stated his determination, on a tour of Kent in December 1483, to see 'every person that find himself grieved, oppressed or unlawfully wronged do make a bill of complaint and put it to his highness, and he shall be heard and without delay have such convenient remedy as shall accord with his laws. For his grace is utterly determined all his true subjects shall live in rest and quiet, and peaceably enjoy their lands, livelihoods and goods according to the laws of this land, which they be naturally born to inherit.'

On 23 January 1484 parliament was summoned and Richard's

title to the throne – the *Titulus Regius* – approved. During the session Richard required the lords and bishops to swear an oath of loyalty to his son. Soon after parliament ended, the king again showed the evidence of his true title to the London livery companies. Through these meetings, Richard was hoping to secure the dynastic future of his son and heir.

But Richard's parliament did far more than that. Its overriding theme was the provision of justice, reflected in the opening address of the Lord Chancellor, Bishop John Russell, which emphasized that the first duty of the prince was 'to give equal justice with pity and mercy'. Laws were passed ensuring the selection of honest jurors, forbidding the seizing of property of those held on suspicion of committing a felony prior to their conviction, and most importantly, authorizing justices of the peace to grant bail to those held under 'light suspicion' – the forerunner of our modern bail system. Legitimate property rights also received greater protection.

Richard now had the chance to develop his vision of kingship. He wanted to bring an end to the climate of sexual immorality prevalent at court and within the realm, writing to his bishops that 'amongst our other secular business and cares, our principal intent and fervent desire is to see virtue and cleanness of living to be advanced, increased and multiplied, and all other things repugnant to virtue, provoking the high indignation and fearful displeasure of God, to be repressed and annulled.'

Dominic Mancini related that Richard had won respect within the realm for his probity, whereas the Woodvilles were disliked for their lax morals. Mancini added that the feud between the queen's son by her previous marriage, Thomas, Marquis of Dorset, and William, Lord Hastings which had marred the last years of Edward IV, was not merely over public office but 'because of the mistresses they had abducted, or tried to entice from one another'.

Richard had at least two bastard children, but it is likely that both were born before his marriage to Anne Neville. His marriage itself appeared a happy one, and the records of the bishopric of Durham and Queens' College, Cambridge, both showed the couple co-operating over spiritual matters and sharing a very similar religious outlook. His condemnation of Woodville immorality was genuine enough and when he attacked the Marquis of Dorset in his proclamation against rebels for having 'many and sundry maids, widows and wives damnably and without shame devoured, deflowered and defouled', we hear not only Richard's adult piety, but also an echo of the violence against his mother that he had witnessed as a child.

Richard's interest in ritual and ceremony had already been shown in his support of the royal heralds, the experts in chivalry. He had overseen ordinances that encouraged heralds to cultivate manners and eloquence, and record contemporary feats of arms and ceremonies. As king, Richard gave them a charter of incorporation and the London house of Coldharbour as their headquarters. He owned a copy in Latin of Aegidius Colonna's *De Regimine Principum* ('The Conduct of Princes'), which was one of the standard fifteenth-century 'mirrors' or advice books, in which a prince could find delineated for him the embodiment of his role.

Pietro Carmeliano, who had come to England in 1480 and found employment as a chancery clerk, had few doubts that Richard possessed the virtues of such a good prince. In 1484 he dedicated a copy of his life of St Catherine to Sir Robert Brackenbury, and in his introduction penned a eulogy of praise to Brackenbury's master: 'If we look first of all for religious devotion, which of our princes shows a more genuine piety? If for justice, who can we reckon with above him throughout the world? If we contemplate the prudence of his service, both in peace and in waging war, who shall we judge as his equal? If we look for truth of soul, for wisdom, for loftiness of mind united with modesty, who stands before our King Richard?'

Two years later, under Henry VII, Carmeliano was one of the first to change his tune, denouncing Richard as 'a murderous tyrant'. Was he merely a court flatterer, churning out praises on demand? Or did he, in 1484, write what he believed was genuinely true?

The king was well-educated, and enjoyed the company of a notable group of Cambridge humanists, men such as William Beverley, John Shirwood and his private chaplain John Dokett, a scholar at King's College, Cambridge, and subsequently a student at Padua and Bologna, where he became a Doctor of Canon Law. Dokett later bequeathed books on canon law and theology to King's, and it is significant that the University of Cambridge not only supported the basis of Richard's claim to the throne, but appointed men to preach the justification of it on his behalf.

Richard was always intelligent. The *Croyland Chronicler* remarked that he 'never acted sleepily, but incisively and with the utmost vigilance'. Even Polydore Vergil praised him as a man 'to be feared for circumspection and celerity', who had 'a sharp wit, provident and subtle'. Richard was able to outwit his opponents in April 1483, surprise or outmanoeuvre Hastings the following June and outface Buckingham and the other rebels in October.

In a famous letter written from Lincoln on 12 October 1483 Richard spoke of his anger over Buckingham's rebellion, castigating him as 'the most untrue creature living'. He had evidently just heard of the revolt, and yet what is notable about the letter – amid all the emotion – is its lucidity of thinking. Richard wanted the great seal to be delivered to him, so that he could more readily control government business. His chancellor, John Russell, Bishop of Lincoln, was unwell, and what was revealing in the circumstances was the clarity and courtesy with which Richard set out the arrangements.

Richard now pulled off another striking achievement, persuading Elizabeth Woodville and her daughters to come out of sanctuary at Westminster Abbey. A solemn arrangement was drawn up on 1 March 1484, whereby Richard promised to provide reasonable marriages for the girls and, above all, made a sworn commitment: 'I shall see that they shall be in surety of their lives.' This telling phrase begged the question, nowhere made explicit, of what had actually happened to the queen's two sons, the Princes in the Tower.

As Richard had left on his progress in July 1483, the princes had largely disappeared from view in the inner recesses of the Tower. Their last servants were dismissed on 18 July. Before Dominic Mancini left London at the end of the month people openly said to him they feared the princes were already dead, but Mancini added that no one actually knew their fate. If Richard regarded his own claim to the throne as a cynical piece of deceit, as the Tudors believed, it would be vital to eliminate the princes as quickly as possible. If he felt that his own title was genuine, it would not be necessary to kill the boys, just to keep them securely guarded. This is what Richard seems to have done.

Then something happened that dramatically changed the situation. A plot was hatched to either rescue or remove the princes from the Tower. It involved attendants actually in the Tower complex itself, and starting diversionary fires around London, but the attempt failed and the ringleaders were rounded up and executed. Richard, on progress, seems to have learned of this on 29 July, when he wrote to his chancellor of 'an enterprise' recently taken against him: 'Whereas we understand that certain persons of such as of late have recently taken upon them the fact of an enterprise, as we doubt not that you have heard, be attached and in ward.' This was the rescue effort, and there now was a substantial risk in leaving the boys alive. Buckingham – who had not been on the first stage of the progress – dramatically rejoined Richard on 2 August at Gloucester. The fate of the princes must have been discussed by the two men. And then there was silence.

On the basis of all the material available we do not know what happened to the princes. (Please note this is an issue where the co-authors disagree – for this, see the debate in Appendix 1.) There is strong circumstantial evidence that Richard now ordered their murder, possibly on the advice or yielding to the persuasion of Buckingham – as most people thought at the time.

This is what Dominic Mancini said:

> After Hastings was removed, all the attendants who had waited upon the king [Edward V] were now debarred access to him. He and his brother were withdrawn into the inner apartments of the Tower proper, and day by day began to be seen more rarely behind the bars and windows, till at length they ceased to appear altogether. The physician Argentine, the last of his attendants whose services the king enjoyed, reported that the young king, like a victim prepared for sacrifice, sought remission of his sins by daily confession and penance, because he believed that death was facing him . . . I have seen many men burst into tears and lamentations when mention was made of him after his removal from men's sight; and already there was a suspicion that he had been done away with. Whether, however, he has been done away with, and by what manner of death, so far I have not at all discovered.

Mancini's testimony is deeply moving – and honest. On 15 January 1484, some six weeks before Richard's arrangement with Elizabeth Woodville was drawn up, the chancellor of France, Guillaume de Rochefort, made this announcement to the Estates-General at Tours: 'Look at what has happened in England since the death of King Edward IV: how his children, already big and courageous, have been put to death with impunity, and the royal crown transferred to their murderer by the favour of the people.'

Robert Ricart put it very simply in his calendar: 'in this year [the year ending 15 September 1483] the two sons of King Edward were put to silence in the Tower of London.' An early London chronicle also gave a key role to Buckingham: 'This year [1483] King Edward V, late called Prince of Wales, and Richard duke of York, his brother, King Edward IV's sons, were put to death in the Tower by the vise [advice/design] of the duke of Buckingham.'

Buckingham's involvement in the murder is entirely plausible; his taking sole responsibility for it far less so. When Nicolas von Poppelau visited Richard's court in 1484 he was interested in the fate of the princes. Many told him they thought they had been done away with, but how they did not know. Others expressed the hope that they were being hidden somewhere, in a dark enclosed room. 'This is what I would like to believe,' said Poppelau. But Richard remains the most likely candidate for their deaths. It may seem extraordinary to us that the widowed queen was now prepared to release her daughters to the man who could have murdered her sons, but what other choice did she have? She could not remain in sanctuary for ever.

If Richard had indeed ordered their deaths (and the evidence is suggestive but not conclusive), and if we allow for the possibility that he genuinely believed in the rightfulness of his own claim, from all that we know of his character, even in this ruthless age it was a course of action he would have embarked upon with reluctance and regret. Events may well have forced his hand – and the survival of his dynasty was at stake.

In the event, Richard's joy at delivering the daughters of Edward IV from sanctuary was short-lived. In April he learned that his only son, Edward of Middleham, had suddenly died, after a short illness. The *Croyland Chronicler* wrote starkly: 'You might have seen the father and mother, after hearing the news at Nottingham where they were staying, almost out of their minds for a long time with sudden grief.'

Richard, after having taken such careful steps to secure his son's succession, now had to begin all over again. He may at first have considered designating Edward, Earl of Warwick, the son of Clarence, as heir to the throne, but Edward was still only a child. Finally the king decided to settle the succession on John, Earl of Lincoln and the de la Pole family, the offspring of the marriage of his sister Elizabeth to John, Duke of Suffolk.

Shakespeare portrayed a king alienated from his family and from society as a whole, but in these difficult months Richard sought solace from his mother, writing to her on 3 June 1484, and asking 'in most humble and affectionate wise [way] of your daily blessing to my singular comfort and defence in my need'. And his reverence for his father grew ever more pronounced. On 10 September he founded a chantry at Wem, nine miles north of Shrewsbury, where the Duke of Buckingham had been captured after his unsuccessful revolt, and instructed prayers to be said specially for the soul of Richard, Duke of York, as if the invocation of his memory would be a shield against his present troubles.

Much of late medieval monarchy was about public display and utterance, but in September 1484 Richard wrote to the Irish Earl of Desmond in highly personal terms, commiserating with him over the circumstances of his father's death, in Edward IV's reign. Richard's letter opened a remarkable window on the king's private thoughts. Desmond's father had been murdered in February 1468, it was alleged, by the Earl of Worcester acting on behalf of the Woodville family. Desmond had told Edward IV that his marriage was entirely unsuitable and the queen had never forgiven him for the remark.

Richard expressed his sympathy, confiding to the earl that 'he had always had inward compassion of the death of his father' and then made a striking comparison with the execution of his brother George, Duke of Clarence, telling the earl 'notwithstanding that the semblable [similar] chance was and happened sithen [since] within this realm of England, as well of his brother, the duke of Clarence, as other his nigh kinsmen and great friends'. Richard's clear inference here was that Woodville influence lay behind both men's deaths. It is intriguing to speculate who the other 'nigh kinsmen and great friends' might have been. It is possible that Richard was referring to the deaths of Richard Neville, Earl of Warwick and his brother John, Marquis of Montagu – in other words blaming the fracture between Warwick and Edward IV, in which Richard had remained loyal to his brother Edward, entirely on the king's Woodville marriage.

Richard remembered the support Desmond's father had given to his own father in Ireland, in 1459–60. And in his letter he chose to style himself as the son of Richard, Duke of York rather than the brother of Edward IV, strongly hinting at his alienation from his brother's court. Richard emphasized that his true feelings had remained 'inward' – that is to say it had been unsafe to show them openly. His recollection mirrored the comments of Dominic Mancini, who portrayed a court bedevilled by suspicion and intrigue. If Richard had been forced to keep his opinions to himself for much of his brother's reign, these were not the actions of a dissembler, but of a man who feared for his own future.

Now times had moved on. In October 1484 the king's sole remaining challenger, Henry Tudor, fled from Brittany and took shelter in France, protected by the minority regime of Charles VIII. The French took the decision to recognize Henry's claim to the throne, and asked him to publicize it. In private, they were unable to ascertain whether he had any right to the throne at all.

In November Henry set out letters condemning Richard as an 'unnatural tyrant and homicide' who had forfeited the right to rule. In the following month, Richard responded, deriding Henry Tudor's pedigree, which he said gave him no right to the kingdom whatsoever 'as every man well knoweth'. At Christmas 1484 Elizabeth Woodville sent her daughters to court. She also attempted to persuade the Marquis of Dorset to renounce his allegiance to Tudor, and return to England to make his peace with Richard. Then on 16 March 1485 Richard's wife Anne Neville fell ill and died of tuberculosis. Rumours began to spread that Richard now wanted to marry his niece, Elizabeth of York. These were unfounded, and Richard vigorously denied them. In fact, after the queen's death, a match between the king and Joanna of Portugal had been planned. The Portuguese ruling house also held – through their descent from one of Henry IV's sisters – what was now the primary Lancastrian claim to the English throne. Through this marriage alliance Richard knew he would further undercut Henry Tudor's credentials and also unite the Houses of York and Lancaster.

It is hard to judge a reign that lasted only a little over two years. As he did not have time to show what manner of king he would be, to a great extent Richard's achievements will always be overshadowed by the way he took the throne. And yet he brought an idealistic vision and considerable energy to his kingship. He pursued a sensible and effective foreign policy, and some of his administrative innovations were notable, including setting up a Council of the North, to provide better government for the region, and establishing a Court of Requests to give the poor better access to the judicial system. The opportunity to continue such policies would now be dependent on Richard defeating his one remaining political opponent.

In May 1485 the French government started cautiously to release funds for Tudor's invasion force. Richard moved to his mother's residence at Berkhamsted to seek her blessing on his enterprise. This seems an unlikely course of action if – as Polydore Vergil later insinuated – Richard had grievously slandered Cecily Neville's reputation with the unfounded allegation that Edward IV may have been illegitimate. Richard – out of reverence for his father and respect for his mother – wished to champion a rightful inheritance from the House of York, not fight as an outsider from its ranks.

Richard then moved to Nottingham Castle and prepared to meet his challenger. The king's military preparations were almost complete. From early in the year he had been purchasing guns and employing specialists from Flanders to manufacture more in the Tower of London. Richard intended to deploy field artillery and numerous hand guns against his opponent and this ordnance was now moved up to the Midlands. Richard had also bought 168 suits of Milanese plate armour; its relative lightness and mobility made it ideal equipment for a cavalry charge.

On 23 June Richard issued a second proclamation against Tudor, amplifying the contents of the first, and specifically stressing that he was of bastard stock in both his paternal and maternal lineages. Henry Tudor's French backers were now showing less enthusiasm for his cause and on 13 July he had to borrow the remainder of the money needed to pay his mercenary troops. By the end of the month his small invasion army had gathered at the Norman port of Honfleur. Events were drawing towards their inevitable climax: a clash of arms on the battlefield.

9

The Identification of the Remains

Thursday, 6 December 2012

I T HAD BEEN an anxious three months. The circumstantial evidence surrounding the remains had been powerful. The chances of finding another set like these, of the right age, sex and condition, with what could be battle wounds and a specific pathology (scoliosis), buried in the choir of the church, had been estimated at a million to one. The odds told us that the remains must be those of King Richard, but in the twenty-first century scientific proof is essential.

The date of the actual founding of the Greyfriars in Leicester is unknown, but a house connected to the friary existed on the site in 1230, with the chapel first mentioned in 1255. As King Richard was buried there in 1485, this gave us a window of two and a half centuries of potential burials at the Greyfriars. We also had two interesting details to work with. First, we had a stop date for the burials in the church in 1538, with the Dissolution of the Monasteries. Further, from what the historic record suggested, Richard III had been the last known recorded burial within the church, which gave another potential window of only one burial in the church in its last fifty years (1485–1538). If the carbon-14 dating placed the remains in the late fifteenth century, these factors would add to the likelihood of the remains being those of Richard III.

Richard Buckley, Lead Archaeologist from ULAS, and Lin Foxhall, Head of Archaeology and Ancient History at Leicester University, had warned me that the identification process would take time: they would be carrying out every possible test to make sure the results were reliable. These tests were numerous and exhaustive. There was the stratification study of the site, with its finds, large and small; the genealogical confirmation and the DNA analysis; the osteology, which included the dental report and CT scans of the remains, pre- and post-wash; the investigation of the scoliosis; and the forensic trauma analysis by a weapons expert. In addition, there was the isotopic and calculus analysis, the parasite sample examination of the soil and of course the big one, the carbon-14 dating.

I'd been asked not to contact ULAS because DSP wanted to capture my first reactions to the results on film. As the client in the project it was a big ask but I'd agreed. I'd only spoken to Richard Buckley in the early stages of the investigation when he had relayed some disturbing news that the sex of the Greyfriars skeleton was in doubt.

With the results in, I headed to ULAS to meet Nick Cooper, the small finds expert and first in a series of specialists I would be consulting. With Simon Farnaby and Dr John Ashdown-Hill present, Cooper quickly brought us up to date regarding the barbed arrowhead. This had been found in the grave at the back of the skeleton between the second and third thoracic vertebrae, although not lodged in the bone. Detailed X-rays now revealed it to be a nail, probably Roman, which had already been in the ground where the body had been laid in the Greyfriars Church. It was not the auspicious start I had been hoping for, but the next result was far more important.

My palms were sweating as Richard Buckley arrived and we moved to his computer. Buckley was about to reveal the results of the carbon-14 tests on the bones. Carbon-14 dating is used to estimate the age of organic material by calculating the rate of decay of the carbon-14 in the material. These tests could get us to within an eighty-year period. For there to be any chance that the Greyfriars remains were Richard III, who was buried in 1485, the carbon dating result would have to fall within the mid to late fifteenth and early sixteenth centuries.

As we gathered round Buckley's computer, I scanned his face for any give-away signs and made a mental note not to go up against him at a poker table. First he told us that the stratification study of the site had shown that the remains were found in the medieval layer. Cut medieval floor tiles had been found nearby, indicating a hastily dug grave. The tiles were at the correct height for a medieval floor, with the grave itself two to three feet deep. Further, the later Victorian foundations had missed the remains by only three inches, near the leg bones.

Two samples of rib bone had been submitted to two specialist radio-carbon dating laboratories to enable the results to be cross-checked. The work was undertaken by the Scottish Universities Environmental Research Centre at the University of Glasgow, and the Oxford Radiocarbon Accelerator Unit, part of Oxford University's Research Laboratory for Archaeology and the History of Art.

Buckley presented the carbon-14 data on screen. It showed a 95 per cent probability that the Greyfriars remains dated from about 1430 to 1460, too early for Richard III but far too late for any of the other known burials in the church. It was a blow. But it wasn't the end. The analysis had thrown up an anomaly. Stable isotope analysis indicated that the person in the grave had had a high protein diet. This diet had been heavily marine-based, and as marine animals absorb significant amounts of carbon-14, the result had been skewed. The recalibrated analysis provided a 68 per cent probability that the age of the skeleton lay between 1475 and 1530, with a 95 per cent probability of a date between 1450 and 1540. Richard had died in 1485. I could hardly believe it. Buckley added that a heavily based marine diet was indicative of a high-status individual, since the usual medieval diet consisted of potage, a vegetable-based soup. I was elated with these results and sure it was Richard III, but the osteology results were still to come. Would these confirm my belief, or dash my hopes?

Friday, 7 December 2012

Dr Jo Appleby had undertaken the osteology examination at ULAS and was waiting to reveal the results to us in one of the ULAS finds rooms, together with Dr Piers Mitchell, a scoliosis specialist and hospital consultant from the University of Cambridge.

I knew that a comprehensive record of this whole process had to be made, but I was worried about the way the DSP footage and the university's photography would be released to the world. I was anxious to avoid a repeat of the humiliating display of his dead body after Bosworth.

Before filming started, Louise Osmond, award-winning director for DSP, tried to allay my fears by explaining what I would see. The remains would be on a table in the centre of the darkened room, positioned on a specially designed light box that would illuminate them gently from beneath. There would be no harsh strip lighting in an impersonal laboratory setting, and the remains would be given as much dignity within the analysis as possible. This explanation was a comfort, but didn't alter my feeling that I was about to do the very thing I had tried to avoid.

I shed quiet tears of despair despite Simon Farnaby gently reminding me that the only option was to display Richard's remains; the world had to see him for itself.

I don't remember the opening words of the session. All I could see was the box that illuminated him, his washed bones bright against the darkness. To me he seemed unprotected and I felt like a ghoul invading his privacy. I saw faces, mouths moving, and then I heard the word hunchback again. It was all too much: I had to escape that dreadful room.

Agreements had been negotiated to prevent the public display of pictures of Richard's body except in museum archives and these were important to me. But now they seemed worthless, buried by the scientific demand for visible proof. I stood outside, wondering desperately how I could prevent pictures of Richard's remains from being strewn over the internet.

I was joined by Sarah Levitt who had become a friend and understood the turmoil I was in; but as Head of Museum Services she also understood the pressure to authenticate the find. She reminded me that the search for Richard had always been about the truth: 'This is Richard's moment to reveal his truth,' she said.

But there was still that awful word, 'hunchback', that I thought had been discarded. Why had the specialist used it – and to describe scoliosis? Simon Farnaby told me to go back in and stand up for myself and make Piers Mitchell explain. I thought about all those who gave to the International Appeal and who had saved this project for Richard; not for me, or any scientists and TV programme. I returned to the room and could now look at Richard so beautifully illuminated, and see his remains for what they were: the evidence he would give to the world.

Jo Appleby and Piers Mitchell stood at the far side of the light box facing Simon Farnaby and me. Appleby was confirming the age of the remains, which were of someone in their late twenties to late thirties (Richard was thirty-two). Lifting the skull with great care away from the lower jaw, the mandible, she tilted it towards us to show the inner cavity. She pointed to the top surface where the bone plates met, her finger indicating a smooth but jagged line. Here the sutures of the skull were still visible, but had fused, thus providing the estimate of age. In addition, the third molars, the wisdom teeth, had erupted which meant the remains were those of an adult, since wisdom teeth normally develop some time between the ages of seventeen and twenty-five. I asked about the rest of the teeth. She said they were in relatively good condition, with some dental calculus (calcified plaque) and a few cavities, with the missing front tooth most likely lost in the grave as there was no evidence of trauma on the bone or healing, but the later dental report would investigate this further.

Next, Piers Mitchell explained the scoliosis. He had measured the remains, and the angle of the curvature of the spine appeared to be sixty degrees, but it could have been as much as eighty degrees in life. Without seeing him in the flesh, it was difficult to tell how severe the scoliosis would have looked. It was idiopathic scoliosis, that is, of no known cause: he hadn't been born with the condition – it had developed later in life. It was most likely progressive and may have led to a shortness of breath, due to increased pressure on the lungs.

The most common cause of scoliosis is hormonal. As puberty began, at around ten to twelve years, the spine would have begun to curve. How long it would have taken to reach its final shape was impossible to tell. The curve was a 'C' shape, in the upper torso, not an 'S' shape, and would have made the right shoulder appear higher than the left. Mitchell now showed us the two clavicle bones, or shoulder bones, and pointed out that the end of the right clavicle was a different size and shape, much bigger than the left. He said that the individual would have been an ordinary child, and, as the lower and upper vertebrae had a straight alignment, would have stood erect and walked normally. The hip joints and the length of the legs also suggested a normal gait. However, without the feet, Appleby added, it might be difficult to prove this conclusively.

Seeing the extent of the C-shaped curvature of the spine, I asked Mitchell if it would have been painful, but he couldn't answer. I cited the example of the DSP cameraman at the dig who had curvature of the spine and had been in great pain after carrying a heavy camera. Mitchell still wouldn't be drawn and moved on to describe the skeleton, again using the word hunchback. He said that, although we knew the person didn't have kyphosis, when bent forward there was probably some form of prominence on the right side. He called this prominence 'hunchback' merely as a commonly understood term.

Jo Appleby resumed her analysis. She said that the remains were in good condition and suggested someone well-nourished in life. The femur (thigh) bones and the bones of the lower leg were strong with good muscular development and attachment. Mitchell added that the arms showed no sign of being withered. The upper arm bones – the humerus – were the same length and symmetrical. The lower arm bones, the radius and ulna, though normal, were gracile – that is, quite graceful and slender.

Appleby then moved down to the pelvis, lifting it gently to reveal the sciatic notches, the circular gaps that indicate the sex of a skeleton. A smaller gap was male; larger was female (for child-birth). In the Greyfriars remains the gap was of medium size, and therefore the gender was indeterminate. It could be female. At this point, Appleby explained the scale against which human remains are measured. At one end is the heavy-set, thick-browed, very male person, and at the other an incredibly delicate female. In between, you have every possible variation, from a very mus-cular female to a delicate male. The Greyfriars remains, with their gracile lower arm bones and pelvis, were around the centre of the scale. I asked if this could be part of the pubescent hormo-nal disturbance that brought on the scoliosis, but they couldn't say. Appleby declared that, on balance, she thought the remains were male, but only the DNA result would confirm it one way or the other. As far as height was concerned, she said the skeleton was five feet eight inches tall, above average for the fifteenth century, but the scoliosis would have taken two or more inches off the person's height. As the lower leg bones showed no evidence of injury or trauma, the missing feet had been removed while the remains lay buried in the grave – most likely by the Victorian builders.

Next, Robert Woosnam-Savage, Curator of European Edged Weapons at the Royal Armouries in Leeds, and Dr Stuart Hamilton, Deputy Chief Forensic Pathologist, East Midlands Forensic Pathology Unit, would reveal the likely sequence of events during the last moments of life, and explain the nature of the fatal blows.

In his research, Woosnam-Savage deals with the most vicious of human behaviour on the battlefield, with the weapons of the era. He could be aptly named, but the sensitivity he and Stuart Hamilton showed helped me get through that day. They had warned me in advance that the presentation would be detailed and possibly distressing. I accepted that; we can't change events, but we have to know the facts in order to understand them.

Woosnam-Savage began by saying that he would call the remains Richard, and that he would start at the top of the skull and work downwards. Hamilton agreed, saying this would reveal the likely sequence of injuries. Jo Appleby tilted the skull towards us, and Woosnam-Savage pointed to a distinct shave wound. A sharp-bladed weapon, a sword or halberd, had been swung directly at the head from behind, with such force that it had taken off a thin slice of skin and bone. It, or a similar blow, had even skipped slightly, and made a second shave wound immediately after. Another blow, also from behind but at a slightly different angle, had been aimed at the head, but again had taken only another small slice of skin and bone. The skull had not taken the full impact of the blow.

From the angle of the strokes, Woosnam-Savage concluded that mere scalping was not intended, and also that Richard's head must have been uncovered to have received such a wound; he was possibly bending or on his knees, though this was not certain. Woosnam-Savage couldn't say whether Richard had ducked and dived away from the blows, so that they failed to connect fully, or whether the attackers' aim was faulty in a frenzied mêlée. But it seems that Richard may have been dazed by these first injuries, because the next wound was close up and on target.

Appleby tilted the skull again. There was a square puncture wound visible at the top. I remembered this from the exhumation and had assumed it had been made by a pole-axe. It hadn't. A much more likely candidate for the weapon that delivered this penetrating injury was a type of dagger with a four-sided blade, such as a rondel dagger. The dagger could have been placed directly above the top of the head and then, using the palm of the other hand on the pommel for extra force, pushed down into the head with brute strength. Appleby moved the skull to show the interior and the two small flaps of bone the knife wound had dislodged inside. The weapon had penetrated the bone, and affected the brain, but it was not a fatal wounding.

Now Jo Appleby turned the skull round to show the back. Here, there was no doubt about the violence wrought upon Richard's head. Woosnam-Savage said it looked very much as if a cutting blade, such as that found on a halberd, had been swung down with force, and sliced off part of the back of the head, taking a portion of the brain with it. This may have proved a fatal blow, and, if so, death would have been almost instantaneous. Hamilton agreed, conjecturing that Richard would most likely have felt nothing but the impact before losing consciousness. The powerful swing had left a flap of skull still attached, no doubt matted with blood, hair and grey matter from his exposed brain. Woosnam-Savage commented on how this slicing motion, along with the other scoops and slices to the skull, agreed so well with the most evocative description found in a 'praise poem' written for the Welsh noble, Rhys ap Thomas, who may have played a crucial role in the battle. The poem was written before about 1493 by the poet Guto'r Glyn, who also fought at Bosworth: '*Lladd y baedd, eilliodd ei ben*' ('Killed the boar, shaved his head').

Appleby turned the skull again slightly to reveal another potentially fatal wound. The tip of a sword, or bladed weapon, had been thrust through the head on the right, penetrating to a depth of just over four inches and marking the inside of the skull on the opposite side. Although there was no way to determine the sequence of the blows this wound alone would have been enough to kill Richard, as it was a stab perfectly capable of felling him almost at once.

Six wounds to the head had made their mark on the bones but death, when it came, had probably been immediate. In the adrenalin rush, Richard would have felt nothing: the shave wounds like bumps and scratches, the knife wound a dull thud in his head.

Woosnam-Savage wanted us to see the face. Appleby put the skull back on the mandible so that it was complete on the light box. On the right of the mandible there was a slash mark, a knife wound, but not very deep, or long. It would need further inves-tigation to tell whether it had been done to remove Richard's helmet strap or was another attack wound, but it looked as if it too could have been delivered from behind. Above the cut was a single stab wound on the cheekbone to the right of the nose, potentially from a four-sided dagger, such as a rondel. It was a clean, square puncture wound similar to that on the top of the skull, so perhaps it was inflicted by the same attacker. Woosnam-Savage showed how an assailant might have come from behind and held Richard's head for purchase as he stabbed the dagger into his face, but not to its full extent. Might Richard have been fighting on his knees?

Woosnam-Savage believed it would be speculation to go any further. Unlike remains from many battle sites, including Towton in 1461, the features were not terribly defaced. It appeared that Richard may have been protected from further damage, perhaps on the orders of Henry Tudor. If Henry was to claim King Richard's throne, he needed his rival not only dead, but seen to be dead, and not just on the battlefield; civilian observers who had known him and could identify him would be essential to Tudor plans.

From the marks on the bones, Woosnam-Savage and Appleby calculated there were a total of eight wounds to the head, all of which had come from behind. The legend that King Richard's head had hit Bow Bridge on his return to Leicester, where his spur had struck on the way to battle, was, it seems, a myth, as there was no mark to suggest the skull could have struck a bridge.

Richard's armour had done its job: his arms and legs showed no attack marks or defensive wounds. But there was a further post-mortem wound, another cut from behind, where a dagger had been slashed across a rib on the right-hand side of his back, although whether this was inflicted with the armour removed, or as it was being cut off the body was unclear. It was suggestive, however, of a probable 'victory' blow.

I felt a sense of relief, as I thought we had come to the end, but the story was not over yet. The body had one final wound to reveal. Woosnam-Savage squeezed my hand, and quietly told me to prepare myself. In his study of human remains from medieval battlefields, he had never come across what he regarded as such blatant physical evidence for the particular and final indignity inflicted on Richard's body.

He asked us to move down the table. Appleby lifted the pelvis and tilted it towards us. Woosnam-Savage pointed to a small but deep cut that went in one side and out the other. Richard had been stabbed in the right buttock, so forcibly that the blade had penetrated the pelvic bone. The weapon used may have been a double-edged sword or dagger, but Woosnam-Savage thought the very fine nature of the trauma indicated it was most likely a dagger.

The atmosphere in the room had been quietly sombre. Now it was charged with shock. I could scarcely take in his words. The acute angle of the cut showed, Woosnam-Savage explained, that it probably couldn't have been made when the armoured Richard was standing, or even lying on the ground. The blow would, however, appear to be consistent with it having been struck when his body was perhaps tilted and at a more readily accessible angle, his rear presenting an easy target. He had most likely been stabbed while slung over the back of the horse that bore him back to Leicester.

This was the final proof Woosnam-Savage needed to satisfy himself that the Greyfriars skeleton was indeed that of Richard III. It was an insult injury. In his years of study into the nature of battlefield trauma he had come across many insult injuries, but it was the placement and angle of this one that had convinced him, and was why he had decided to name the remains throughout his presentation. Stuart Hamilton had seen this kind of insult injury in the backside inflicted by today's football hooligans. Nothing is new, he remarked. He too was convinced by it that the skeleton was that of Richard III.

Richard had revealed his story. His bones didn't record any other wounds or insult injuries, only his ignominious burial.

In Jo Appleby's opinion the grave was hastily dug as it was too short for the body, and as a result the head was discovered at a higher level during the exhumation. His hands and arms were still together but positioned over his right pelvic area, suggesting his hands had been tied. With his hands bound, the chances were that his body had not been washed or properly prepared for burial. He might not have been given a shroud either. Was it Henry Tudor's henchmen who shoved the corpse into the earth naked and despoiled? And did Henry Tudor choose the site in the friars' sanctum deliberately so that the grave would not become a House of York shrine?

I shared the quiet journey back to the hotel through the dark, wintry streets of Leicester with the DSP team. We dropped Bob Woosnam-Savage off at the station to catch his train, and he squeezed my hand again before he jumped out. The day was over, and I felt a sort of relief: at least we wouldn't have to go through that again and nor would Richard.

I drank and laughed that night. It's true what they say: when the dark times pass, people need to remind themselves that they're alive. Just for a short while I certainly did, but I had more weeks of worry ahead of me. Professor Caroline Wilkinson at the University of Dundee was to carry out the facial reconstruction and much would be revealed at the end of that painstaking process. And the DNA testing would establish the most important facts of all regarding the identity of the Greyfriars remains. Suddenly all my certainty that they were those of Richard Plantagenet was thrown into the air again.

Wednesday, 16 January 2013

With the cost of the university's analysis work mounting, it looked as if the facial reconstruction would have to be abandoned. But Dr Phil Stone, chairman of the Richard III Society, declared that the society would commission and fund this part of the project. To see the face of the remains discovered at the dig would be a crucial part of the society's investigative work. For me it would be a further step in the quest for the real Richard III. Finally to see the face of the last warrior King of England, the man I had sought for the last four years, would be the culmination of a long and difficult journey. It would also be an enormous personal relief since after all the research it would have seemed wrong not to proceed to the project's visual conclusion. For purposes of veracity, DSP would administer the facial reconstruction process whilst filming it and then hand over the completed reconstruction to the society at the end of the project.

The surviving portraits of Richard are all sixteenth-century copies of lost originals. The only possible contemporary portrait is a drawing in historian John Rous's *The Rous Roll*, which was completed during Richard's reign, some time between 1483 and 1484 when his son was still alive, as it depicts Richard with his wife and son. Richard is standing upright in his armour wearing a crown, his dark hair arranged in the style of the period, akin to a bob. The face echoes typical sixteenth-century portraiture, being quite compact, with a strong jaw and chin and well-defined features. Rous's drawing, however, is a brief, ethereal representation and with no particular detail to go on, Richard's face remained as enigmatic as ever.

I had asked Dr Turi King, DNA expert at the University of Leicester, whether the tests would divulge the colour of Richard's hair and eyes. King said that if we were successful in isolating the ancient DNA then advances in this technology meant that information as to colouring would probably be available in the future.

In the meantime, Richard's facial reconstruction was complete. Professor Caroline Wilkinson, a leading expert in facial anthropology, had worked on TV programmes *Meet the Ancestors* and *History Cold Case*, bringing to life many deeply human projects. She had used photography and detailed 3D CT scans of the skull to create an accurate reconstruction and was assisted by Janice Aitken, a specialist artist and lecturer at the University of

Dundee's Duncan Jordanstone College of Art and Design, who added the final skin tones and colouring.

Before I was to see the reconstruction, Professor Wilkinson talked Simon Farnaby and me through the preliminary stages of the process using computer graphics. Wilkinson first examined the orbital structure to determine the depth and size of the eyes, adding the eyeballs. The reconstruction then followed a process based on the anatomical formations of the head and neck, where scientific standards are used to interpret the facial features. Computer-generated pegs are placed on the skull to act as guidelines for soft tissue depths. This data, taken from living individuals, is used to predict the amount of fat and skin over the muscle structure. Once this was done, the finished head was replicated in plastic and the hair, skin and eye colour added.

The reconstructed head was set up in the centre of the main archaeological finds room at the Archaeological Institute, University College London. To enable DSP to record me meeting Richard for the first time, I was asked to close my eyes as Simon Farnaby led me in. After a few moments' hesitation, I opened my eyes. Richard's face took me completely by surprise. I don't know exactly what I had expected but it wasn't this. I was not confronted by a stern face marred by thin lips and narrow eyes; nor features worn down by worry and grief. Instead it was the face of a young man who looked as if he were about to speak, and to smile. I searched in vain for the tyrant. I can't describe the joy I felt. I was face to face with the real Richard III.

Sunday, 3 February 2013

It was the afternoon of the day before the University of Leicester was to announce the results of all the tests to the world's media. Unlike modern DNA which can be isolated in a matter of days, ancient DNA is incredibly delicate and difficult to deal with. Dr Turi King led the investigation, making it a model of excellence by using a double-blind test. Four molars from the skeleton had been carefully removed in a sterile lab and ground to a fine powder. If the DNA was there, it would have been protected inside the tooth's enamel. The powder was divided between the Université Paul Sabatier in Toulouse, France, and the University of York, and by using two samples and two laboratories Turi King was hoping to reduce any possibility of error.

A sample of Michael Ibsen's DNA had been taken at the beginning of the dig and King had sequenced it in her labs, identifying its particular code. If Richard's DNA matched that of his alleged seventeenth-generation nephew, it would be the final piece of evidence that the Greyfriars remains were those of the king. The test would also check for the male Y-chromosome since it was feasible, though unlikely, that the remains could be those of a female. Evidence of gender had yet to be found.

Michael Ibsen had asked for the result of the investigation to be revealed to him first privately. Turi King met him in an office in the university then brought him to meet Simon Farnaby, Richard Buckley and me.

As Michael entered he was in shock, his face ashen. King began with the news that a Y-chromosome had been found, meaning that the Greyfriars skeleton was male. She then revealed that the mitochondrial (female line) DNA was a complete match. This confirmed that Michael was a direct genetic descendant of Richard's elder sister, Anne of York, and that he carried the same rare genetic subgroup as the Greyfriars skeleton – his seventeenth-generation great uncle, Richard III. Moreover, with the help of Morris Bierbrier, genealogist and author Kevin Schurer, a historian at Leicester University, had traced a second line of maternal descent from Richard's sister, Anne of York. Michael Ibsen not only had a new cousin, but the DNA of this person was also a perfect match, and could be triangulated with Ibsen's line from the original research by Dr John Ashdown-Hill.

The remains we had found on 25 August 2012, in the Leicester City Council Social Services car park, were those of King Richard III (1452–85).

Was I surprised the DNA was a perfect match? Yes and no. The project had run so smoothly, from the finding of Richard's remains on the first day, exactly where I thought they would be, to the carbon-14 dating, the osteology, scoliosis, insult wound and facial reconstruction. Although I believed from the very beginning that the remains were those of Richard, I had been assailed by fears and doubts throughout the process. Now, after confirmation of the identity of the remains, I was unmoved. Perhaps it was exhaustion. Perhaps it was a new concern.

Leicester University wanted to publish pictures of the remains, including the skull. However, I didn't want the skull to be shown full face, as a mark of respect to the man, and the university had agreed that no images would be shown that might be considered prurient. The university had also assured me that I would be allowed to attend its scientific announcement as they would be inviting Sir Peter Soulsby, the Reverend David Monteith from the cathedral, and the team from Channel 4 and DSP, but there was no invitation for Dr John Ashdown-Hill. University scientists would form the panel issuing the statement but I would be allowed to speak at the end.

Monday, 4 February 2013

At 11 a.m., the University of Leicester made its historic announcement. The investigative work of the scientists had been exemplary, their conclusions compelling and I was thrilled that Richard Buckley was asked to declare the identity of the remains.

He said: 'It is the academic conclusion of the University of Leicester that the individual exhumed at the Greyfriars in August 2012 is indeed King Richard III, the last Plantagenet King of England.'

That evening Channel 4 in association with Darlow Smithson Productions, premiered the documentary that had taken nearly two years to bring to fruition. *Richard III: The King in the Car Park* told the story of the search for the king's grave.

10

Bosworth

I N AUGUST 1485 events moved rapidly. Henry Tudor embarked
from France with a small invasion force at the beginning of
the month and reached Milford Haven in south Wales on 7
August. When Richard heard the news of Tudor's landing he
immediately set about recruiting his army, and then, with preparations nearly complete, moved his forces from Nottingham to
Leicester. Tudor, who had marched through Wales gathering
recruits to his cause, and had reached Shrewsbury on 17 August,
was now fast approaching. Contemporaries realized that a major
battle was not far off, and the anxious citizens of Nottingham
sent out a rider to shadow the king's army and report back on the
outcome of events. They would not have long to wait.

Richard III and his army rode out from Leicester on the
morning of 21 August 1485. Richard's force had been recruited
quickly and purposefully, and was around 8,000 strong. The king
had learned from his scouts that his rival Henry Tudor had dis-
embarked in Wales with little more than 2,000 men. Although
he had gathered further reinforcements, these were not numerous. Tudor's army was now on the Warwickshire-Leicestershire
border near Atherstone, and as yet no major English nobleman
had thrown in his lot with the challenger. The king now had the
opportunity to crush the smaller force of his opponent.

Richard was responding to this threat against his rule with
urgency. If he delayed, he knew that Tudor had a chance to

increase his strength considerably, forging an alliance with the powerful Stanley family. The head of the family, Thomas, Lord Stanley, was married to Tudor's mother, Lady Margaret Beaufort. Margaret had plotted on her son's behalf during an earlier rebellion against Richard's rule, in 1483, but on that occasion the Stanleys had stayed loyal to the king. However, in the summer of 1485 Richard openly suspected Stanley's younger brother, Sir William, of being in treasonable communication with his opponent. If Sir William Stanley and his retainers from Cheshire and the Welsh Marches joined Tudor's cause, it would more than double the strength of his army.

Richard had taken precautions against such a danger, keeping Sir William's nephew as a hostage within his own force. Mindful of this, and aware that Tudor's chances did not look good, Stanley brought his men into the vicinity of Atherstone, but did not join Henry. Stanley's temporizing offered Richard a chance to strike hard and fast against the weaker army of his rival, and it was one that he now seized upon. Moving westwards out of Leicester, the royal forces covered some fifteen miles that day, reaching the area around Market Bosworth in the evening. Richard and his men then camped on the nearest high ground surrounding Ambien Hill. The king's attention was fixed firmly on the road south, the old Roman road running through Atherstone, and then on to London. It was the route Henry and his followers – now gathered close to Atherstone in the grounds of Merevale Abbey, eight miles to the west – would take the next morning. When they did so, they would find Richard's army firmly blocking their path.

In the summer of 1485 the realm of England had already seen thirty years of civil war. Long periods of relative peace and prosperity were interspersed with bouts of sudden, violent fighting. The armies approaching each other were of very different character. Tudor's was predominantly a mercenary force from

France, Brittany and Scotland, with smaller contingents of Welsh and Englishmen. He had experienced war captains with him, including the Lancastrian exile John, Earl of Oxford and the French soldier of fortune Philibert de Chandée. And there were those who had joined his cause repelled by Richard's violent accession to the throne. The majority of these men would fight with grim professionalism.

By contrast, Richard III's army was fully English, recruited from the royal household and the retinues of major aristocrats such as John, Duke of Norfolk and Henry, Earl of Northumberland. Both men had strongly supported him when he took the throne, and in the first major rebellion against his rule. Richard had also brought up an artillery train.

In the fifteenth century gunpowder weaponry was transforming the face of medieval warfare. Cannon were now routinely used in sieges, and smaller field guns and hand arms were also beginning to be deployed on the battlefield. Artillery was rarely seen in earlier civil war clashes, but Richard – always interested in the latest military technology – this time brought guns from the royal arsenal in the Tower of London, and some were even transported from the English garrison at Calais. The king's intention, as far as we can gauge it, was to place his artillery ahead of Tudor's advancing forces and, as they approached, let off a series of volleys to demoralize his army.

We cannot of course know what was going on in Richard's head as he prepared for battle. He left no personal account of his actions, and those of his closest followers who survived wisely said little about them during the reign of Bosworth's victor, Henry Tudor (who after Richard's death became Henry VII, the founder of the new dynasty). But Tudor chroniclers were quick to second-guess Richard's state of mind – a characterization that culminated with William Shakespeare's dramatic portrayal of man and battle. In these accounts, which grew more and more exaggerated, Richard was nervous and uneasy, afflicted by terrible nightmares in which his victims rose as one to curse him and his army. Sinister prophecies circulated, including one found pinned to the king's own tent flap, foretelling that the monarch and his followers would be betrayed, just as they had betrayed so many others. Henry Tudor was the avenging angel, poised ready to administer this divine punishment.

According to Tudor sources, Richard went into battle with desperate resolve. This, however, was not shared by his army, who quickly began to desert him. Seeing the battle spiralling out of his control, Richard then attempted to find and overcome his Tudor opponent – but instead was left, isolated and alone, overwhelmed by a mass of his enemies. Tudor Bosworth was thus a morality play, where the forces of good enjoyed a rightful and inevitable triumph.

But there was nothing inevitable about the outcome of a medieval battle. Instead of resorting to a series of moral judgements about Richard III and his army, it is vital to consider what the king's real intentions might have been, from what we know of him as a man and from the battle experience of the Wars of the Roses. We must put him firmly back into the context of his times.

Richard was going into battle against a man he had never met, and whom he knew little about. His rival and challenger Henry Tudor was twenty-eight years old, five years younger than Richard. But most of Tudor's adult life had been spent out of the country, as an exile in Brittany, and then in France. In Tudor accounts – and in Shakespeare's play – Henry's apparent anonymity was cast as a virtue, his inoffensive demeanour becoming a mirror to reflect back all the more strongly the horror of Richard's crimes. But bland and anodyne leadership was not a virtue on the battlefield. In an age where charismatic leadership was an essential prerequisite of military success, Tudor – during his advance into the English Midlands in August 1485 – had contrived to lose touch with the rest of his soldiers for a whole day. Fearful and disorientated, he was relieved to find them again at nightfall. A challenger to the throne who managed to lose his entire army could also easily lose the confidence of his followers. The clash of personalities at Bosworth was far less clear-cut than Tudor accounts would have us believe.

Richard had ample time to think about this confrontation. From the autumn of the previous year, Tudor, sheltering in the court of the young French king Charles VIII, had claimed the throne of England, sending out a stream of letters and proclamations, styling himself in the manner of a king, and urging his supporters to rise up and join him when his invasion was launched. Now that time had come.

This was an age where one's ancestry, one's family pedigree, was thoroughly scrutinized in lavish genealogies commissioned by ruling dynasties and aristocratic houses. But, despite the support of the French, Henry Tudor's own claim to the throne was very weak, as Richard had made clear in his proclamations of 7 December 1484 and 23 June 1485. His lineage, from his mother, Lady Margaret Beaufort, linked him to the royal blood of the House of Lancaster, but the Beauforts were of bastard stock, and although legitimated at the end of the fourteenth century they had been specifically barred from succession to the throne. Henry's grandfather, Owen Tudor, had married Henry V's widowed Queen Katherine, connecting him to the French House of Valois, but the circumstances of this secret marriage to a man of lowly rank and status were disreputable, and the couple's first child, Edmund (Henry Tudor's father), may well have been born before the ceremony took place. Beyond this, Tudor had a supposed descent from a distant Welsh prince and a hoped-for marriage to Elizabeth of York, the eldest daughter of Richard's brother, Edward IV. But Henry would have to win at Bosworth for such a marriage to come about.

He therefore drew his chief credentials from relentless attacks on Richard and the violence he had used in taking the throne. Henry had repeatedly denigrated the king as a murderer and homicide, who no longer had the right to rule the country. Here lay the genesis of Tudor mythology about Richard III. The new dynasty was forced to attack Richard's reputation because its own claim to the throne was so weak. And yet, for this strategy to be effective, its accusations had to be founded upon at least some measure of fact. The Princes in the Tower had disappeared shortly after Richard had taken the throne, and many believed the rumours that they had been murdered by the king. Richard had certainly executed a number of noblemen as he took power, on charges of treason that looked contrived and unconvincing to others; it is more likely that they were seen as threats to Richard and so were summarily removed. But after the bloody events of the summer of 1483 Richard ruled moderately and with merit. Tudor's accusations therefore carried some weight, but whether they would be enough to unseat the king in battle was far from clear.

This was a ruthless and self-interested age, where loyalty and moral scruple were tempered with pragmatism. Richard III had disposed of one serious uprising, in the autumn of 1483, and the majority of the English peerage had stayed loyal to him. However, one thing was clear: Henry Tudor was now the king's only serious challenger. The Tudors were keen to stress Richard III's anxiety on the eve of battle. But Richard would have known that if he could decisively defeat Henry and his invading army, his own rule would then be secure.

Both men had much to gain through seeking the death of their opponent in combat. In the bloody clashes of the Wars of the Roses, decisive victory rested not only in winning on the battle-field, but by ensuring the death of one's challenger. Bosworth did not happen in isolation – it was part of a series of battles where vendettas were pursued and old scores settled. As we have seen, in the first engagement of the civil war, at St Albans in 1455, fighting ceased once Richard, Duke of York, Richard's father, had slain his bitter rival, Edmund, Duke of Somerset, chief councillor to the Lancastrian King Henry VI. In the cruel clash at Wakefield in 1460 the roles were reversed: it was now a Lancastrian army that surrounded and cut down the Duke of York, and in the aftermath of battle despoiled his body. These were events that Richard had learned of as a child, and they were central to the story of his family, the House of York, and its claim to the throne of England. It was a claim that had to be fought for repeatedly – and that fight reached its culmination at Bosworth.

Brutal realpolitik was paramount when Richard, now a young man, was able to participate in battle himself. After a misguided policy of leniency and conciliation in the early part of his reign, his brother Edward IV had faced a renewed assault on the throne. He was at first driven out of the country, but returned with an army to turn the tables on his opponents with a vigorous campaign and victories at Barnet and Tewkesbury in April and May 1471. In the latter battle and its aftermath Edward deliberately killed all his principal challengers, even those who had found sanctuary at Tewkesbury Abbey. Some chroniclers believed Edward IV perjured himself, solemnly promising those inside a pardon if they left the abbey; others that he had desecrated holy ground by hauling them out by force. But the message from the House of York was clear: when faced with dynastic challenge, no mercy would be shown to any future opponent.

Richard at this troubled time does not come across as nervous and tormented, but rather as a man of action – decisive and uncompromising. We have spoken of his support for Edward IV at Barnet and Tewkesbury. His performance in the battles that restored his brother to the throne in 1471 demonstrated he was a warrior of considerable bravery. Some years later, in an endowment to Queens' College, Cambridge, Richard remembered those who had fallen by his side in battle, recalling each by name, even the most humble of his retainers. Such careful commemoration was unusual in late medieval society – and notable. Richard had positive values of his own, prizing courage as the standard to attain for himself and those around him.

The Tudor portrait of an amoral tyrant is countered by Richard's strong interest in the chivalric code – the code of honour that bound medieval knights together – and to the ritual of chivalry, owning ordinances about the conduct of knightly affairs. He was fascinated by the crusades, the greatest examples of martial endeavour in the medieval age, and this fascination was linked to a genuine and deeply felt piety. We know that he owned a small collection of chivalric texts, and one of his books, a beautifully illuminated manuscript, depicted a king of ancient times, Alexander the Great, seeking out and dispatching his rival Porus in mounted combat. These two crowned leaders were shown in a fight to the death, while the majority of their followers looked on.

With such a background, it is entirely plausible that Richard III wished to imitate this action at Bosworth, and strike down his challenger himself. If so, he would think carefully about the shape of the engagement ahead of him, not defensively and fearfully, as the Tudors would have us believe, but boldly and aggressively. Richard would need to anticipate the contours of the battle, plan his tactics, anticipate how Henry Tudor would arrange his army, and, above all, imagine where his opponent might place himself within it.

In medieval combat, armies were organized in three main units: a vanguard, main division and rearguard. A courageous commander, wishing to lead by example and inspire his troops, would position himself in the main division, amid the principal grouping of his men, and make himself clearly visible. As an additional demonstration of resolve, he would dismount and fight on foot, showing he would never flee the field and that battle would end in victory or death. Some seventy years earlier, England's great warrior king Henry V deliberately placed himself in the middle of his main battle grouping at Agincourt. Henry V was wearing a richly adorned battle crown and fighting under the royal standard – a target for his enemies but a fighting example to his men. And that fighting example had been crowned with success: a crushing defeat of a numerically superior French army.

But Henry Tudor was no Henry V. His only experience of battle had been as a frightened twelve-year-old, witnessing, at a safe distance, the overthrow and devastating defeat of the forces of his guardian William, Lord Herbert at Edgecote in 1469. In the aftermath of this debacle, young Tudor had been led away to safety by a Shropshire knight, Sir Richard Corbet. It was hardly propitious that as Tudor's invading army crossed Wales and entered England at the town of Shrewsbury, Corbet and a small body of followers were once more there to greet him. Corbet had reminded the challenger, if reminder was necessary, of this act of service – giving Henry an unhappy premonition of the battle he was about to face against King Richard III.

Richard may well have heard about Henry's flight from the field from his guardian and mentor, the Earl of Warwick, whose retainers had crushed Herbert's army, although he would not have read much into it at the time; Tudor after all was only twelve. But the image presented here – of a hapless and frightened bystander, at the mercy of events he is unable to control – would be repeated in Henry's adulthood, in two further incidents Richard most certainly knew about. With little other experience of his challenger, these may have formed, over time, his opinion of Tudor's character and mettle.

The first had occurred in November 1476, during the second reign, after his brief period of exile, of the Yorkist Edward IV.

Richard was prominent at court and in the counsel of his brother the king; Tudor, by contrast, was an exile in the Duchy of Brittany. Edward was now eliminating all potential challengers to the throne, and the previous year had devised a most convenient 'accident' for one of them, Henry, Duke of Exeter, whom he arranged to be pushed off a boat and drowned on his return from the king's French expedition. He then turned his attention to another possible threat – Henry Tudor – and an embassy was sent to the Breton court demanding he be handed over to the English king.

Once again, this was Edward IV, not his brother Richard, demonstrating absolute ruthlessness in order to safeguard his rule. Unluckily for Tudor, his protector, the Duke of Brittany, had fallen ill. During this illness the duke's principal adviser – temporarily governing the duchy – was amenable to negotiating a deal with the English. As a result, Tudor was handed over to Edward's men and forcibly escorted to the Breton port of Saint-Malo. Nineteen-year-old Henry imagined that he was about to suffer a similar maritime mishap to that of his unfortunate predecessor. Fearing this prospect, and clearly in terror of his life, he succumbed to a violent burst of stomach cramps, exclaiming he was unable to proceed any further. During the ensuing confusion, the invalid suddenly regained his mobility and fled into one of Saint-Malo's churches, claiming the right of sanctuary. Edward IV's men then tried to extricate him from his new-found ecclesiastical shelter. It was a strange echo of the denouement of the Battle of Tewkesbury some five years earlier, where Edward IV's opponents also sought refuge in consecrated ground, but had been forced out and executed. But for Tudor – unlike the Lancastrians at Tewkesbury – there was a happy ending to the drama.

For the townspeople of Saint-Malo, watching events with considerable interest, now strongly took against the activities of the English. Resenting foreigners forcing their way into one of their own churches, a mob of irate Bretons rallied to the assistance of Tudor. An uneasy stand-off followed. At this very moment the Duke of Brittany made a sudden recovery from his illness, and hearing what was happening, sent a party of riders to overtake the English ambassadors, rescue Henry from sanctuary and secure his return to the Breton court.

It was a dramatic adventure, and young Tudor was certainly lucky to have survived it. His story would have been told with wry humour at the Yorkist court. At the age of eighteen Richard had fought his way out of trouble in battle, demonstrating presence of mind and bravery, and at Tewkesbury he had commanded a Yorkist division. His opponent – when faced with a threat to life and limb – had collapsed with stomach pains. Tudor's retreat into sanctuary was only too understandable. But it was also undignified and even, in retrospect, darkly comic.

Richard would have remembered this story. Another incident, which took place after he had secured the throne, gave it greater force. In the autumn of 1483 Richard faced the first major rebellion against his rule. The conspirators staged a series of uprisings: in Kent, Wales and the West Country. Richard and his supporters responded quickly and confidently to this threat. John, Duke of Norfolk, who would be chosen as commander of Richard's vanguard at Bosworth, had speedily overwhelmed the Kentish rebels. The West Country rising was more dangerous, and Richard resolved to deal with it in person. The West Country rebels were supposed to be supported by Henry Tudor, who had raised a small force in Brittany and set sail to assist them.

As Richard bore down on the rebel stronghold at Exeter, Tudor's ships hesitantly appeared off the Devon coastline. Tudor's intervention was less than heroic. He sent a small boat to the shore to ascertain the progress of the uprising. Judging that it was not going well, he then quickly turned tail and fled back to Brittany, never actually setting foot on English soil in support of the rebellion. Richard – prizing courage as a virtue above all others – may well have decided at this time that Henry Tudor was a coward.

In August 1485 Henry Tudor had finally managed to land – though in Wales not the West Country – and was marching towards Richard. As the king sent out spies and informers to gather intelligence on his rival's advance, he was struck by the news that one of Tudor's principal supporters, his uncle Jasper, who had shared Henry's Breton exile and landed with his force at Milford Haven, was no longer accompanying him. It was hard to explain such an extraordinary absence, unless his opponent was so despairing of his chances that he had deliberately left Jasper behind in Wales to safeguard an escape route if the battle went badly. The king would have drawn much encouragement from this. His opponent hardly seemed to be spoiling for a fight. And if this was so, Richard could expect that the cautious and militarily inexperienced Tudor, rather than dismounting and making himself a target in the centre of his army, would remain on horseback and position himself well to its rear.

Here we now have a different Richard on the eve of battle. Far from being paralysed with indecision, he sought to exploit the battle initiative. And if he believed Tudor was primed to flee at a moment's notice, Richard would need to counter this, and thereby scotch all threat of rebellion once and for all.

There is evidence that Richard had already devised a plan to prevent his challenger rapidly departing from the battlefield. Richard ordered some of his men to gather at Leicester 'horsed and harnessed' – ready to fight either on horseback or on foot. And he had within the ranks of his solely English army one foreign adviser, a Spaniard, Juan de Salazar, an experienced military professional who may have been skilled in the organization of cavalry attacks. Richard, it seems, was envisaging the launch of a sudden, mounted charge against the rearguard of his opponent, to overwhelm his force and cut him down before he could flee from the field.

These are not the actions of an uneasy and apprehensive villain. If we put Richard back into the context of his times, we gain a different sense of him, in which the king had decided – in advance of actual battle – to destroy his challenger, and had drawn up a clear plan for doing so. Richard was an avid reader of chivalric romances, and within these a cavalry charge was extolled as the epitome of valour, so he knew that if he achieved success in this fashion, he would win martial kudos as well as destroying all opposition to his rule, kudos that might serve to offset the damage done to his reputation by the way in which he had taken the throne. In this scenario, Bosworth, far from being a moral judgement on his character, would become an act of redemption defining his right to rule.

It was, in purely military terms, a risky course to undertake because timing and co-ordination on the battlefield would become difficult after the charge was launched. Once again, there were military precedents for this. The Battle of Towton, in 1461, was the Yorkist victory that put Richard's brother, Edward IV, on the throne. It was the bloodiest clash of the entire civil war, fought for an entire day in a blinding snowstorm, and during the course of this the Yorkists were at first worsted. Their Lancastrian opponents then launched a cavalry charge to finish them off. But the charge was not supported by the infantry behind, who moved too slowly to back it up, giving the Yorkists the opportunity to repulse the attack and regain the initiative. Again at Tewkesbury, in 1471, a battle where Richard was present and in command of the Yorkist vanguard, his opponents once more charged his position – only to find that others had failed to join them. On this occasion, one of the Lancastrian leaders, the Duke of Somerset, became so irate that he returned and smote off the offending captain's head. Unsurprisingly, this

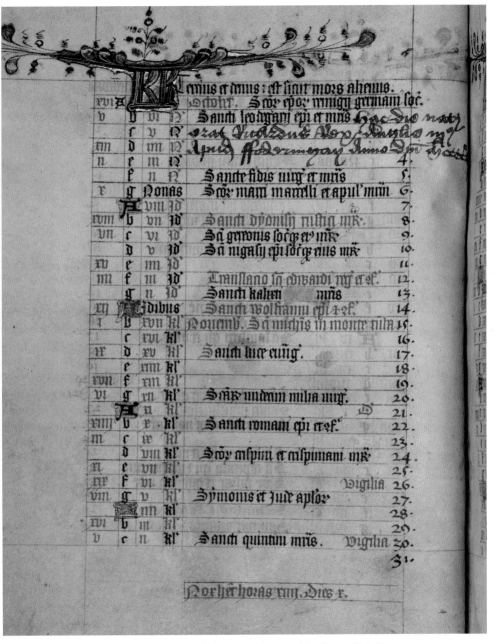

Richard's book of hours – showing his date of birth
at Fotheringhay (2 October 1452), written in his own hand

Fotheringhay Church

Tomb of
Richard's
father, Richard
Duke of York

Baynard's Castle – the London residence of Cecily Neville, where Richard stayed during much of his Protectorate in 1483

Cecily Neville's seal – both her piety and her political acumen would be inherited by her youngest son

Portrait of Richard's older brother, King Edward IV

Middleham Castle – where Richard was brought up and later a favourite residence of his as Lord of the North

Richard's signature as Duke of Gloucester and one of his mottoes (*tant le desiree* – 'I have longed for it so much') at the bottom of his manuscript copy of *Ipomedon* – the story of 'the best knight in the world'

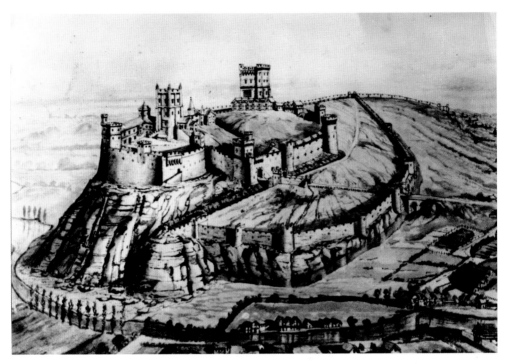

Nottingham Castle – enlarged by Richard, and where
he stayed before the Battle of Bosworth

Richard's opponent
and rival to the
throne, Henry Tudor

The likely battlefield area – remnants of the marsh, with
the high ground of Crown Hill rising above it

Recent artillery
finds at Bosworth

The boar badge found on
the edge of the marsh –
where Richard was probably
overwhelmed by his foes

0   30mm

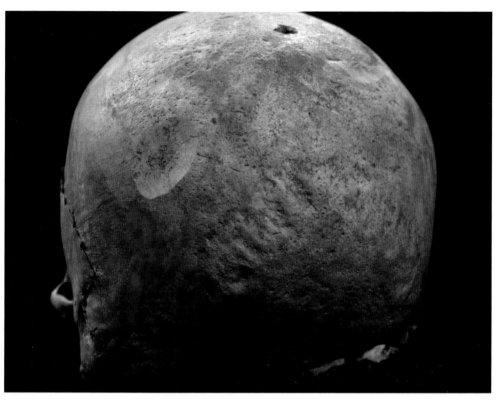

Close up of Richard's skull showing battle wounds

The death of a king: the three weapons used to kill Richard
(sword, halberd and rondel dagger)

Effigy of Sir John Cheney, Salisbury Cathedral, the man who protected Henry Tudor as Richard's last charge came so close to killing his opponent

Memorial brass of Sir John Sacheverell of Morley (Derbyshire), recording that he fought at Bosworth for Richard III

Richard's final moments of combat, from the carved bed lintel of Rhys ap Thomas. The king's horse is to the left of the halberdier

action quickly led to the entire Lancastrian line dissolving into chaos.

As Richard was well aware of such danger, we can assume he consciously chose to take the risk, aiming to enact his cavalry manoeuvre successfully, and thereby prove his right to be king through courage on the battlefield. Such a bold course would also pre-empt any intervention by the Stanleys. With Sir William Stanley's forces close by, the sooner Richard could finish the battle, the better his chances of victory.

It was Tudor, not Richard, who had most reason to be nervous and fearful on the eve of combat. While Richard marched to battle, Henry had spent the day in Atherstone, locked in fruitless discussions with Sir William Stanley. As the king's army was so near, it was vital that Tudor and Stanley now combine their forces, but Sir William would not commit to doing so. He was of course still worried about the fate of his nephew, who Richard would surely execute as soon as Sir William joined Tudor's army. He may also have been pessimistic about Henry's chances of securing victory. Stanley would only promise to advance in the direction of the king's forces, but keeping his men separate and at a distance from Tudor's, with a vague assurance that he would intervene directly when the opportunity was right. Henry may or may not have believed him, but he had to act as if he did, for without Stanley's assistance he was outnumbered three to one by the royal army and facing almost certain defeat.

On his return to Merevale Abbey that night Henry consulted with his principal captains, the Earl of Oxford and Philibert de Chandée, and together they decided on their battle tactics. Unusually, they would advance towards Richard's army with the largest part of their strength concentrated in the vanguard, including many of the French mercenaries. The hope was to force an early advantage, which would persuade Stanley to commit himself at last to Tudor's cause. This was a desperate gamble, and all knew that if it failed, their forces would be overwhelmed and destroyed. Accordingly, it was agreed that Henry would place himself among the rearguard, and this would be positioned a substantial distance from the main battle line – almost a mile behind it – to give him a chance of escaping the field. These battle dispositions could hardly have filled Tudor's men with confidence, and yet it seems that this forlorn hope was embraced with grim determination. With Henry so far from the majority of his troops, he would be unable to exercise any meaningful control over his army and the command was instead given to Oxford. Once again Tudor was relegated to the role of a helpless bystander, watching while his fate was decided by others.

Henry's inner feelings at this critical moment can be glimpsed from his later donation of a stained-glass window to Merevale Abbey, in commemoration of the battle. The window was of St Armel, a little-known Breton saint adopted by Tudor at an earlier time of crisis, when his ship was caught in a storm and buffeted by winds off the coast of France, and seemed certain to sink. Henry had appealed to Armel, and credited his survival to the saint's miraculous intercession. The window portrait of Armel – a fourth-century bishop – uniquely depicted him in plate armour, strongly suggesting that Tudor had prayed to him for assistance in the forthcoming battle. Henry was once more in mortal danger, and very much at the mercy of events.

The mood in the royal camp was rather different. On the morning of 22 August Richard assembled his army and, once it was fully gathered, paraded before it, displaying to them in a procession along the battle line 'the rich crown of England', part of the coronation regalia – and possibly the crown of Edward the Confessor. This was a solemn ceremony that required time and careful preparation to enact. The king wished to show his men, through this ritual, that success in battle would at last firmly establish the Yorkist dynasty and mark a new beginning to his reign. This powerful statement of intent by the ruling monarch belied later Tudor claims that Richard awoke troubled and demoralized, with his men in disarray. Rather, the king was confident and ready for the fight. After the ritual was complete, he led his men out on to the Roman road, and, moving westwards, took up battle positions several miles along it, between the small villages of Fenny Drayton and Dadlington, there to await the arrival of Tudor's army.

Tudor's forces had further to march, and after leaving the vicinity of Merevale Abbey they struck out over its adjoining fields. It was harvest time, and Henry later paid out compensation to the parishes of Atterton and Fenny Drayton as his troops, fanning out towards Richard's expected position, trampled down the crops. They then formed up along the road, and pushed forward towards the village of Fenny Drayton. Beyond it lay the royal army.

Battle began in the middle of the morning, when Richard's guns opened up on Tudor's approaching vanguard. It must have been a demoralizing moment for Oxford and Chandée, seeing for the first time the full size of the army deployed against them and now on the receiving end of an artillery bombardment. But in this desperate situation they responded with skill and ingenuity. To lessen the effect of Richard's guns they resolved to close with his troops quickly, devising a flanking attack that took advantage of the protection of a nearby marsh, which enabled them, with the benefit of the strong morning sun behind them, to bring their full strength down on the wing of Richard's vanguard. The king's forces – commanded by the Duke of Norfolk – were taken aback by the force of this attack and, while fighting stalwartly, began to be pushed back by their assailants. Now Stanley's troops could also be seen – drawn up some distance from the fighting – but despite the initial success of Tudor's army Sir William made no attempt to intervene.

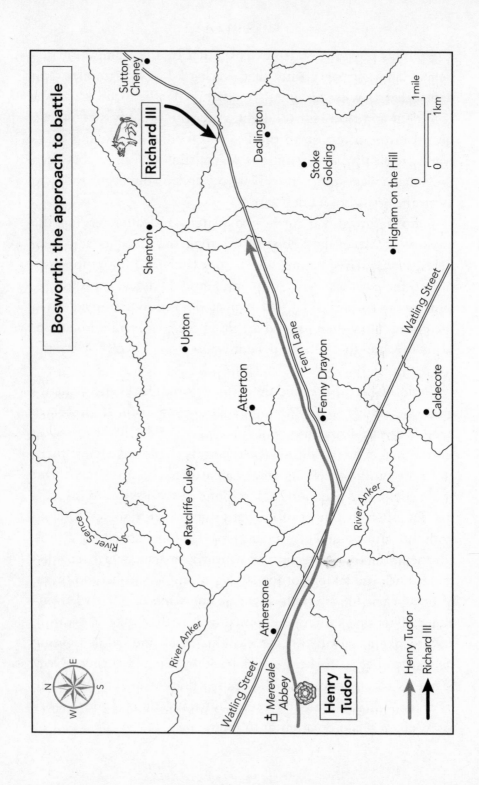

Bosworth: the approach to battle

It was at this opening stage of the battle that Richard III first caught sight of his Tudor challenger. Henry and his rearguard had now appeared, at a considerable distance behind the main body of his forces. In Richard's eyes, a battle-winning opportunity was opening up before him. The two vanguards were still closely engaged, Stanley's forces stood immobile and seemingly removed from the fighting and Tudor and his small contingent were now in view, dangerously isolated from the rest of his army. Richard quickly made his decision. He had the opportunity that he had hoped for. He would launch a massed cavalry charge at his opponent, and finish with Tudor once and for all.

Tudor sources later derided Richard's charge as an impulsive gamble, one that was prompted by the discovery of treachery amid his followers. They imply that – after the clash of the vanguards – the king was rapidly losing control of his army, which showed little stomach for the fight, and that his attack on Tudor was an ill-prepared and desperate act that stood no chance of success. But these accounts are unconvincing, for Richard gathered his cavalry force with calm deliberation. We have already invoked Richard's ritual preparation for battle. A signal was given to the chosen men of his main division, the king placing a loose-fitting robe displaying the royal coat of arms over his armour. His followers mounted up. Richard then donned a battle crown, a specially made helmet with a circlet crown welded to it. His men readied themselves for the charge. Finally, the king lifted his battle-axe. The line of horsemen began to move forward, slowly at first, then with increasing momentum, swinging wide past the clashing vanguards before gathering speed to close on Henry's position.

Tudor was taken completely by surprise by this bold attack, and pandemonium broke out among his retinue when Richard's force was suddenly sighted. It was now too late for the challenger to flee, and an account by one of the French mercenaries in Henry's army related how Tudor instead decided to dismount and was then hidden among the men of his personal bodyguard, to present a less visible target. 'He wanted to be on foot – in the midst of us,' the soldier said candidly. But once again, at a moment of crisis Henry was blessed by good fortune. A small body of French pikemen was standing nearby, placed there by Oxford – in reserve – as an additional precaution. There were few of them, but they were well-trained, and, following a desperate appeal for help, these men quickly dropped back and enclosed Henry in a mass of bristling weaponry.

The pike was an eighteen-foot-long wooden stave with a steel head. It was formidable in tight, unbroken formation. These troops had been a special parting gift to Tudor from the French king. And, luckily for Henry, they were trained in a recently adopted Swiss technique to counter a cavalry charge, in which a front rank would kneel with their weapons sloping up, the second standing behind them with their pikes angled, the third with their weapons held at waist level. It had been found that a mounted attack would be considerably slowed by such a formation. But this was only a small force; the majority of the pikemen had been deployed with the Earl of Oxford in the vanguard of Tudor's army. King Richard still had the chance to fight his way to victory.

The majority of Tudor's forces were still on horseback and Richard and his followers ploughed straight through them. There must have been a terrible collision between the king's mounted troops and Tudor's retinue, the clattering shock of impact followed by sheer chaos as riders crashed into each other, and those behind into their fellows. Tudor stood dismounted, protected by his French soldiers, as the king drove his way towards his standard.

King Richard was close to victory. But the phalanx of pikemen formed around Henry had bought him precious time. Richard was fighting with extraordinary determination, but he was also cut off, far from the main part of his army, his picked body of horsemen isolated and vulnerable. Sir William Stanley, watching proceedings from higher ground nearby, was being offered a most tempting target. As Richard sought out his opponent, one of Henry's mercenaries recollected the king crying out in rage and frustration, cursing the body of pikemen: 'These French traitors are today the cause of our realm's ruin.' This has the ring of a genuine memory from someone close enough to hear. Although it is impossible to know the exact sequence, it seems likely that Stanley now decided to commit his forces against the king. The battle was nearing its awful climax.

Richard now faced a crisis. Most sources agree that the king's supporters urged him to flee at some stage of the fighting, and this appears to be the likeliest moment. Richard was told to quit the battlefield and save his life. Richard spurned the opportunity. His reply was grimly defiant. He would finish the matter, and kill Tudor, or die in the attempt.

This was a heroic way to fight. All contemporaries, even the most critical, now spoke with admiration of Richard's courage, that he 'bore himself like a gallant knight' and he 'fought manfully to the very end'. There was a sense of awe as he and his men now hurled themselves into the thickest press of their opponents. But Stanley's men were approaching; there was so little time. The king's men seemed to have joined in a body around his banner and smashed their way through Tudor's forces towards the slender pike wall that offered Henry his last protection. The rival standards were only yards apart as this ferocious surge carried Richard towards his challenger.

At this critical point in the battle, Richard reached Tudor's standard, cutting it down and killing the standard-bearer, Sir

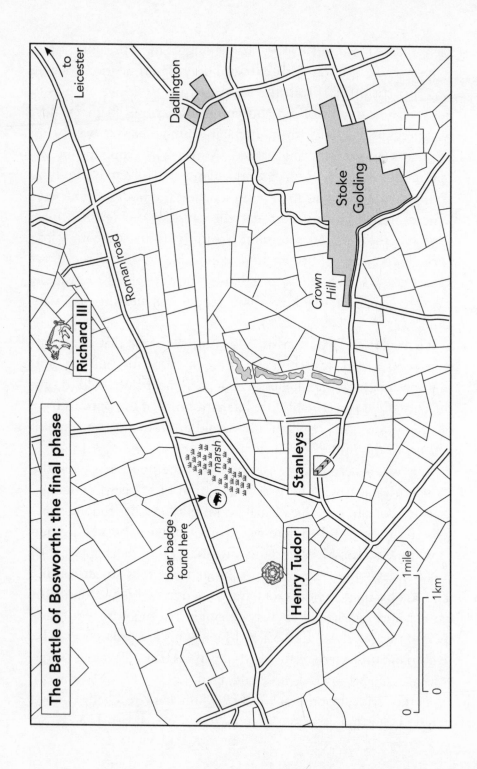

The Battle of Bosworth: the final phase

to Leicester

Dadlington

Stoke Golding

Roman road

Richard III

Crown Hill

Stanleys

marsh

boar badge found here

Henry Tudor

0   1 mile

0   1 km

William Brandon. He was now tantalizingly close to Henry himself. Tudor – still dismounted – made no attempt to engage his opponent, and it was left to others to try to fend off Richard's attack. A flux of horsemen was now swirling around Henry's pike position. A strong knight, Sir John Cheney, rode in front of them, blocking Richard's way, and further protecting his master. The king flung him aside. Tudor would have been only a few feet from him, but Richard no longer had time to cut his way through the screen of pikemen and strike him down. Stanley's men had arrived and as they pitched in to assist Tudor's beleaguered force it was now Richard's followers who were being overwhelmed. In the battle's terrible climax the royal standard-bearer was brought to his knees, his legs cut from underneath him.

The king fought on, engaging another of Henry's followers, Sir Rhys ap Thomas, in fierce mounted combat. But he was being pushed further and further away from Tudor by the sheer press of numbers. On the edge of some nearby marshland, several hundred yards from Henry Tudor's position, Richard turned to rally his troops. In the desperate mêlée his horse lost his footing and plunged into the marsh. The king was thrown to the ground. He gathered himself, but he was now surrounded by his enemies.

It is here that the dramatic discovery of the king's body opens a compelling window on the last few minutes of the battle. The pattern of injuries found on Richard's recently discovered skull powerfully recreates the last agonizing moments of the king's life. (For details see Chapter 9.) His foes closed in on him. Two wounds to the chin show his helmet straps were cut off by his opponents and his helmet then flung away. Richard fought on, but a rain of blows was now falling upon his unprotected head. The king was struck repeatedly: a puncture mark from the head of a sharp-bladed weapon – probably a dagger – forced him to his knees. And then, the fatal strike from a halberd, slicing off the bone and cutting through to the skull. With Richard finally on the ground, a sword was thrust through his head.

Richard's remains confirm the account of the Burgundian Jean Molinet – who almost certainly gleaned his information from French mercenaries in Tudor's army – that the king was killed by a Welsh halberdier after his horse lost its footing and plunged into a nearby marsh. A later, seventeenth-century life of Sir Rhys ap Thomas also alluded to the family tradition that Rhys and Richard engaged in fierce mounted combat, forcing the king further and further away from Tudor; and a Welsh praise poem by Guto'r Glyn described the deadly blow that 'shaved his head'. But the most striking evidence is found in the beautifully carved bed lintel Rhys ap Thomas later commissioned in Henry VII's reign. It showed Bosworth's culmination, with Rhys and Richard clashing on horseback and captured the moment when the king's mount lost its footing – rearing up, with a horseshoe coming off its hoof. Between the two combatants a foot soldier had been placed, carrying a halberd – symbolically depicting the blow that killed Richard.

However, Molinet also related that at the very end Richard sought to flee the battlefield. If this had been true, the Tudors would have made much of it. A Spanish account of the battle, written by Diego de Valera, conveyed something very different: that Richard had been offered a fresh horse by his followers and told to make good his escape, but had resolutely refused to do so. 'God forbid that I retreat one step,' Richard had exclaimed. 'I will either win the battle as a king – or die as one.' Polydore Vergil also caught the king's defiant response, 'that this day he would either make an end of war or of life', adding reluctantly 'such was the great fierceness and force of his mind.'

It is here that even sources highly critical of Richard provide a firm rebuttal. Polydore Vergil described how the king fought and died in 'the thickest press of his enemies'; John Rous said simply, 'he bore himself as a gallant knight and acted with distinction as his own champion until his last breath.' And the *Croyland Chronicler* – an implacable enemy of the king – was moved to offer this remarkable tribute: 'For in the thick of the fight, and not in an act of flight, King Richard fell in the field, struck by many mortal wounds – as a bold and most valiant prince.'

The fight was over – Bosworth was now a Tudor victory. 'We were in part the reason the battle was won,' the French mercenary acknowledged. Moments later, a relieved Henry was greeted by his battlefield saviour, Sir William Stanley. Richard's cut-away helmet had been recovered from under a thorn bush, and its circlet crown was hacked off in an impromptu ceremony and presented to the victor. But Henry's exhilaration at surviving these last frenzied moments of combat quickly turned to spite. He ordered that his rival's body be stripped of its armour and clothing, trussed up with the hands tied together and then flung naked over a horse. Richard, who had so valued the power of dignified ritual in life, was to be granted little of it in death.

Examination of Richard's bones shows that one of Tudor's followers now stabbed the dead king in the buttocks, in an act of ritual humiliation. Henry wished to prove to all and sundry that his opponent was dead, and at the same time – still shocked and frightened by how close Richard had come to winning – he vindictively encouraged his men to disparage his corpse. Richard's naked and disfigured body was then carried to Leicester and publicly displayed for two days in such shocking fashion. Afterwards the new king began his victorious progress to London, and, as his men departed, the corpse – unwashed with the hands still tied – was hurriedly interred in the Church of the Greyfriars, without coffin or shroud. No ritual respect was to be offered to the fallen leader; his body was forced into a crudely excavated hole beneath the choir. And when the gap was too short, and the remains did not easily fit it, the corpse was left hunched in the grave. The hasty burial complete, Henry's followers rushed off to join their master. The Tudor dynasty had begun.

II

The Man Behind the Myth

My PROJECT, TO find Richard III and his grave, seems complete. A battery of experts have subjected the skeleton found in Leicester City Council's Social Services car park to a bewildering array of scientific tests and concluded, beyond reasonable doubt, that these are the remains of Richard III. But this is not the end of his story, or the reason my search for Richard began.

The Looking for Richard project had four clearly defined phases: research and development, archaeology, identification, reburial. The reburial was planned from the outset and was the reason the project had been created. Why was this? Richard III was deeply religious, with a keen sense of justice. These two strands of his character are powerfully woven around his reverence for the dead and provision for their spiritual welfare. For Richard, burial and reburial held a deep significance. At Towton he had ensured that the dead of that conflict, on both sides, were afforded proper burial, founding a chantry chapel to commemorate the slain. And although Richard executed William, Lord Hastings, he subsequently gave him a tomb in the royal mausoleum at St George's Chapel, Windsor, beside Edward IV – as Hastings had requested in his will.

The reburial of his father, Richard, Duke of York, strongly demonstrated Richard's own spirituality. In July 1476 Richard undertook the role of principal mourner for the translation of his father's remains from Pontefract to Fotheringhay. The poignant event took nine days. Richard oversaw the exhumation, and at each stop along the way, as the coffins rested in a chosen church for the night, took part in the masses said for the souls of his father and older brother Edmund. At Fotheringhay Church – the mausoleum of the House of York – the family laid its loved ones to rest. The ritual allowed a full and final commemoration of the Duke of York's achievements.

The similarity between the lives of the Duke of York and his youngest son, who carried his name and strongly resembled him, was striking. Both men mounted cavalry charges to take the fight to their enemy – at the battles of Wakefield and Bosworth – and both would be cut down in the fierce hand-to-hand combat that followed. The bodies of both men would then be mutilated and denied proper burial by their enemies.

With the discovery of his remains, we now know something of the treatment meted out to Richard III at his own burial. It would take Henry VII ten years before he honoured him with a tomb, and in so doing publicly recognized the former king. At the time it may have been politically expedient to do so. A pretender, 'Perkin Warbeck', claimed to be the younger son of Edward IV (one of the 'Princes in the Tower') and rightful King of England. By modestly commemorating his predecessor, Henry may have hoped to finally draw a line under the Yorkist dynasty.

But Henry VII's gesture only went so far. Moving the remains of a former king to a more distinguished resting place was a way of fully making peace with the past. In 1413, as a mark of reconciliation, the young Lancastrian King Henry V moved the remains of Richard II (the monarch deposed and almost certainly murdered on the orders of his father, Henry IV) from King's Langley to Westminster Abbey. Henry V hoped through this very public act to atone for this sin and to heal the divisions of civil war that had plagued his father's reign. Richard himself undertook a similar symbolic reburial. As king, he had exhumed the remains of the saintly Henry VI from Chertsey Abbey and reburied him with honour in the royal mausoleum at St George's Chapel. According to John Rous, 'the king's body was taken out of his grave in Chertsey in August 1484 and honourably received in the new collegiate church at Windsor, where it was again buried with the greatest solemnity to the south of the high altar.' The treasurer's accounts of the College of St George provide a window on this event, recording money paid 'for the removal of King Henry VI from Chertsey'.

There would be no such consideration for King Richard from either Henry VII or his son and successor Henry VIII. They left him exactly where he was. In reburying this last Yorkist king, the Looking for Richard project could now offer him the same spiritual care that he had shown others in his lifetime and in so doing give him what had been denied him in 1485.

Now we are in a position to honour the remains of Richard III in a fitting ceremony of reinterment. Before we had found his remains, in anticipation of that day, in September 2010, the Looking for Richard project commissioned the design of a tomb based upon Richard's life and what was important and meaningful to him. Undertaken by a team of Ricardians, it is hoped that the finished design, welcomed by so many, may form a part of the innumerable deliberations in the busy months ahead as we move inexorably towards the reburial when the last warrior King of England will finally be laid to rest.

The discovery of King Richard is a historic moment when the history books will be rewritten. A wind of change is blowing, one that will now seek out the truth about the real Richard III. Already the project has challenged many of the myths that surround him. We now know that his remains were not dug up and carried through the streets by a jeering crowd to be thrown into the River Soar. We also know he had no 'withered arm', nor did he suffer from kyphosis, a debilitating condition where the head is thrust onto the chest, inappropriately termed 'hunchbacked'. Richard's limbs were straight, so he probably walked normally, and indeed no one before Shakespeare suggested otherwise. None that saw him, or knew him, described him as being 'lame', a well-known medieval description for those that walked with an abnormal gait. What is clear is that Richard's scoliosis, first shown when his body was stripped naked at Bosworth, has been deliberately exaggerated and used against him. Might this have been why his body was thrown over a horse, to display the unevenness of his back when bent forwards?

During the project I was described as a 'fan' of Richard III, trying to recast him as something of a saint. That was certainly far from the truth. But as a screenwriter I wanted to delve behind the caricature Shakespeare has given us and gain psychological insights into the man himself and his reality.

Contemporary writers agreed that Richard, as Duke of Gloucester, was a man of good reputation, a skilled arbitrator and respected dispenser of justice. It seemed he was a man to be relied upon, and trusted, and by none more so than the king, his brother. I wanted to understand Richard's motivation, what got him out of bed in the morning and defined his character. As the youngest son of a great lord his life's work was already determined: to devote himself to loyalty, duty and service. He could have chosen to rebel against this path, as others had done before him, but he chose to carry out his duties to the best of his ability.

So it seems rather out of character that Richard decided to take the crown, particularly in the way that he did. Until, that is, one considers Edward's disastrous marriage, the declared illegitimacy of his children and the power of the Woodvilles. In that light it is not entirely fanciful to suggest that Richard transferred his loyalty, duty and service to the kingdom since he could not commit his allegiance to Edward's illegitimate sons. But from what I could see of the man, I doubted it was in his character to murder children. It was much more likely for him to send them to a place of safety.

The enlightened laws he enacted showed that Richard was clearly willing to defy convention. I came across an earlier example of this behaviour when in April 1482, when he was Duke of Gloucester, a citizen of York had visited his castle at Middleham but had been insulted by Thomas Redeheid, a servant of the castle treasurer. Richard was informed about the insult, which in itself tells us he was someone who was approachable, unlike many another lord. But it is what happened next that intrigues. There were two courses open to Richard: to ignore the incident, or punish the servant himself. Richard did neither, but chose a third option. He sent the offending servant to York with a letter authorizing the city fathers to punish him in a way they deemed appropriate. It is a story reminiscent of the wisdom shown by King Solomon in the Old Testament. Richard showed principle, insight and sensitivity, as well as a strong sense of fairness and absolute trust.

I consulted two further sources whom I believed would help clarify Richard's character. First I decided to take a slightly unusual tack. While some may doubt the reliability of graphoanalysis it is a scientific system for assessing an individual's character from their handwriting and is used as a tool by many respectable organizations, including the police. In 2000 I therefore approached master graphologist Bridget Hickey who had no previous knowledge of Richard. For the purposes of analysis, I chose the postscript, in Richard's own hand, in a letter to Chancellor Bishop Russell, dated 12 October 1483, denouncing the treachery of his former ally, the Duke of Buckingham. I chose this partly because it is the longest example of Richard's writing, and partly because it was composed at a time of great stress. It seemed likely to me that, given the circumstances, any viciousness of character would be clearly revealed. But Hickey's graphoanalysis emphasized the likelihood of illness – a possibility I had originally rejected as the historical record showed quite plainly that he was a physically able and active man. Then the dig revealed Richard's scoliosis, and I returned to the analysis which said:

> There is nothing to indicate a repressed childhood, but there appears to be suffering and mental unhappiness. He suffers and is plagued with conflicts. There is stability much of the time but a swing from withdrawal to charming extrovert can suggest sickness, unhappiness and suffering. Both physical and mental. Optimism is not evident and he may easily resort to a gloomy view. This could further suggest health problems. It is possible in childhood he had a fear he might not succeed or too much was expected of him. (Perhaps health or competition.) He might have lost confidence. Though full of courage, he would avoid chancey risks. In early childhood there may have been a feeling of self-castigation, guilt or even self-pity. Poor health might have played a part in this. However, most things were overcome, not on physical strength, but on his mental abilities, willpower and determination. Criticism of a personal nature could hurt him. There appears to be some sadness and a desire to withdraw into the self. Suffering in silence may have been endured. He is not a manipulator, liar, deceiver, selfish or mean with others. He faces facts and knows himself. What he sees is another matter. Conflicts. One could almost picture the actor clown, concealing unhappiness and depth of feeling. The clown's make-up hiding perhaps illness, sadness, despair and suffering. Both mental and physical.

The conclusions were interesting pointers to the potential effects of scoliosis. If the condition had worsened during his lifetime, Buckingham's rebellion may have exacerbated its effects.

The second resource I decided to explore was psychological profiling, and for the Looking for Richard project I had commissioned Professor Mark Lansdale and Dr Julian Boon of the University of Leicester to carry out what, to the best of my knowledge, was the first academic study of Richard's psychology.

To assess Richard's mindset they first explored whether he was a murderous psychopath. According to their findings, the reverse appears to be the case. (For a summary of the conclusions, see Appendix 2.) Key aspects of psychopathy were examined including narcissism, cowardice, thought disorder and Machiavellianism. The latter was a favourite accusation by his detractors, but no evidence was found to support it. In terms of the overall personality portrait, three psychological approaches were explored, each of which offered a different key to understanding: the effect of Richard's scoliosis; the possibility of an anxiety disorder; and the elevation in his status from Lord of the North to monarch.

Reading Lansdale and Boon's analysis, it seemed to me as if Thomas More's description of Richard biting his lower lip and constantly drawing his dagger from its sheath were not the quirks of a cunning murderer, but of someone with heightened levels of anxiety, and a need for order and security.

So, from all this we have a man whose turbulent childhood provoked a fundamental need to create a stable, dependable world, but was ejected from that safe haven into an unpredictable and challenging world of life-threatening responsibility where he was forced to tame a crowd of determined, and therefore dangerous, courtiers, who did not share his worldview.

One of the main difficulties in studying the last Plantagenet is there are relatively few contemporary accounts of his reign. Those who knew him often spoke well of him, but most of our information comes from later sources who hadn't met him and tend to be either foreign or openly hostile. Why there is such a dearth of information on Richard is unclear. It may be that the Tudors destroyed much of it. The end result is that for any personal insights we are dependent upon scraps of generally private correspondence to and from those who knew him.

There are letters from him that reveal a well-developed sense of humour such as the one he wrote in summer 1483 to Chancellor Russell asking him to try to dissuade Thomas Lynom, one of the king's solicitors, from marrying Elizabeth (Jane) Shore. In it Richard's understated humour at Lynom's captivation with Shore is apparent. Richard may have been infuriating and frustrating, but his true friends were unfailingly loyal and supported him to the death.

After the news of Richard's death at Bosworth, the Welsh bard Dafydd Llywd, who knew Henry Tudor, but not Richard, set to work. He composed the first piece of Tudor's propaganda against the last Plantagenet. It was a damning indictment, regaling its readers with images of the former king's deformity of body, mind and spirit. This new story about Richard came from the top down even though Henry Tudor had never met Richard. The Tudor regime, it seemed, needed a bogeyman.

Happily, the Looking for Richard project has begun to expose the propaganda that underlies the centuries-old vilification of the last Plantagenet king. It has not only succeeded in finding Richard III's body, it has also brought the real Richard III back on to centre stage. Shakespeare's evil and misshapen tyrant, and the psychotic murderer beloved of Tudor writers, should now be seen as a great dramatic invention, not a fully rounded historical portrait.

Richard III wasn't a saint. He was a man, who played the hand he was dealt loyally and, as far as he could within the limitations of his time, humanely. Above all, whether on or off the battlefield, he never failed to display courage. In this, I am reminded of the words of Winston Churchill: 'Courage is the first of all human qualities because it is the quality that guarantees all others.'

12

The Man and his Times

O N 22 AUGUST 1485 the body of Richard III was stripped naked, thrown over the back of a horse and carried from Bosworth battlefield to Leicester. There the remains of the king were put on public display. Even in the mid-Tudor period, the chronicler Edward Hall still found the treatment of the corpse shameful. 'Our bruised arms hung up for monuments,' Shakespeare had Richard declaim. Three days after the battle, on 25 August 1485, Richard III was hurriedly buried in the Church of the Greyfriars, Leicester. Polydore Vergil related that this burial took place without any funeral rites.

While he had lain on display, his victorious challenger, Henry Tudor, chose first to celebrate his victory not at Leicester but Coventry, travelling there on 24 August, and holding a banquet, before returning to Leicester the following day, and then journeying on to London. Henry stayed in the house of Coventry's mayor, Robert Onley, where money was paid for 512 penny loaves of bread, and, in a choice of beverages that would have pleased the French mercenary contingent in his army, 110 gallons of red wine and a relatively modest four and a half gallons of ale.

Before he left Leicester Henry executed three of Richard's followers, William Catesby and John Bracher and his son. Bracher had betrayed news of Henry's West Country landing in 1483 to Richard III. Catesby's mission to Brittany in September 1484 had been to offer the duchy military assistance – a picked body of English archers – if in return it withdrew its support for Henry Tudor. Catesby's arrival in Brittany and the onset of these negotiations was worrying enough to provoke Tudor's hurried flight from the duchy into France. Francis, Duke of Brittany had been prepared to support Henry as rightful claimant on the basis of his promised marriage to Elizabeth of York, in other words through the right of his future wife. The French government made Henry play a different role.

In contrast to supportive Brittany, Henry's exile in France had been an unhappy one. The minority government of Charles VIII had forced him to set out a claim to the throne in his own right, then, finding itself unable to discern what that right was – as the chronicler Philippe Commynes bluntly put it – made him play the part of an impostor, a younger son of the murdered Lancastrian King Henry VI. That claim had jeopardized Henry's pact with the Woodvilles – and nearly lost him the very marriage to Elizabeth that was vital to buttress his claim to the throne. The executions showed how bitter Tudor felt about that turn of events, a bitterness caught well by Commynes, who heard from Henry at their meeting in November 1484 how he had spent most of his life as an exile or fugitive.

In Shakespeare's *Richard III*, Henry benignly made provision for proper burial of the slain at Bosworth. But in a treatise on the sweating sickness, a disease that had made its appearance in England at the same time as the arrival of Tudor's largely foreign army, the French doctor Thomas Forestier described something rather different. Forestier, who wrote his tract in London in October 1485, only two months after Bosworth, reported the widely held belief that most of the slain had simply been left on the battlefield. His candour was unwelcome to the new Tudor dynasty; he was promptly arrested and locked up in the Tower of London. All manuscript editions of his work were confiscated.

Richard as king had planned a chapel at Towton in memory of those who had died in battle there. It was, as Archbishop Rotherham of York later described it, a most impressive building, 'expensively and imposingly erected from new foundations'. The archbishop said that the chapel had been deliberately sited 'upon the battleground where the bodies of the first and greatest in the land, as well as great multitudes of other men, were first slain and then buried and interred in the fields around'. Richard had been concerned not only to commemorate the fallen, but to ensure that the bodies of those killed in the battle, on both sides, received proper Christian burial. In a grant of an annuity to the nearby parish church of Saxton on 19 February 1484 Richard made this explicit, recalling that in this bloody clash of arms, fought in a blinding snowstorm on 29 March 1461:

> the people of this kingdom, in a plentiful multitude, were taken away from human affairs; and their bodies were notoriously left on the aforesaid field and in other places nearby, thoroughly outside the ecclesiastical burial places, in three hollows. Whereupon we, on account of affection, contriving the burial of the deceased men of this sort, caused the bones of the same men to be exhumed and left for an ecclesiastical burial in these coming months, partly in the parish church of Saxton in our said county of York and in the cemetery of the said place, and partly in the chapel of Towton aforesaid, and in the surroundings of this very place.

Henry was not prepared to treat the fallen at Bosworth, largely from Richard's army, with the same respect. News of his victory had now reached London, where an anxious city council – aware of the loans leading city members had made to Richard III in recruiting his army – at once named a party of eight leading citizens to ride towards the new king.

But they had nothing to be worried about, since London had not contributed any of its levies to Richard's defeated army. And it was Richard's army only that Henry Tudor – now Henry VII,

King of England – particularly distrusted. Bosworth had, after all, been almost too close to call.

In the aftermath of the fighting the battle name itself remained in a state of flux: Redemore, Dunnesmore and Dadlington Field were some of the early attributions. Bosworth was only used for the first time – in a deed drawn up by one of Henry's soldiers – in 1500, more than halfway through the first Tudor king's reign. Henry VII always honoured service performed for him at the battle, and one of his followers, Thomas Gregory of Ashfordby in Leicestershire, recorded proudly on 26 October 1500 that he had been with the Tudor king 'at Bosworth Field'. There was little fixity of battle naming in the early years after Bosworth. And who can say whether on some dark and windy nights, when Henry slept uncomfortably in one of the royal palaces he had inherited from the vanquished Yorkist dynasty, it could have seemed that the battle result itself might reverse just as easily?

During that clash, Richard's loyal lieutenant John, Duke of Norfolk had fought and died for his master; his son, Thomas – who fought by his side – was captured and imprisoned. The *Croyland Chronicler* noted that the Earl of Northumberland's rearguard did not engage with Tudor's force, but battlefield terrain rather than treachery seems the most likely explanation for this – and Northumberland was also imprisoned by Henry in Bosworth's aftermath. The tributes paid to Richard's bravery in all the sources were a powerful and painful reminder to the new dynasty of how close the battle's outcome had been. When Henry VII's staunch supporter Sir Rhys ap Thomas celebrated his election to the Order of the Garter in 1505, he commissioned a series of fine carvings showing scenes of martial valour – and within it, his personal combat with Richard III took pride of place. In private at least, Rhys – whose courage had done much to save his Tudor master – believed Richard's charge worthy of chivalric renown.

'In that charge', Polydore Vergil related, Richard III 'killed several men and toppled Henry's standard'. Others had intervened to protect Tudor and buy him precious time, as Sir William Stanley's forces – likely to have been stationed on nearby rising ground, close to Crown Hill – rode to his rescue. Richard had flung Sir John Cheney to the ground, a remarkable feat of strength and horsemanship. Cheney (a former standard-bearer of Edward IV) was, according to Vergil, a warrior 'of surpassing bravery' and may have been, on the evidence of bones found in his own tomb, no less than six feet eight inches tall – a giant of a man.

And Richard had killed Henry's own standard-bearer, Sir William Brandon, chosen for his physical toughness, whose brother and then his son became notable jousters at the Tudor court. Forty-four years before Bosworth, on 20 July 1441 at Pontoise, Guillaume Chastel had sacrificed his life for his royal master, allowing the French king, Charles VII, narrowly to escape the clutches of Richard's father, the Duke of York. Charles VII never forgot that sacrifice, instructing that Chastel be buried in the royal mausoleum at Saint-Denis, an exceptional mark of honour. Henry VII remembered William Brandon's sacrifice in similar fashion, allowing his infant son Charles to be brought up in the royal household in the company of the king's own children. At the court of the Tudor king's son and successor, Charles Brandon would be elevated to the dukedom of Suffolk and become one of Henry VIII's closest companions.

The description of Richard's army in the first parliament that Henry VII summoned was telling. We hear of a great force, well-armed, with banners unfurled, ready to wage 'mighty battle'. Henry had decided to date the beginning of his reign to 21 August 1485, the day before Bosworth, thereby making all those who had fought for Richard there traitors, who would have to petition for a return of their lands. To do so successfully, they would need to accuse the last Plantagenet king of coercion, claiming that he had forced them to fight against their will. In this fashion the parliament of November 1485 – on Henry's prompting – deliberately set out to create an image of Richard III that was cruel and vindictive.

This was, in fact, a highly unpopular move by the new monarch. A diarist of the sessions in the House of Commons noted that it was the subject of heated, angry debate. A contemporary letter of the Yorkshire Plumpton family added that many were opposed to it, but as it was the king's strong wish it was eventually pushed through. Even the *Croyland Chronicler*, no supporter of the memory of Richard III, attacked the decision. What would happen when a future King of England summoned an army to attend him, the chronicler wryly observed: would his subjects, instead of responding loyally and wholeheartedly, calculate that if their sovereign lost they were likely to forfeit lands, goods and possessions – and stay at home? Yet the measure had its desired effect.

The king now attainted for treason no fewer than thirty persons who had been in Richard's army, including five peers and eight knights. Others could be proceeded against later. Geoffrey St Germain had died the day after Bosworth from wounds received in the fighting. His daughter and heir claimed that he was only with the royal army through fear, because he was so threatened by Richard's summons 'that unless he came to the said field he should lose his life'. Roger Wake of Blisworth (Northamptonshire) claimed that it was against his 'will and mind' to fight for the late king. Wake was in fact the brother-in-law of Richard's staunch supporter William Catesby. The command that had now allegedly so worried both men merely followed the standard form used by all medieval monarchs to muster troops before battle.

But parliament passed up the chance to dissect Richard's claim to the throne, the *Titulus Regius*, by questioning its author and architect, Robert Stillington, Bishop of Bath and Wells, who had initially revealed the pre-contract that had invalidated Edward IV's marriage. Rather than allow Stillington to be subjected to questioning, Henry gave the fortunate bishop a free pardon, and ordered that all copies of the *Titulus Regius* be destroyed. And destroyed they mostly were, although John Stow unearthed one, more than a century later.

As for Henry's own rightful title, the *Croyland Chronicler* frankly admitted that it would be better to say little on this matter, and instead wait for the king's marriage to Elizabeth of York. This took place in January 1486, although Elizabeth's coronation as queen was delayed until the following year – as if the new king did not want to seem too beholden to his wife for the right to rule.

Henry had won the throne by killing the reigning king on the battlefield. For this reason, Tudor was anxious to display the body of his rival for two days at Leicester, to demonstrate to all that Richard had fallen at Bosworth. The bodies recently excavated from the Towton grave had had their faces hacked away, either in the last stages of the fighting or as spite wounds after death. But a study of Richard's skull showed that he had not suffered this form of injury. In the last terrible moments of the battle an order must have gone out not to disfigure Richard's face – Tudor had to prove that his rival was dead. But Henry VII's struggle to assert his authority had only just begun.

The Tudor poet Bernard André likened the first twelve years of his reign to the labours of Hercules, as plots and conspiracies abounded. Henry's position remained terribly vulnerable. Rumours persisted that the younger of the Princes in the Tower might have escaped, a part played by the Yorkist pretender Perkin Warbeck, and as the story spread, Warbeck attracted considerable international support. Plotting on his behalf was no less a person than Sir William Stanley, the king's chamberlain, who was executed for treason less than ten years after decisively intervening for the Tudor monarch at Bosworth.

In Henry VII's first parliament a number of petitioners referred to Richard III's cruelty. Richard's anger could be frightening, but the charge of cruelty implied something different, a cold-blooded relish in the suffering of others. Such cruelty as there had been was now heavily distorted by the new regime. Richard's ruthlessness when as duke he bullied the helpless Countess of Oxford was now recounted in a Tudor parliament and portrayed in the most hostile light. But ruthlessness in pursuit of one's 'livelode', one's rightful inheritance, was a feature of late medieval life.

For instance Margaret Beaufort, mother of Henry VII, was renowned for her piety and educational benefactions. Yet she deliberately ignored the pious request of her great-uncle Cardinal Beaufort to endow his hospital of St Cross in Winchester, and instead diverted the lands for her own use. And the Stanleys pursued a feud against the Harrington family to enhance their landed power in northern Lancashire, and intimidated and imprisoned the Harrington heiresses to secure their interests, eventually marrying them off against their wills.

Richard displayed dynastic ruthlessness as Protector when he summarily executed Lord Hastings. If he believed that Hastings was now opposed to him, or was plotting against him, it was necessary dynastic ruthlessness. He subsequently treated his widow with respect and allowed Hastings the burial in St George's Chapel, Windsor, that he had wished in his will. Since we do not know what happened to the Princes in the Tower after he took the throne, Richard, as a man of his times, is the most likely suspect for their murders. This may, however, be true without bringing with it the wholesale besmirching of his character. Was he really a Machiavellian, a master of dissimulation?

Machiavelli wrote his famous treatise, *The Prince*, from which our present-day understanding of the term Machiavellian is itself derived, in the early sixteenth century. Yet late medieval England was already becoming more Machiavellian in its political standards, even before *The Prince* gave the definitive description of such behaviour. In 1399 the Lancastrian Henry Bolingbroke returned to England from exile merely claiming his ducal lands. This clever subterfuge allowed him to gather support and then depose the reigning king – Richard II – and claim the throne for himself, when the time was right. This sleight of hand would be repeated in 1471 when Edward IV returned to England from exile in Burgundy practising subtlety and deceit, and *The Arrivall*, the official account of the king's return, praised him for doing so. When Edward approached the city of York, *The Arrivall* tells us that the returning Yorkist king instructed his followers to pretend that he came 'only to claim to be duke of York', in other words to claim his aristocratic inheritance, not the crown of England. This dishonest declaration got him into the city unopposed, and *The Arrivall* described the tactic with wry amusement. The Earl of Northumberland was also praised for dissembling, refusing to commit himself openly one way or the other, and thus doing the king a good service.

The arch dissemblers in the Wars of the Roses were of course the Stanley family. At the Battle of Blore Heath in September 1459 Sir William Stanley joined the Yorkist army while his older brother Thomas, Lord Stanley committed himself to the Lancastrians, even though he found all manner of excuses to avoid joining their army. This family strategy was repeated in 1470–71, when the Stanleys first supported the Earl of Warwick and then changed sides, throwing in their lot with Edward IV. In 1483, during Buckingham's rebellion, Lord Stanley's son, George, Lord Strange, raised an army in Lancashire; contemporaries were unable to discern what he intended to do with it. The Stanleys' hesitant and puzzling behaviour during the Bosworth campaign in 1485, rather than being directed against Richard III, was entirely consistent with their survival strategy practised during the entire civil war.

But Richard himself had not dissembled when he supported the Harrington family. He did this in 1470, when the Stanleys first attempted to seize the Harringtons' residence at Hornby Castle in Lancashire. He did this again as king, when he considered overturning the arbitration award that finally delivered Hornby to the Stanleys. If he was practising the art of realpolitik, assisting the Harringtons made little sense; the Stanleys were far more powerful and far more necessary for Richard's political survival. Here Richard's favourite motto, 'loyaulte me lie', 'loyalty binds me', had a clear meaning. The Harringtons were in this predicament because the head of the family and his son and heir had died supporting Richard, Duke of York at Wakefield. Richard was loyal to the memory of his father and loyal to those who had fought and died in his cause.

A similar loyalty can be seen in his grant to Queens' College, Cambridge, on 1 April 1477, where humble soldiers who had died fighting with him in the Battles of Barnet and Tewkesbury were remembered by name. Richard garnered no political advantage by such acts; they appear heartfelt and genuine and without contradictory evidence must be assumed to have been so.

And if Richard could be as ruthless as his contemporaries, he was also brave, loyal and charismatic. We now know more about him: more about his incredible courage in the last few moments of Bosworth; and more about the pain he probably suffered from the scoliosis of his spine. 'Deformed' was a word readily used by medieval and Tudor writers to pass judgement on others. We would use different words, 'disability' or 'condition', and draw no moral inference from them. (For details on Richard's scoliosis see Chapter 9.)

The condition left him with one shoulder higher than the other, which some contemporaries noticed while others did not. The disparity could have been disguised by the tailored clothes Richard wore; he is also likely to have had his own armour made for him. Richard was physically active and strong, and particularly enjoyed the hunt. But interestingly, despite his love of chivalry, he did not enjoy the tournament, where court jousters such as Anthony, Earl Rivers were prominent: it is likely that he found the frequent changes in armour and costume off-putting. And Richard's awareness of his physical condition may understandably have heightened his distaste for the sexual debauchery of the latter years of Edward's court.

In June 1483 we do have evidence that Richard suffered from a level of pain that was briefly disabling. In the period from 10 to 13 June Polydore Vergil related that Richard suffered from a debilitating torpor, where he was overcome by lethargy and unable to eat or sleep. Thomas More acknowledged that Richard believed he was under attack from witchcraft in the council meeting of 13 June. These Tudor sources did not take these symptoms particularly seriously. We should, however. They would account for the sense of danger Richard felt menaced by when he appealed to his northern followers for aid, believing the Woodvilles were using witchcraft against him. They help to explain the tumultuous council meeting of 13 June too.

Richard was also afflicted the night before Bosworth. The *Croyland Chronicler* related that the king's face was unusually white and drawn on the morning of the battle, and that he complained of terrible dreams where he had been assaulted by demons. But Richard cast away the pain and psychological distress with extraordinary resolve. We can only admire his courage. His physical condition makes the bravery and valour of his conduct on the battlefield all the more remarkable.

The ritual that Richard enacted to his followers before the

clash with Henry Tudor, where he displayed the 'rich crown' of England, thereby enacting a second coronation on the field of battle, demonstrated an exceptional belief in the rightness of his cause. He rode against Tudor with a battle crown welded to his helmet, and fought with an incredible determination.

Richard III – in death as in life – divided opinion, and did so with a remarkable intensity. Symbolic of this division was Richard's own badge or emblem, the boar. This boar, which was recently and movingly found on the edge of the marsh at Bosworth, was the device by which this fascinating and controversial man was recognized. Its mark can still be seen in some of the places most closely associated with Richard's life; one, the oriel window in Barnard Castle overlooking the Tees, almost allows one to feel his presence. It was the badge worn by his supporters, followers such as Ralph Fitzherbert, whose magnificent tomb effigy adorns Norbury Church in Derbyshire and was also the image deployed by his opponents to denigrate him. In Richard's choice of the boar, we learn more about the inner thinking and self-identity of the man.

Richard's boar badge made a pun on the Latin for York (Eboracum), his favourite city, the place that mourned him with such feeling and courage after his death. For 'bore' – an alternative spelling of the animal in the late Middle Ages – was an anagram of 'Ebor', the contracted form of the city's Latin name. But even in York Richard could divide opinion. The civic records showed that in 1491, in a drunken argument, a schoolteacher called Richard a 'hypocrite and a crookback', declaring of his unseemly death and burial, 'he died like a dog in a ditch' – as if he thoroughly deserved it. Others rushed to Richard's defence, and in a way we have never stopped replaying this debate.

To Richard's opponents, the boar – by which they both identified and denigrated Richard – was a wrathful and impulsive creature, and features in hunting manuals as an angry and dangerous animal. Polydore Vergil may have drawn upon the image of the enraged boar as he described Richard, about to launch his last, fateful charge against Tudor, 'overcome with ire'.

But the discovery of the boar badge at Bosworth is a timely reminder that Richard's supporters wore this emblem with pride, and were prepared to die for this king and the cause he championed. Richard's own attraction to this badge may have been much deeper than a pun on the city he loved.

One of the saints Richard venerated was St Anthony, who, exiled in the wilderness, had been protected by a boar. This boar drove off threatening animals, kept demons and evil spirits at bay and protected Anthony from sexual temptation. Here we can see a different man, the one caught in Dominic Mancini's portrayal, alienated from the sexual debauchery of Edward IV's court, and forging his own morality – and the religious and chivalric values that overlaid it – largely in isolation from it.

Richard III's brief reign was mired in controversy. The hostility of Thomas More – which so influenced Shakespeare – was in turn inspired by the real-life enmity of John Morton towards Richard. Morton was Bishop of Ely at the beginning of Richard's reign, and subsequently a political exile and strong supporter of Henry Tudor, rising to Archbishop of Canterbury under the new Tudor dynasty. Morton witnessed – and never forgot – the terrifying council meeting of 13 June 1483, and was imprisoned after it. Morton's view was slanted by the allegiances he subsequently chose, but there is no doubt that he hated Richard III.

However, others were as positive as Morton was negative. Thomas Barowe, who got to know Richard during his patronage of Cambridge University, and afterwards served him as duke and king, was a valued member of his legal counsel and rose to become Richard's master of the rolls. Barowe was still prepared to honour Richard's memory – and the battle in which he had died – in a grant to the university in the reign of Henry VII. In an indenture of 19 January 1495 Barowe asked that the name of Richard III be remembered and masses said for his soul on 21 and 22 August each year, the eve of Bosworth and the anniversary of the battle itself.

There are no winners and losers in a vicious civil war. All suffer. If Richard genuinely believed in the legitimacy of his right to rule, and killed to enforce it, so did the Tudors. Henry VII locked up the young Edward, Earl of Warwick, son of the Duke of Clarence, and then executed him on trumped-up charges. Warwick's 'crime' was to have a better claim to the throne than Henry VII. The likely fate of this innocent prince was a cause of concern throughout the first half of Henry's reign, although we hear little about this third Prince in the Tower, and much about the two sons of Edward IV.

Yet the injustice of Warwick's imprisonment by Henry VII featured regularly in the newsletters of the time, even though the Tudor regime discouraged speculation about him. On 29 November 1486 Sir Thomas Bateson reported that in London 'there is little speech of the Earl of Warwick, but after Christmas they say there will be more of this'. There was not. On 17 December 1489 Edward Plumpton witnessed four royal servants hanged on Tower Hill for an attempt to rescue him, organizing a plot 'to take out of the king's ward [custody] the Earl of Warwick'. Warwick remained incarcerated in the Tower. And on 21 November 1499 John Pullen bluntly noted that the earl had now 'confessed of treason', and had been tried and executed.

That left Clarence's daughter, Margaret, who married into the Pole family. In 1539 Henry VIII decided they were all a dynastic threat, and executed Margaret's son. He also arrested Margaret and her twelve-year-old grandson. On 27 May 1541 this sixty-eight-year-old woman, now frail and ill, was led to her execution still roundly protesting her innocence. She was dragged to the block, and as she refused to lay her head upon it, was forced down. When she struggled, the inexperienced executioner mistimed his blow, making a gash on her shoulder instead. Ten additional blows were required to complete the execution. One account stated that she leapt from the block after the first clumsy blow and ran, being pursued by the executioner, and was struck eleven times before she died.

Contemporaries expected that her fourteen-year-old grandson, Henry Pole, would be executed at the same time. Instead, in a sequence eerily reminiscent of the possible fate of Edward V, he was withdrawn into the recesses of the Tower, deprived of his tutor and other servants, and then vanished completely. It was rumoured that he had been starved to death some time in 1542.

Today, we know little of this last prince of the House of York. Our ruling dynasties were quite ruthless in protecting their own survival – by our standards, horrifyingly so. Richard III, whatever the fate of the two sons of Edward IV, must be put firmly back into the context of his times.

It was all too convenient for the Tudor writers who followed Thomas More to blame Richard for the death of his brother, George, Duke of Clarence, although no contemporary source ever made that accusation. It was Clarence and his lineage that the Tudors were most worried about. Richard's designated successors, the de la Pole family, also gave them a run for their money. John de la Pole, Earl of Lincoln, made heir presumptive by Richard in 1484, died fighting against Henry VII at the Battle of Stoke, two years after Bosworth, in 1487. Two of his brothers were subsequently imprisoned by Henry VII in the Tower of London. And even forty years later, the death of the youngest of them, the exiled Richard de la Pole, the 'White Rose', who on a number of occasions had threatened to lead a foreign invasion against the Tudors, was greeted with relief and celebration by Henry VIII and his court.

A genealogy drawn up for the de la Pole family early in the reign of Henry VII diverged sharply from the official Tudor view. The pedigree was dominated by a fine portrait roundel of Richard III in the centre of the roll. The sons of Edward IV were dealt with in perfunctory fashion, no title being accorded to Edward V, the elder of the Princes in the Tower, who was said simply 'to have died without heirs in his youth'. The accession of Henry VII received scant respect, accommodated by the addition of a thick black line in the right-hand margin, thus appearing peripheral to the roll's content.

The purpose of the pedigree was to extol Richard III's legitimate right to rule – a remarkable statement to make in the early Tudor period. His coronation was described, and his subsequent nomination – after the death of his son, Edward of Middleham – of John de la Pole as his heir presumptive. It was emphasized that this had been done with the consent of all the nobility of the land. The male de la Pole offspring were clustered around Richard III; Henry VII had been pushed to the margins.

The issue did not die away. Late in the reign of Henry VIII – in March 1541 – an insulting tale was recounted about Henry Tudor's ancestry. Richard Fox of Colchester was charged with making slanderous statements about the House of Tudor and its right to rule, in which Katherine of Valois's liaison with Owen Tudor, Henry VII's grandfather, was described in less than flattering terms. Fox told how Katherine (Henry V's widow) took Owen to bed, 'baying like a very drunken whore', and through this conceived a child, Henry's father, Edmund Tudor. Henry's own career was then given an unenthusiastic résumé, described as a little-known exile, brought up largely outside the country, who invaded England in 1485 and only secured the throne by killing the reigning king, Richard III, in battle. He had 'no right to it', Fox concluded bluntly.

Fox's tale was embarrassing for the Tudors, one of a number

of skeletons in their genealogical cupboard. Once again, the spectre of the belated Valois-Tudor marriage had been raised. A secret marriage had probably taken place between Katherine and Owen Tudor some time in late 1431, probably after the dowager queen had borne her first child. The couple subsequently had four children – three sons and a daughter. But remarkably the English council remained blissfully unaware of developments, although Katherine had been forbidden by statute to marry anyone of such low rank as Tudor. The council only found out about the relationship in 1437, after Katherine of Valois's death. Owen was subsequently arrested, but pardoned and released in 1440. His two oldest sons, Edmund and Jasper, were placed under the care of the crown. This secret and scandalous marriage bore an unhappy resemblance to Edward IV's own union to Elizabeth Woodville. Richard III's attack on the validity of this match in the *Titulus Regius* was thus doubly painful for the Tudor dynasty that supplanted him.

Speculation about the relationship between Henry VII's grandfather and Katherine of Valois was common currency in the early Yorkist period. One Welsh poem mockingly said that Owen, 'once on a holiday, clapped his ardent, humble affection on the daughter of the king of the land of wine'. This cryptic statement contained the seed of a story current in the sixteenth century that Owen caught Katherine's attention at a ball, when he was so unsteady on his feet that he fell into her lap.

At the time of Fox's table-talk, a more elevated but equally worrying conversation was taking place within the walls of Dublin Castle. The king's master of the rolls, Sir Anthony St Leger, stated that prior to his marriage to Elizabeth of York, Henry VII had only the most slender title to the throne, passing over Henry's Tudor lineage completely. When a companion pointed out that Henry had a title of sorts through his mother, Lady Margaret Beaufort, St Leger was unimpressed. Henry had no rightful title, he emphasized, and that was why his supporters had urged him to marry Elizabeth of York without further delay.

Early Tudor sources were reticent about Henry VII's personal background, and details of his exile, first in Brittany and then in France, were scarcely alluded to. There was a similar reticence over his family background – unsurprising given that his mother's Beaufort lineage was tainted by bastardy and his father's by a clandestine marriage. The issue of legitimacy was the shadow over the Tudors' right to rule, and it fuelled their attacks on Richard III. By relentlessly pointing up his villainy, they hoped to distract the political community from the weakness of their own dynastic position.

To remember the legacy of Richard positively in the Tudor period took real courage. In around 1525 Jane Sacheverell decided to erect a memorial brass to her first husband, Sir John Sacheverell of Morley in Derbyshire, on which she specifically stated that he had died in Richard's service at Bosworth Field; Sacheverell had almost certainly fallen in that last brave cavalry charge against Tudor. It was the only memorial of its kind in existence.

And the widowed Jane Sacheverell showed further mettle, for in the aftermath of Bosworth she was abducted and forced to marry against her will. In a bill of complaint she later brought, Jane described the awful occasion, on 11 November 1485, when she and her party were ambushed by Richard Willoughby of Wollaton with a band of over a hundred followers 'riotously arrayed, as if for war'. Jane was assaulted, robbed and bound, and then carried off by Willoughby, 'there to do his own pleasure with her, at his own will, without her consenting or being agreeable'. But Jane Sacheverell was a survivor. In May 1486 she obtained a divorce from Willoughby, and went on to marry another. In 1485 the forcible abduction of a woman was a mere trespass under the law; in 1487, in response to a petition

Sacheverell brought to parliament, Henry VII made it a felony, passing an act 'against the taking away of women against their wills'.

In his proclamation against the rebels of 1483, and in the *Titulus Regius* the following year, Richard III had spoken out in favour of the sanctity of marriage and against sexual immorality and the mistreatment of women. It was fitting that the sole existing Tudor memorial brass to name a king scarred by seeing his mother assaulted and raped was put in place by a woman who had suffered exactly the same experience.

Our history books are full of heroes and villains. But real-life experience sometimes defies such convenient generalizations. People, then and now, are complex – and in a violent age genuine concern for justice and deeply felt morality can coexist alongside political ruthlessness. For Shakespeare, Richard's book of hours, his personal prayer book, was a prop in a theatre of deceit, and Richard's reading from it a clever ruse to assist his seizure of the crown. Richard – in this version – was acting a false part of modesty and piety to cloak his naked ambition for the throne. Yet Richard's piety was genuine and deeply felt, and his prayer book, carried with him to the battle where he fought and died, was later found in his war tent at Bosworth Field.

Richard III had a cause that he believed in. Some were repulsed by the way he took the throne; others remained loyal to him to the very end. When we finally lay Richard to rest we do not seek to make him 'bad' or 'good'. Rather, we put a stop to the stigmatizing and vilification and allow for complexity. We also grant him the dignity of resting in peace, a dignity that 500 years of history have denied him.

The Fate of the Princes in the Tower

Introduction

THE FATE OF the two sons of Edward IV, the Princes in the Tower, is one of the great mysteries of Richard III's reign and a controversy so powerful and compelling that it has often overshadowed all other aspects of Richard's life and kingship. It is also an issue where the two authors disagree. Because of this – and also because the issue has still not been solved, and may never be – we have added this brief debate as an appendix to our book. This issue is complex, and in truth one could write many pages on the subject. But it is our hope that this brief discussion will be a pointer to ongoing debate and research.

And such ongoing debate and research is necessary, because there is no proof that Richard III killed the Princes in the Tower. If Richard were put before a modern law court he would almost certainly be acquitted, as we saw in Channel 4's 1984 staging of Richard's trial. But it is equally the job of the historian to deal with probabilities not certainties. The survival of archive and chronicle information from the late Middle Ages is frequently fragmentary and incomplete – and new material often emerges that forces us to reassess our opinions. New material may still be discovered that will cast fresh light on this particular mystery.

It is important to remember that people at the time also lacked clear knowledge of what had happened. No less a person than Sir William Stanley, who had been steward of Edward, Prince of Wales's household in the 1480s, whose intervention was so decisive on the field of Bosworth and who subsequently became chamberlain of Henry VII's household, was not completely sure of their fate. In 1495 Stanley was overheard saying that if the younger of Edward IV's two sons, Richard, Duke of York, had in fact survived he would be bound to support him – words that cost him his head. At the time of Stanley's statement the pretender Perkin Warbeck was claiming to be Richard, and this claim was attracting considerable European interest and support and, importantly, was authenticated by Richard's sister, Margaret, Dowager Duchess of Burgundy. If Stanley could not be completely certain of the princes' fate, neither can we.

Henry VII was surprisingly sluggish in investigating what had happened to the princes. The first parliament of the reign made no specific accusation against Richard, but rather employed inference, 'the shedding of innocents' blood'. It may have been difficult to ascertain their fate in the immediate aftermath of Bosworth. However, there was a cynical and self-interested reason for the lack of urgency. If Henry had declared the younger of the two princes dead, he would have been forced to release his substantial estates, as Duke of York, to the three younger sisters and co-heiresses of his queen, Elizabeth. The lands of the Duchy of York were highly lucrative and, after endowing his queen, Henry chose instead to keep the remainder and enjoy their profits.

The first specific indication of what had happened to the princes only emerged, or apparently emerged, in the last decade of Henry VII's reign. Sir James Tyrell had been one of Richard III's most trusted servants. He was then retained in the service of the first Tudor king, but in 1502 was convicted of treason for conspiring with members of the de la Pole family. Facing execution, Tyrell also allegedly confessed to his involvement in the murder of the Princes in the Tower. Yet strangely, details of this confession were never circulated, and the confession itself was only reported in a London chronicle some ten years after it had happened. This supposed confession formed the basis of Sir Thomas More's investigation into the princes' fate, and his work gives the first dramatic account of how they met their deaths. More's verdict was clear: Richard III was guilty.

In Charles II's reign the bones of two children were found in the Tower of London, and these bones – immediately assumed to be those of the princes – were subsequently reinterred in Westminster Abbey. They were later examined by two experts in the 1930s and as a result declared to be the remains of the princes. For some this was, and is, good enough. But modern science has advanced greatly, and it is fair to say that the majority view among historians is that this evidence is no longer conclusive. More's testimony is shot through with inaccuracy and ambiguity. And the evidence of the bones is now seen as unsatisfactory. They could be those of the princes – but equally they could not. It is important to stress here that neither More, nor the evidence of the bones, can be dismissed. But they do not offer proof. Ongoing debate is valuable – indeed essential.

Before we commence, it is important to define more clearly what we are debating about and what we are not. There are three views on Richard III and the princes. The first is that he planned to kill them from the outset. That of course was the viewpoint of the Tudors and ultimately William Shakespeare. It is also an interpretation held by many modern historians. To complicate matters, there are two alternative versions of this view. The first, and most extreme, is that Richard was always plotting to take the throne, certainly from the death of his brother Edward IV in April 1483, if not even earlier. The adherents of this interpretation consider that Richard was motivated by ruthless ambition, his claim to the throne, advanced in June 1483, and subsequently set out in the *Titulus Regius*, being a transparent falsehood that neither Richard nor those around him really believed.

The second interpretation is that Richard was not always planning to take the throne, but the political uncertainty in the aftermath of his brother's death, and his fears for his future once Edward V was crowned, forced his hand. This view is more moderate; both sets of adherents believe that Richard's claim to the throne, and the pre-contract upon which it was based, was opportunist and had no real plausibility – and thus it was never taken seriously. But in both versions, Richard was compelled to kill the princes because they held the rightful claim to the throne and he did not – and these views cannot be dismissed. They were held by many people at the time, some of whom actually believed, or suspected, that Richard had killed the princes before his accession on 26 June 1483. And, as stated earlier, it is the conviction of many present historians. Yet it is not the belief of either of the co-authors of this book.

Our common ground can be simply put. We believe that Richard III's claim to the throne should be taken seriously. We believe that he himself saw it as genuine, in other words that he felt, or came to feel, that he was rightfully king. We believe that he saw no necessity to kill the princes to establish that claim. And finally, from everything we know of Richard's character, we believe that he would have been most reluctant to have authorized their murder.

Where we differ can also be summarized simply. The view of Michael Jones is that the attempt to rescue or remove the Princes in the Tower, conducted in late July 1483 while Richard was on progress, forced his hand. He came to realize that he could no longer guarantee the viability of his succession with the princes still alive, and ordered them to be disposed of, a course of action he only undertook with the utmost reluctance and with the deepest regret. Philippa Langley disagrees that the July plot forced Richard's hand: it was a scheme, easily thwarted, so there was no impetus for the measures suggested, nor were they in Richard's interests at such a sensitive point at the very outset of his reign.

One final point needs to be made. It is the conviction of both authors that the life and reign of Richard III deserves a positive reassessment and that Richard is deserving of such a reappraisal whether he ordered the princes' deaths through dire and cruel necessity, or whether he was innocent of such a charge. And both authors recognize that the state of existing evidence only allows conclusions based on balance of probability and does not permit a definitive statement – one way or the other.

The Argument for Richard III's Innocence Regarding the Deaths of the Princes in the Tower

All anyone can truly say regarding the fate of Edward IV's sons, the Princes in the Tower, is that they disappeared. Who was responsible for their disappearance, and how it occurred, is not known.

We don't know how, why or when, or who moved them, or where to. The widespread belief that they were killed is purely tradition – an assumption based on two things. First, gossip and rumour spread during a (failed) uprising aimed at killing Richard and replacing him on the throne. And second, uncorroborated statements put out by the French-backed invader Henry Tudor and his partisans, to justify the deaths of Richard and so many other loyal Englishmen at Bosworth. Traditional belief also telescopes the events of that summer before they disappeared, supposing that people thought the boys dead at a time when we know the Woodvilles were actually forming alliances to restore them to the succession. The Tudor version would have us believe that the queen mother heard that her sons were dead, accepted the fact unquestioningly, and immediately started plotting to promote the dangerously ambitious Tudors. Real life is not so neat and tidy, and unless she saw their bodies with her own eyes, you have to wonder what evidence of their death would be sufficient to convince her to abandon their cause. This is why we have to be so wary of unsupported claims by Tudor writers.

The speculation has always been that it was Richard III himself who killed his nephews, an allegation based on hearsay and gossip originating, in the most part, after King Richard's death. During Richard's lifetime, there are four sources who quote gossip accusing Richard, all foreign. In 1483 the story was circulating at the court of the French king, England's enemy Louis XI, but at the time the boys were very much alive. Then, later in 1483, Dominic Mancini, a foreign visitor to England with contacts at court (including the princes' own doctor) made enquiries but admitted he wasn't able to discover anything.

In January 1484, again in France, the French Chancellor, Guillaume de Rochefort, addressing the Estates-General, accused Richard of the murder. With a vulnerable new boy-king on the French throne, and attempting to counteract a backlash against royal authority, his speech was a calculated rallying cry urging his listeners not to emulate the dreadful English and their 'regicidal proclivities' as one historian has put it. The reciting of catalogues of murdered English monarchs seems to have been a favourite theme in French politics, and one needs to bear in mind Franco-English hostility before taking Rochefort's accusations at face value. Moreover, this speech came after Buckingham's rebellion when many of Richard's enemies had fled to Henry Tudor in nearby Brittany. The fourth contemporary reference is one from the visiting German knight Nicolas von Poppelau, who spent several days in Richard's company. Recording his thoughts in his private journal, presumably for his eyes only, Poppelau noted down some rumours he had heard, including one that said Richard had killed the princes, but added that he didn't believe it.

Indeed, if Richard were indicted with the crime today no court would, or could, convict him. In 1984 Channel 4 broadcast a unique programme, *The Trial of King Richard III*, which put him in the dock on the charge of murder. After four hours of deliberation, Richard was declared not guilty.

There had been a shift in the speculation that Richard killed his nephews, from suspicion that he carried out the murders himself to supposition that he ordered others to do it. The princes were last heard of in the summer of 1483: Richard was then in the north on his royal progress around the kingdom. Would he be likely to send men south to do his dirty work for him, and trust that no one in the Tower of London, a busy royal palace, got word of it? This seems not only illogical, but inordinately risky. Richard was the anointed king, declared as such by the Three Estates, the Lords, Church and Commons, whereas the boys had been declared illegitimate. But he was also newly crowned, and yet to make his mark. To order the murder of the sons of Edward IV, even if he felt able to divert suspicion away from himself, would lay him open to the danger of the worst kind of odium at the vulnerable start of his reign. Is it reasonable to assume he believed his nephews were such a threat that it was worth taking this risk? Did the failed attempt to rescue (or abduct) them from the Tower in the summer of 1483 change Richard's perception of the threat they posed?

Let's imagine that it did. Does this reckless act fit with everything else we know about Richard? Certainly he could be decisive, brutal even, and authorize executions. In his role as Constable of England under Edward IV he had sweeping powers, including those of conviction and sentence without appeal in cases of insurrection and treason.

However, he is not known to have executed anyone who in his day would have been presumed innocents – women, priests, children – or against whom no proof of guilt could be found. Summary executions would only become a regular means of disposal during the reigns of the Tudor monarchs. In fact, there are at least two occasions when Richard showed clemency, possibly even naïvety. In autumn 1483 Margaret Beaufort, wife of Thomas, Lord Stanley and mother of Henry Tudor, was found guilty of conspiring against Richard during Buckingham's rebellion. As the act of a traitor this warranted the death penalty. Instead she was simply confined under house arrest under the control of her husband.

In 1483, at the Council meeting of 13 June that led to the execution of William, Lord Hastings for treason, there were seven arrests. These included Beaufort's husband, Thomas, Lord Stanley, Thomas Rotherham, Archbishop of York, and John Morton, Bishop of Ely. All were released, Morton into the care of the Duke of Buckingham. Rotherham and Stanley remained in government circles, and Morton was offered a pardon. The latter two, though treated mercifully by Richard, later acted against him. With hindsight, had Richard considered executing such 'innocents', it could be argued that he might never have needed to fight the Battle of Bosworth.

The princes' mother, Elizabeth Woodville, is known to have made her peace with Richard early in 1484 when she emerged from Westminster, where she had taken sanctuary, and Richard promised to treat her well and arrange appropriate marriages for her daughters. Richard acted honourably in this, and the following year negotiated a marriage for Elizabeth's eldest daughter, Elizabeth of York, to the Portuguese Duke of Beja, who later became King Manuel I. Elizabeth of York was the princess who, according to Henry Tudor, was supposedly promised to him by her mother. After Richard's death the marriage negotiations were halted. Richard treated the women fairly, especially since the Yorkist claim to the throne came through the female line, and Edward IV's daughters could be perceived as a threat to him.

Not only did Elizabeth Woodville reconcile herself to Richard, but she also wrote to her eldest son, Thomas, Marquis of Dorset, who was in France with Henry Tudor, asking him to return to England so that he too could make his peace with Richard. Dorset tried to do so, but was caught and imprisoned by Henry Tudor before he could escape. It seems most unlikely that if Elizabeth believed Richard had murdered the two princes, she would risk the life of a third son. And if she was under duress, after Richard died she would surely have denounced him for murdering her sons.

But Elizabeth Woodville said nothing about the fate of her sons. However, she did take action; she immediately supported a rebellion against Henry Tudor, now King Henry VII, in the name of Lambert Simnel, a possible stalking horse for the return of Edward V. This, when her eldest daughter Elizabeth of York was Tudor's wife and Queen of England. The rebellion against Henry Tudor failed and as a result of her involvement, Elizabeth was imprisoned by Henry in Bermondsey Abbey where she died in poverty. Elizabeth Woodville's actions tell us two things: she either had incontrovertible knowledge that her sons were alive, or not enough proof that they were dead; either way she knew that Richard hadn't killed them.

There is another point. For the deaths of the two boys to be of any benefit to Richard, he had to show their bodies. Without visible proof that Edward IV's sons were dead (of some suitable illness, of course) it would always remain open to pretenders to assume their identities and lead rebellions against Richard.

The third prince, Richard's other nephew, Edward, Earl of

Warwick, son of George, Duke of Clarence was legitimate but his father had been attainted so leaving no inheritance and certainly no claim to the throne. But attainders could be reversed by a simple Act of Parliament: the taint of illegitimacy was much more difficult to reverse. So it follows that if Richard had believed that the removal of his illegitimate nephews would secure him his throne, he would have had to remove Edward of Warwick too who was legitimate and living in the royal nursery in Richard III's household in the north. But Richard did nothing of the kind. It was Henry Tudor who sought out and imprisoned this prince immediately after the Battle of Bosworth, eventually executing him on trumped-up charges in 1499 after he had languished in the Tower for at least twelve years.

The two independent studies I commissioned for the Looking for Richard project, to try to understand Richard's character, both dealt with the princes and whether or not Richard killed them. The first was by master graphologist Bridget Hickey, whose findings were published in the September 2000 issue of the *Ricardian Bulletin*:

> If there is something so provoking, so tremendous, then everyone is capable of murder, and according to their temperament would set about it differently. I cannot see him setting out, without provocation, to do harm to anybody. My gut feeling after doing this analysis, after living with this man for three weeks, is that he could not have killed the Princes in the Tower without a *very* good reason. He was so analytical; he would have asked so many questions, he would not act on impulse. He was not emotionally deranged. There is a side which didn't like the business of the day – the executions etc. – but of course he would do them when it was necessary, or when he was threatened.

My second commission was the Psychological Analysis by Professor Mark Lansdale and Dr Julian Boon of the University of Leicester, which they undertook in great detail and with considerable professional interest. The result was a lengthy article in the *Ricardian Bulletin* of March 2013.

Their conclusions as to the likelihood of Richard having the princes put to death were contextualized within their overall psychological profile, which is summarized in Appendix 2. They were careful to review the possible necessity for the boys' removal against the historical background of the time. Elimination of deposed kings had been done by previous monarchs, and Richard might have found himself in similar circumstances and compelled, albeit reluctantly, to follow that precedent. The key questions were why he might do so, and whether his psychology provided a clue.

As to why, this seemed problematical for two reasons: first, he may have believed his legal position as rightful king was very strong compared to theirs; and consequently he may not have seen them as a major threat. Second, at the time they were said to have disappeared he showed no sign of perceiving any serious threat from them.

As to Richard's psychological impetus, the over-riding assessment was that he seemed to have been, above all other things, a controlled and careful person. Thus, if the princes ended up dead (however it happened), it would be out of character for him to leave the matter untidy, uncertain and unexplained. Nor would he derive any particular benefit from keeping it to himself. Looking at the alternative proposition of sending them to a secret place of safety, in such a scenario utter silence was the only way to make it work. This, they felt, was more in keeping with his personality than complicity in their death.

For me the mystery of the Princes in the Tower is crucial. For more than 500 years, Richard has been held responsible for their murder. This belief has shaped the study of both the man and his reign. If we could apply the principle of innocent until proven guilty, rather than convicting him on a balance of probabilities, it would open up serious research which may well shed new light on an ages-old mystery.

The Argument for Richard III being responsible for the deaths of the Princes in the Tower

In July 1483 the two sons of Edward IV disappeared into the inner recesses of the Tower of London. Their servants were dismissed and they were never seen again. A rebellion against Richard's rule in October 1483, which involved a coalition of those who had previously been implacable enemies – on the one hand Lancastrians, on the other loyal members of the household of Edward IV – was clearly grounded in the conviction that the princes were no longer alive. As a result, all parties had become willing to advance the little-known Lancastrian exile, Henry Tudor, to the throne, on condition that he marry Edward IV's eldest daughter, Elizabeth of York.

If the princes were at this stage still alive, Richard III could have quashed this conspiracy by parading them through the streets of London, a course undertaken by Henry VII in 1487 when the pretender Lambert Simnel announced that he was the Earl of Warwick, the Duke of Clarence's son and heir. Henry immediately produced the real Earl of Warwick – held in custody in the Tower of London – and publicly displayed him. It is telling that Richard never undertook such an action.

Richard III's responsibility for the deaths of the princes was not fabricated by the Tudors. It was the belief of many contemporary or near-contemporary sources. It is important to say that this verdict is not unanimous – a few sources implicated the Duke of Buckingham, or confessed that the ultimate fate of the princes was not known. But the majority believed that Richard was responsible for their deaths, including Dominic

Mancini, our earliest source, along with the *Croyland Chronicler* and other near-contemporary London or foreign chronicles. And when new accounts are unearthed they tend to substantiate the same conclusion.

Such a survey needs to be nuanced. In his main narrative, the Croyland Chronicler was circumspect, reporting the general belief by September 1483 that the princes were dead, but also making clear that no one knew exactly what had happened to them. But elsewhere the chronicler revealed his own suspicion that Richard had 'suppressed his brother's progeny'.

Dominic Mancini was present in London in the summer of 1483 and vividly reported the fear of many ordinary citizens for Edward V's fate. He recalled that the subject was so distressing that some would burst into tears when considering it. Mancini gave us a remarkable window on these events and caught the contemporary mood in the capital. He also had access to one of the closest attendants of Edward V, his physician John Argentine, who was dismissed from his service in July. Argentine poignantly reported how Edward now believed his death was approaching, and had received mass and confession every day in imminent expectation of such a fate. It was a chilling testimony. Mancini was honest enough to say that when he left London at the end of July 1483 the actual fate of the princes was not known. But his clear inference that they were either dead or in immediate danger of death is all the more convincing as a result.

Mancini provides us with a contemporary account. It was based on events of the summer of 1483 he personally witnessed or reported on and thus predated the Tudor tradition. So too was the accusation that Richard had done away with his nephews, made by the French chancellor Guillaume de Rochefort to the French Estates General at Tours in January 1484. This was a remarkable comment for de Rochefort to make. He has been described as a learned and rather staid personality, and his testimony cannot be dismissed merely as an anti-English diatribe. It may have been based on specific intelligence. When the German Nicolas von Poppelau visited Richard's court in 1484 he was also interested in the fate of the princes. Some told him candidly that they had been done away with; others that they were still being held in some safe and secret place. Poppelau chose to believe the latter – unsurprisingly perhaps, since he dined regularly with the king. But it is striking that others had been so open with him.

Then there is the behaviour of the princes' mother, the dowager queen Elizabeth Woodville. At the beginning of March 1484 she had come to an agreement with Richard III where she emerged from sanctuary at Westminster Abbey, and chose to deliver her daughters to the king's safe-keeping. At first glance such an agreement seems incomprehensible if Elizabeth felt that Richard was guilty of her sons' deaths. But we have to look carefully at the broader political context.

In the autumn of 1483 Elizabeth had chosen to support a rebellion against Richard III that sought to place Henry Tudor on the throne, on condition that he married her eldest daughter, Elizabeth of York. It is hard to countenance her embarking upon such a course – which would automatically disinherit her sons by Edward IV – unless she believed the princes already dead. The rebellion failed, and in its aftermath the dowager queen had to consider her political future. Richard had crushed the uprising with ease and Henry Tudor's attempted invasion in its support had proved abortive. In its immediate aftermath, it must have seemed unlikely to Elizabeth that Tudor or anyone else would challenge Richard for the throne.

Nor was she secure in sanctuary at Westminster. The Yorkists had broken the rights of sanctuary before, when political necessity demanded it. Richard's father, Richard, Duke of York, had forcibly taken Henry, Duke of Exeter from sanctuary at

Westminster in 1454; Edward IV had done the same to those Lancastrians sheltering in Tewkesbury Abbey in 1471. And in the event, she only left Westminster Abbey on the security of the most solemn and public promise that Richard could provide. Placing his hands on the relics of the Holy Evangelists, the king swore in the presence of the lords and bishops of the realm, and the mayor and aldermen of London, that he would fully protect her and her daughters.

We may be surprised or repelled by such realpolitik. But these were violent and ruthless times, and we need to remember that Margaret of Anjou had made a similar deal in 1470, when she came to terms with her arch-enemy Warwick the Kingmaker, the man who had done so much to bring about her husband Henry VI's deposition and the deaths of so many of her kinsmen and friends. Margaret was now a penniless exile in France, and in the hope of a return to political influence she agreed to the marriage of her son, the Lancastrian Prince Edward, to Warwick's daughter Anne (who would subsequently – after Edward's death at Tewkesbury – become Richard's wife). This was an act of cynical realism that surprised even the hardened contemporary observer Philippe de Commynes.

By December 1484 relations between Elizabeth Woodville and Richard had thawed. Elizabeth sent her daughters to Richard's court for Christmas and in February 1485 tried to persuade her son by her first marriage, Thomas, Marquis of Dorset, to abandon the cause of Henry Tudor and return to England. Again, the political context is all-important. A month earlier Tudor had fled from the protection of the Duke of Brittany to the French court of Charles VIII, and – on French encouragement – had subsequently proclaimed his right to the crown of England, styling himself as if he were already king. This proclamation reneged on Tudor's earlier agreement with the Woodvilles that his right to the English throne rested solely on his marriage to

Elizabeth of York. Again, this was realpolitik in action, and however remarkable it may seem, Tudor's proclamation probably drove the Woodvilles closer to Richard III.

In the Middle Ages, English monarchs would publicly display the dead body of a rival adult claimant or political opponent to scotch all further insurrection on their behalf. Henry Tudor himself, lacking a legitimate claim of his own, went to great pains after Bosworth to display the remains of Richard III. But the princes were not adult rivals – they were innocent children. If Richard had decided to kill them, even with the greatest reluctance, it is hard to imagine him advertising the fact. King John was widely suspected of killing his young nephew Arthur of Brittany and Henry VIII of disposing of his young dynastic rival Henry Pole; neither monarch then chose to exhibit their bodies.

The Tudors portrayed Richard III as a merciless killer. I do not think he was. He was remarkably lenient to Margaret Beaufort, who organized the rebellion of 1483; Henry VIII had Margaret Pole, Countess of Salisbury, executed for far less. And Richard did not harm his other nephew, Edward, Earl of Warwick. But Richard saw Clarence's son and heir as part of the legitimate Yorkist family and even, according to John Rous, considered vesting the succession on him after the death of his own son, Edward of Middleham. Once the marriage between Edward IV and Elizabeth Woodville had been declared invalid, their two sons – the Princes in the Tower – were cast from its ranks and Richard regarded their claims to the throne, which would nevertheless have commanded support, as illegitimate and damaging.

I do not believe Richard wished to kill the princes. But after the failed attempt of July 1483 to rescue them from the Tower of London – an attempt that was recorded by the contemporary chronicler Thomas Basin and confirmed by the later researches of the antiquary John Stow in the early seventeenth century –

what other choice did he have? Leaving them alive imperilled the future of his dynasty.

Some contemporary chroniclers implicated the Duke of Buckingham in the decision. That Richard took the decision on the advice of the duke, perhaps some time in early August 1483, is entirely plausible. For Buckingham to have done the deed on his own authority is far less so. It is widely accepted that even if Richard were present in the Tower on the night Henry VI was murdered, in 1471, the responsibility for that decision rested with the reigning monarch, Edward IV. A similar logic must be applied to the events of 1483.

It is important to look for historical parallels. We need to remember that when Henry IV deposed Richard II in 1399, Richard's subsequent murder took place not after the deposition itself, but after the first attempt to rescue him, made around Christmas of that year. Faced with a rebellion against his rule, one that sought to put Richard back on the throne, Henry took the decision to kill an anointed king – cruel though it was – to safeguard the future of his own Lancastrian dynasty.

The argument here is based on probability not certainty. And there is much about Buckingham's behaviour in the summer of 1483 that we do not fully understand. But the historical evidence as it stands indicates the likelihood of Richard taking the decision to kill the princes, however reluctantly. It is important that the debate continues and we continue to think and enquire openly about the issue. Here the evaluations of graphology or psychological profiling can add to our broader thinking about the man and his times. But on this crucial issue they can never be a substitute for historical methodology. At present, that methodology points to Richard's guilt.

Richard III: A Psychological Portrait

Historical debate and psychological profiling

I T IS THE intention of this book to open out the debate about Richard III. As such, the commissioning of a psychological analysis of Richard is of real interest. A précis or short summary of this is offered in this appendix. The intention is to offer a fresh perspective on Richard's life and allow the reader a different way of engaging with him. It is not being offered as a substitute for historical argument, rather to complement some of the ideas in this book.

Psychological profiling of historical figures is still in its infancy. Professor Mark Lansdale and Julian Boon do not bring a preconceived agenda to their assessment – and the openness of their approach breaks some of the moulding of Richard's life and personality that took place under the hostile Tudor dynasty. But they have also acknowledged that their approach has its limitations as well as its strengths.

We can find much common ground with figures from the medieval past, but in a number of important respects they were also very different from us. They had a far stronger collective sense of family and saw themselves as actors on this family stage, rather than individuals operating independently from it. Psychological profiling is a system that we in the twenty-first century can easily identify with – and it offers us a bridge to the past. Its values would be more alien to a medieval audience and we need to be aware of this.

Late medieval society operated under a different belief system to our own. It was a far more violent era, where life expectancy was shorter and much more fraught with risks. And yet it also had its own certainties: a way of seeing the world – whether through the lens of a Catholic religion yet to be challenged by the Reformation, or the warrior code of chivalry – that allowed an individual a sense of destiny and the possibility of redemption that we in our modern era would struggle to comprehend.

We ask the reader to remember this. And once again, the précis of the profile is not being offered as a replacement for a historical assessment of Richard's life and death. However, it is hoped that its fresh frame of reference and insights will be stimulating and thought-provoking.

The following is a précis by a member of the Richard III Society of an article published in the Ricardian Bulletin *in March 2013.*

In 2011, as part of the Looking for Richard project, Philippa Langley commissioned two leading psychologists, one specializing in forensic psychology, to use their science in an experiment to see if we could learn anything new about Richard III and the kind of human being he really was.

They first explored one crucial issue: was he a murderous psychopath? For him to be so, he would be likely to exhibit a number of traits. The first of these is narcissism, a characteristic which manifests itself in extreme egotism combined with indifference to the feelings of others. Richard, however, appeared to be appropriate in his dress and was a natural leader of his people. Secondly there is cowardice, a quality conspicuous by its absence in the battles in which he fought. If Richard had displayed this characteristic, no doubt the Tudor historians would have seized upon it to denigrate him further. Machiavellianism, the use of cunning and duplicity in political dealings, was also considered. Richard's open disapproval of his brother's dealings with the French in 1475 was not in keeping with such an attitude. Finally, Richard's interpersonal relationships were studied. A psychopath has no conscience in exploiting and manipulating people, yet Richard was able to form trusting and positive relationships.

A number of psychological approaches were then considered that might lead us to the 'real' Richard. In medieval times a physical disability might be seen as an outward manifestation of inner wickedness. The extent of Richard's scoliosis was severe and, despite possible attempts at concealment, they conjectured that it was probably visible. Richard could have believed his condition was a failing within himself and therefore may have had feelings of guilt which could have made him defensive and behave with caution. He might have accepted it as the will of God; alternatively he could have felt rage and defiance, but Richard was known for his piety. His condition may have affected his dealings with others though, as we have already seen, he had no difficulty in forging strong relationships with others, a characteristic that continued during his reign as king.

Richard may have suffered from what is known in modern psychology as the 'Intolerance of Uncertainty' syndrome, an anxiety disorder characterized by excessive worry. He might have displayed some signs of this, perhaps most strongly seen in his sensitivity to possible threat and danger. Associated with this syndrome is extreme self-control which can lead to inflexible moral and religious beliefs.

The final part of the psychological analysis was an examination of Richard's transition from Lord of the North to king. For a decade Richard had a clearly defined role in the north; he was his own man and got on with the job. Subsequently, the executions of Hastings and Buckingham could be seen as Richard's need to assert control in an unfamiliar and rapidly changing situation.

In summary, we believe it was unlikely that Richard was a psychopathic murderer. Rather, the analysis shows him as a man with good and bad qualities, some attractive, some less so, perhaps including an excessive need or desire for control.

Five questions were then raised and speculative answers provided:

What does Hastings's execution tell us? Although the nature of Hastings's crime was not clear, it would have been entirely plausible for Richard to have acted with impetuosity if he believed that he had been betrayed. We see no inconsistency in the fact that he treated Hastings's widow with respect.

Could Richard have murdered his nephews? No deposed medieval king of England subsequently survived for long. Richard may simply have followed in the footsteps of his predecessors. However, Richard had a claim to the throne of his own – one that he and others may have believed in – as a consequence of which his nephews were declared illegitimate. If this was true Richard did not necessarily have to kill the princes to succeed to the throne. Later, renewed threat of civil war may have forced his hand, obliging him to order their death; alternatively he may simply have resolved to move them to a safer location. As a cautious and judicious man we believe it was more in character for him to hide the princes than murder them.

Was he Machiavellian? We see Richard imperilled to think and act by what he believed in. He was not a mere opportunist.

Did he take the throne opportunistically? Richard had a real sense of justice. Once the illegitimacy of the princes was raised as an issue, Richard may have felt that he was justified in staking his own claim to the throne. His record of loyalty to his brother Edward IV leads us to believe that he did not nurture a secret ambition to be king for years before his brother's death.

Why did he die at Bosworth? At the battle's climax Richard chose to make a dramatic charge against his opponent Henry Tudor. As an experienced soldier he probably believed this manoeuvre stood a good chance of success, and his belief in the legitimacy of his rule and his consciousness of being God's anointed representative as monarch would have further motivated his action.

Acknowledgements

T HIS BOOK HAS involved two parallel journeys: one about finding Richard III's physical remains, the other around exploring his historical reputation. In the course of this, the authors would like to acknowledge the help and support they have received. These debts are many, and more specific instances of thanks are also given in the Notes.

Philippa Langley would like to start with an apology: for four years this search was my passion, and I am aware that I can't possibly mention all those individuals without whom it would not have been possible. If your name is not recorded here, I ask your forgiveness.

I thank my co-author whose critically acclaimed *Bosworth 1485: Psychology of a Battle* re-ignited my quest for the real Richard III and led to my 2004 visit to a car park in Leicester. I had two wingmen at the 2012 dig, firstly Dr John Ashdown-Hill. His long years of painstaking research guided all our efforts, and everyone involved in this project is deeply indebted to him. Annette Carson, my other support, was the first writer I encountered who stated her belief that Richard III still lay where we found him. Her study of the contemporary sources propelled the search for the real Richard. Two founding members of the project, Dr David and Wendy Johnson, contributed unstinting commitment plus years of research to crucial tasks including the design of the tomb and formulating the Reburial Document. Dr Phil Stone, Chairman of the Richard III Society, personally saved the project on four separate occasions, demonstrating belief and vision of truly Ricardian proportions.

The part played by Leicester City Council has been much overshadowed, and I hope this book may help put that right. They graciously granted permission to excavate, for which my appreciation goes especially to Sir Peter Soulsby, the City Mayor, for unwavering support, and Sarah Levitt, lead on the project, whom I have the honour to count as both colleague and friend. To the utterly brilliant Richard Buckley and his dedicated team at University of Leicester Archaeological Services whose skill and expertise shine through in these pages. To that remarkable centre of learning, Leicester University, particularly Professor Mark Lansdale, Dr Julian Boon and Dr Turi King for their many kindnesses, and Richard Taylor, Deputy Registrar, for his decision to support the project. To the Dean, the Very Reverend David Monteith and all at the Cathedral who have preserved and honoured the memory of King Richard. To Julian Ware, Simon Farnaby, Simon Young, Louise Osmond, Pete Woods, Alex Rowson and the entire production team at Darlow Smithson, together with John Hay, Julia Harrington and Ralph Lee at Channel 4. To many other partners and donors: Martin Peters at Leicestershire Promotions, Michael Johnson and Colin Cook at Leicester Adult Schools, and numerous private investors including Raymond Bord, David Fiddimore, Gerry Martin, Fiona Nicolson and Jack Thomson. To Martin Traynor OBE at Leicestershire Chamber of Commerce, Heather Broughton at Leicestershire County Council and Stuart Bailey and Ben Ravilious at Leicester Civic Society. To all at the Richard III Society, its dedicated Secretaries Sue and David Wells, Relations Officer Richard Van Allen and its Deputy Chair Wendy Moorhen, plus local members Sally Henshaw and Richard

Smith, for their long years of commitment. To my friends and family for their unfailing support, particularly Sheila Malham and Geoff Akers, and of course my two sons Max and Raife and their father, John. My final thanks must go to all those Ricardians around the world who stepped in when the dig was threatened with cancellation. The search for King Richard was yours.

Michael Jones would like to express gratitude to his co-author for sharing his vision of putting Richard III back into the story of his family, the House of York, rather than casting him out from its ranks. I would like to thank fellow scholars Professor Michael Hicks, Dr Rosemary Horrox, Drs Sean Cunningham and James Ross at the National Archives, Dr Malcolm Mercer at the Tower Armouries, Professor Colin Richmond and Dr Philip Morgan at the University of Keele, Dr Rowena Archer, Cliff Davies, Diana Dunn, Keith Dockray, Margaret Condon and Anne Crawford for their support over years of working on Richard III, and particularly Professor Tony Pollard and Dr David Grummitt for the advice and help they gave as this present book got underway. To Peter and Carolyn Hammond, who for many years put the resources of the Richard III Society library at my disposal: I am appreciative of their personal kindness and hospitality.

Richard Mackinder of the Bosworth Battlefield Centre has walked the battlefield with me and discussed the latest archaeological finds there. Tobias Capwell, Curator of Arms and Armour at the Wallace Collection, has given helpful advice on the logistics of armour and Richard's cavalry charge. Bob Woosnam-Savage of the Royal Armouries, an expert on late medieval weaponry and wounding in battle, has provided invaluable support around interpreting the battle wounds on Richard's remains and reconstructing the king's final moments at Bosworth. In the case of both the archaeological finds and battlefield terrain,

Richard and Bob have stressed that their conclusions at this stage can only be provisional.

Sioned Williams, Curator of Furniture at the National History Museum, Cardiff, has kindly provided information on Rhys ap Thomas's bed lintel, and Professor Paul Moroz, Orthopedic Surgeon at the Children's Hospital of Eastern Ontario, on the likely effects of Richard's scoliosis. Geoffrey Wheeler has provided valuable assistance with the picture research. I am also grateful to my friends and family for their support – and to my two sons Edmund and Rufus and to their mother Liz.

We both would like to thank our agent, Charlie Viney, who has encouraged us every step of the way, and Roland Philipps, Caroline Westmore, Becky Walsh and everyone at John Murray, who have given us such great support, as well as Morag Lyall, our copy-editor, and Christopher Summerville who has compiled the index. My final debt is to my supervisor, Professor Charles Ross, who first kindled my interest in Richard III. Charles's major biography of Richard was completed whilst I was his post-graduate student and we discussed it on many occasions. His depth of scholarship and personal generosity inspired my love of medieval history – and I have thought of him often as this book was written.

Picture Credits

Bosworth Battlefield Centre: 14. Darlow Smithson Productions Ltd: 4 above, 5 below, 8 centre. Lambeth Palace Library: 9. *Looking for Richard* project 2013: 8 below. National Museum of Wales: 16 below. Private collection: 2 below, 3 above, 5 above, 6 above. Royal Armouries, Leeds: 15 below. Stratascan Ltd: 1 above (Claire Graham), 2 above. Dr Phil Stone, Richard III Society: 1 below. University of Leicester: 3 below (Colin G. Brooks), 4 below, 7 above, 7 below (Colin G. Brooks), 8 above (Colin G. Brooks), 15 above. University of Leicester Archaeological Services: 6 below. Geoffrey Wheeler: 10, 11, 12, 13, 16 above left and right.

Notes

Introduction: The Inspiration

The quotes about Richard come from the York City Records, 23 August 1485 and 14 October 1485.

Chapter 1: The Road to the Dig

For Richard's burial in the Greyfriars Priory in Leicester see Peter Hammond, 'The Burial Place of Richard III', in *Richard III. Crown and People*, Richard III Society, 1985, p. 31 (also *Ricardian*, IV, 59 (December 1977), pp. 30–31). For Richard's tomb, see Rhoda Edwards, 'King Richard's Tomb at Leicester', in *Richard III. Crown and People*, pp. 29–30 (also *Ricardian*, III, 50 (September 1975), pp. 8–9). For John Speed's report on the site of King Richard's grave, see John Speed, *History of Great Britain*, 1611, p. 725. For Wren's account of the memorial pillar in Herrick's garden in Leicester see *Parentalia, or Memoires, of the Family of the Wrens* (London, 1750), p. 144. See Ashdown-Hill, *Last Days of Richard III*, pp. 114–23, for full details on the discovery of Richard III's mtDNA sequence. Ashdown-Hill's discovery was made in 2005 and published in John Ashdown-Hill: 'Finding the DNA of Richard III', *Medelai Gazette*, August 2005. Ashdown-Hill also published full details of Richard III's mtDNA sequence for HVR1 and HVR2 (subsequently confirmed in the Leicester bones, 2013) in 'Margaret of York's Dance of Death: The DNA Evidence', *Handelingen van de Koninklijke Kring voor Oudheidkunde, Letteren en Kunst van Mechelen*, 111, 2007, pp. 193–207. The site of the lost Greyfriars Church was believed to be close to Grey Friars Street in the north-east of the Greyfriars precinct. See Ken Wright, *The Field of Bosworth*, 2002, pp. 142–3, 146. David Baldwin, 'Is there a King under this bridge?' *Leicester Mercury*, October 8 2002. For the assertion that Richard may have first been buried in the Church of the Annunciation in the Newarke in Leicester, see Anne F. Sutton and Livia Visser-Fuchs, 'The Making of a Minor London Chronicle in the Household of Sir Thomas Frowyk (died 1485)', *Ricardian*, X, 126, (September 1994), pp. 86–103. For John Ashdown-Hill's new evidence to confirm the Greyfriars burial see his 'The Epitaph of Richard III', *Ricardian*, 18 (2008), pp. 31–45. Also see Ashdown-Hill, *Last Days of Richard III*, Appendix 4, pp. 134, 168. For Ashdown-Hill's conclusion that Richard's body was still at the Greyfriars site see his *Last Days of Richard III*, pp. 106–9. For the law on burials, see the Burials Act 1857, section 25. The heraldic emblem of a boar has long antecedents, at least back to Roman times. It signified a fighter. Live wild boar do not seek out humans but when hunted, as they were in medieval days, will turn and fight. Richard's best known motto was 'loyaulte me lie' – loyalty binds me. The former grammar school was owned by William Davis Ltd, Loughborough, who very kindly gave permission to carry out the GPR survey (2011) and archaeological investigation (2012). Thanks to Adrian McInnes, Technical Director, and Paul Watkins, Project Co-ordinator. Thanks to Dr Raymond Bord, David Fiddimore, Dr David and Wendy Johnson, Gerry Martin, Fiona Nicolson, Dr Phil Stone, Jack Thomson for funding the GPR survey. The Mira Scanner for the GPR survey was provided by LTU. Englezo's search had been successful; eight pits containing the mass grave of two hundred and fifty British and Australian servicemen from the Great War were discovered. The servicemen were reburied with honour in a new cemetery opened in France by the Prince of Wales. Using DNA profiling and forensic analysis, by 2010–11 over ninety of these remains had been successfully identified.

Chapter 2: The Great Debate

On Richard's use of cavalry against Tudor, I am indebted to Richard Mackinder of the Bosworth Battlefield Centre and Tobias Capwell, Curator of Arms and Armour at the Wallace Collection. My survey is derived primarily from the introduction to Charles Ross's *Richard III*, Keith Dockray's *Richard III* and David Hipshon's *Richard III*. For a chivalric reading of the Richard's final battle see Jones, *Bosworth 1485*, and Tim Thornton, 'The Battle of Sandeford: Henry Tudor's Understanding of the Meaning of Bosworth Field', *Historical Research*, 78 (2005). Such was the power of Tudor and Shakespearean propaganda that when a copy of the Act of Attainder against Clarence was found in the Tower archives in the late eighteenth century, the manuscript annotation of the discovery suggested that rather than being drawn up by Edward IV, 'this instrument was formed by Richard duke of Gloucester': University of Nottingham Archives: Me 2L2/12.

Chapter 3: So It Begins

Edward of Middleham's investiture as Prince of Wales in York from *Berdern College Statute Book* p. 48. Translated by Peter Hammond and Anne Sutton. I have taken Richard's interment in the Greyfriars Church in Leicester as being 25 August 1485 based on the accounts of Polydore Vergil and Diego de Valera and the will of William Catesby, dated 25 August 1485. The Exhumation Licence from the Ministry of Justice also applied this instruction to shield human remains from the public gaze for the protection of the public.

Chapter 4: Yearning for a Noble Cause: Richard's Early Career

The document is Christie's Lot 47/Sale 5960. For the chivalric dimension to York's clash with Henry VI's government see Michael Jones, 'Somerset, York and the Wars of the Roses', *English Historical Review*, 104 (1989) and Mercer, *Medieval Gentry*. York's solemn oath at St Paul's Cathedral in March 1452 is recorded in Durham Cathedral Muniments, Register IV, f.92v. The significance of Richard's experience at Ludlow in 1459 has rightly been emphasized in Wilkinson, *Richard*. On York claiming the throne see Michael Jones, 'Edward IV, the Earl of Warwick and the Yorkist Claim to the Throne', *Historical Research*, 70 (1997). Keith Dockray and Richard Knowles, 'The Battle of Wakefield', *Ricardian*, 9 (1992) give us the best account of the terrible death suffered by Richard, Duke of York, Richard's father. For the suspicion of Warkworth's Chronicle that Richard had executed Thomas Fauconberg after he had received a royal pardon see Richard Britnell, 'Richard Duke of Gloucester and the Death of Thomas

Fauconberg', *Ricardian*, X (1995). For a different view, of Richard executing Lancastrians in the aftermath of Tewkesbury on the authority and orders of the king, see The National Archives (TNA), SC1/44/61 (4 July 1471). Richard's expansion of retaining, in the aftermath of the settlement of the dispute between him and Clarence, is well described in Horrox, *Richard III: A Study in Service*, and Pollard, *Richard III and the Princes in the Tower*. Richard's letter to William FitzWilliam is in Sheffield City Archives, WWM/D/98. Richard, Duke of York's astonishing feat of arms on 20 July 1441 is recorded on Guillaume du Chastel's tomb in the Abbey of Saint-Denis. The commission for the monument is from Honoré Champion, *Prigent de Coëtivy, Amiral et Bibliophile* (Paris, 1906). For the importance this would hold for his son Richard see Richard Firth Green, 'An Epitaph for the Duke of York', *Studies in Bibliography*, 41 (1988). On Richard's literary interests see Sutton and Visser-Fuchs, *Richard III's Books*. For Richard and his brother Clarence acting in common cause against Edward IV's foreign policy, and its perceived manipulation by the Woodvilles, see Michael Jones, '1477 – The Expedition that Never Was: Chivalric Expectation in Late Medieval England', *Ricardian*, XII (2001). The important new evidence of Richard mass-recruiting retainers within weeks of Clarence's arrest is recorded in Durham Cathedral Muniments, Halmote Court Rolls, 1476–7 (which I owe to Professor Pollard). Chunxiao Wei, 'Richard Duke of Gloucester's Petition, 1478, and the Fate of Clarence', *Notes and Queries*, 58 (2011) reminds us that Richard receiving a share of Clarence's lands does not mean he was complicit in his death. On Richard's arbitration awards see Pollard, *Richard III and the Princes in the Tower*. Richard and his brother Edward sometimes clashed over Richard's aggressive stance over Scotland, particularly in 1474–5: Peter Booth, 'Richard Duke of Gloucester and the West March towards Scotland, 1470–83', *Northern History*, XXXVI (2000). But his resumption of aggressive raiding tactics late in the reign was highly praised and his conduct of the 1482 campaign a triumph. For an important reappraisal of the latter: Jackson Armstrong, 'Local Society and the Defence of the Frontier in Fifteenth-Century Scotland: The War Measures of 1482', *Florilegium*, 25 (2008).

Chapter 5: The Discovery of the Church and the Location of the Nave

Thanks to Peter O'Donoghue, York Herald at the College of Arms, London, for supplying the artwork for Richard III's banner and standard. In 2000, Ken Wallace discovered the Hallaton Treasure in Leicestershire, the largest hoard of Iron Age coins.

Chapter 6: Seizing the Throne

For the general outline of events see Charles Ross, *Richard III*; Pollard, *Richard III and the Princes in the Tower*; Cunningham, *Richard III*; and Hicks, *The Prince in the Tower*. John Gigur's comments are from Colin Richmond, 'A Letter of 19 April 1483 from John Gigur to William Wainfleet', *Historical Research*, 65 (1992). For Richard, Duke of York's use of a reduced retinue of 300 men in 1450 see the letter of Humphrey Stafford, Duke of Buckingham, recently discovered in Surrey County Record Office, LM/ COR/1/19, and discussed in Ralph Griffiths, 'Richard, Duke of York, and the Crisis of Henry VI's Household in 1450–51: Some Further Evidence', *Journal of Medieval History*, 38 (2012). A fresh insight into the politics of this period is offered in Carson, *Richard III*. For Richard's genuine fear of witchcraft see John Leland, 'Witchcraft and the Woodvilles: A Standard Medieval Smear?' in *Reputation and Representation in Fifteenth-Century Europe*, ed. Douglas Biggs, Sharon Michalove and Albert Compton Reeves (Leiden, 2004); for his reaction to the sexual immorality of Edward IV's court: David Santiuste, '"Puttyng Downe and Rebuking of Vices": Richard III and the Proclamation for the Reform of Morals', in *Medieval Sexuality: A Casebook*, ed. April Harper and Caroline Proctor (London, 2008). Cecily Neville's well-deserved reputation for piety in her later life does not preclude the possibility of an indiscretion in her youth. The issue of an adultery hearing is echoed in the one book of Cecily's she dispensed with before her death: Mary Dzon, 'Cecily Neville and the Apocryphal *Infantia Salvatoris* in the Middle Ages', *Medieval Studies*, 71 (2009); and for the papal indulgence found in her coffin: Sofija Matich and Jennifer Alexander, 'Creating and Recreating the Yorkist Tombs in Fotheringhay Church (Northamptonshire)', *Church Monuments*, XXVI (2011).

Chapter 7: The Discovery of the Skeletal Remains

At the time of writing, the unidentified female remains discovered in the charnel in Trench Three would, after investigation, be reinterred in a nearby church in Leicester. For the physical description of Richard see Chapter 8. Information on the former grammar school building in Leicester from Leon Hunt, *Archaeological Desk-Based Assessment for Land at Greyfriars, St Martins (NGR: SK 585 043)*, ULAS, 12 April 2013, commissioned by Philippa Langley for the Looking for Richard project. The 10,000-square-foot neo-gothic building was built as Alderman Newton's School in 1864 and extended in 1887 and 1897. In 1979 the buildings became Leicester Grammar School. See also I.A.W. Place, *The History of Alderman Newton's Boys School, 1836–1914*, University of Leicester (1960). In December 2012 Leicester City Council announced its purchase of the former grammar school for £850,000: *Leicester Mercury*, Monday, 3 December 2012. It seems that the sarcophagus found in Trench Three had been located on the Ground Penetrating Radar Survey. Its shape is clearly marked in the central area of the former grammar school car park: Robbie Austrums, *Geophysical Survey Report, Greyfriars Church, Leicester, for Philippa Langley*, Stratascan, September 2011. On 1 April 2013 it was announced that a four-week dig would take place at the Greyfriars site, Leicester in July 2013. The dig will now be part of the city council's continuing work on the new Richard III Visitor Centre that is due to open in spring 2014 in the former grammar school building. The work is to be undertaken by Richard Buckley and the team at ULAS who hope to uncover much more about the Greyfriars Church and its buildings.

Chapter 8: Richard as King

For Richard, Howard and Berkeley see Hicks, *The Prince in the Tower*. On the coronation: Sutton and Hammond, *Coronation of Richard III*. The witness list is Berkeley Castle Muniments (BCM)/A/5/5/2. On Richard's kingship see Charles Ross, *Richard III*; Pollard, *Richard III and the Princes in the Tower*; Hicks, *Richard III*; Horrox, *Richard III: A Study in Service*. On the fate of the princes I have followed Charles Ross, *Richard III* and Pollard, *Richard III and the Princes in the Tower*. For more recent sources see John Ashdown-Hill, 'The Death of Edward V – New Evidence from Colchester',

Essex Archaeology and History, 35 (2004), and Nigel Saul, *The Three Richards* (London, 2006), citing Bodleian Ashmole 1448, a source written in the immediate aftermath of Bosworth, with Henry Tudor still referred to as 'earl of Richmond': 'Richard . . . removed them from the light of the world . . . vilely and murderously.' Some believed they had already been killed before Richard took the throne; others, shortly afterwards: Philip Morgan, 'The Death of Edward V and the Rebellion of 1483', *Historical Research*, 68 (1995). On the legal rights of Elizabeth of York's three surviving younger sisters in the Tudor period, which inhibited Henry VII from thoroughly investigating the princes' survival, see T.B. Pugh, 'Henry VII and the English Nobility', in *The Tudor Nobility*, ed. George Barnard (Manchester, 1992). On Richard's increasing identification with his father: Shropshire Record Office, 3365/67/60, a memorandum of the king's instructions for setting up a perpetual chantry at Wem (10 September 1484). Ashdown-Hill, *Last Days of Richard III*, is valuable on Richard's marriage negotiations with the House of Portugal. Richard's gathering of artillery is from Ross, *Richard III*; information on the Milanese armour has kindly been provided by Tobias Capwell.

Chapter 9: The Identification of the Remains

Mathematics students at the University of Leicester calculated that the archaeologists had a less than 1 per cent chance of finding the grave, with chances of discovery on the very first day at just 0.0554 per cent, or odds of 1,785 to 1 against: University of Leicester, Press Office, 11 March 2013. The dental analysis was of particular interest as we have the dental record of some of Richard's relations: Anne Mowbray, Eleanor Talbot and the bones in the urn in Westminster Abbey, reputed to be those of Richard's nephews, the Princes in the Tower. Later, I approached other scoliosis specialists who confirmed that severe scoliosis, particularly in later life, is painful. And the Scoliosis Association in the UK confirmed that the word 'hunchback' is very distressing and no longer used. The skeleton is missing the left fibula (lower leg bone). Apart from a few small hand bones (twelve missing out of a total of fifty-four, which is a good recovery rate), the feet and a few teeth, the remains were complete: University of Leicester, March 2013. A rondel dagger is a modern term for a type of dagger with a circular, round cross-guard towards the blade, which could be single or multi-edged, and often a pommel of similar form. The rondel dagger was used by knights between the fourteenth and early sixteenth centuries and was so named because of the distinctive shape of its grip. After this examination of the bones, a third wound on the face was discovered: a tiny nick in the mandible also on the right and an inch or so above the other, making a total of nine identified wounds on the skull, with the possibility of more to be confirmed. At the time of writing it was unclear whether this new wound could support the theory that King Richard's helmet was cut off him. The lack of trauma to the face further strengthened my conviction that Henry Tudor did not leave Richard's body on the battlefield as it was his prize. At the time of writing, Jo Appleby confirmed that the soil analysis beneath the body for parasitic sample, the isotopic report and the dental analysis are not yet available, but should be included in the archaeological report some time towards the end of 2013. The facial reconstruction process has been blind-tested at the University of Dundee using living people, CT scans and photography, and the accuracy tested using recognition levels and anthropometry (scientific study of the measurements and proportions of the human body). The second living relative of Richard III who gave a sample of their DNA for the tests wishes to remain anonymous.

Chapter 10: Bosworth

An excellent survey on the sources is provided in Bennett, *Battle of Bosworth*. For a recent archival discovery about the battle see John Alban, 'The Will of Thomas Longe of Ashwellthorpe, 1485. A Yorkist Soldier at Bosworth', *Ricardian* XXII (2012). For Nottingham's intelligence gathering before and during Bosworth, see Penelope Lawton, 'Riding Forth to Aspye for the Town', *Ricardian Bulletin* (September 2012). My ideas on Richard's personal duel with Henry Tudor owe much to conversations with Cliff Davies and are also developed in Michael Jones, 'The Myth of 1485: Did France Really Put Henry Tudor on the Throne?', in *The English Experience in France 1450–1558: War, Diplomacy and Cultural Exchange*, ed. David Grummitt (Aldershot, 2002). The French mercenary's account, written at Leicester on 23 August 1485, is from Jones, *Bosworth 1485*, and my views on the battle have been modified by the important archaeological finds summarized in Glenn Foard, 'Bosworth Uncovered', in *BBC History Magazine*, 11 (2010). On Richard's courage, and his final moments in battle, the provisional ideas of Bob Woosnam-Savage are from 'The Violent Death of the King in the Car Park', a talk given at the Royal Armouries, Leeds, on 27 March 2013. For another who may have struck Richard in those final, terrible moments: Raymond Skinner, 'Thomas Woodshawe, "Grassiour" and Regicide', *Ricardian*, IX (1993). Rhys ap Thomas's duel with Richard is recounted in the seventeenth-century family history: Ralph Griffiths, *Sir Rhys ap Thomas and His Family: A Study in the Wars of the Roses and Early Tudor Politics* (Cardiff, 1993). The history attributed Richard's death to Rhys himself, but it was one of his followers who almost certainly killed him. For the praise poem: Edward Rees, *A Life of Guto'r Glyn* (Aberwystwyth, 2008). Information on the Rhys ap Thomas bed has been kindly provided by Sioned Williams, Curator of Furniture at the National History Museum, Cardiff.

Chapter 11: The Man Behind the Myth

For the story of Thomas Redeheid see Paul Murray Kendall, *Richard III* (London, 1973) p. 136. For Richard's sense of humour: from Leicester Castle, on 18 August 1483, Richard sent an important letter to the French king, Louis XI. The letter was carried by Richard's groom of the stable: 'I pray that by my servant, this bearer, a groom of my stable, you will let me know in writing your full intention . . .' Kendall, *Richard III*, pp. 255–6. For the letter to Chancellor Russell see Kendall, *Richard III*, p. 324. Kendall remarks on the generosity of the letter. For the full text of the poem see Andrew Breeze, 'A Welsh Poem of 1485 on Richard III', *Ricardian*, XVIII (2008), pp. 46–53. For analysis indicating the Tudor instigation behind it, see Annette Carson, 'Dafydd Llwyd's Poem', *Ricardian Bulletin*, autumn 2008, pp. 35–49.

Chapter 12: The Man and his Times

William Bracher, yeoman of the crown, owed his promotion to royal service through informing Richard of the uprising in the West Country in 1483: *Calendar of Patent Rolls, 1476–85*, pp. 373, 390 (grants of lands and offices in Devon, Somerset and Dorset for 'good service against the rebels'). Catesby's role as agent of Richard III in Brittany was crucial in precipitating

Henry Tudor's flight from the duchy at the end of September 1484: Cliff Davies, 'Richard III, Brittany and Henry Tudor', *Nottingham Medieval Studies*, 37 (1993). For the revealing wording of Richard's grant of an annuity to Saxton Church on 19 February 1484: Tim Sutherland and Armin Schmidt, 'Towton 1461: An Integrated Approach to Battlefield Archaeology', *Landscapes*, 4 (2003). For Thomas Gregory's pride in his service 'cum Henrico Septimo apud Bosworth Field', in the earliest use of the actual battle name: the Shakespeare Centre (Birthplace Trust), DR10/1349, a deed of 26 October 1500. Henry VII's first parliament is described in Cavill, *English Parliaments*. Material on the Stanley-Harrington dispute is drawn from Michael Jones, 'Richard III and the Stanleys', in *Richard III and the North*, ed. Horrox. For the political climate of the time see Paul Strohm, *Politique: The Languages of Statecraft Between Chaucer and Shakespeare* (Notre Dame, Indiana, 2005) and Grummitt, *Short History of the Wars of the Roses*. Thomas Barowe's bequest is from Anne Sutton and Livia Visser-Fuchs, 'Richard III and the University of Cambridge', in *Richard III and East Anglia*, ed. Visser-Fuchs. On legitimacy and the Tudor claim to the throne: Michael Bennett, 'Table Tittle-tattle and the Tudor View of History', in *People, Places and Perspectives: Essays on Later Medieval and Early Tudor England*, ed. Keith Dockray and Peter Fleming (Stroud, 2005). For the de la Pole pedigree see Philip Morgan, '"Those Were the Days" – a Yorkist Pedigree Roll', in *Estrangement, Education and Enterprise in Fifteenth-Century England*, ed. Sharon Michalove (Stroud, 1998). Cliff Davies, 'Information, Disinformation and Political Knowledge under Henry VII and Early Henry VIII', *Historical Research*, 85 (2012) provides an important reassessment of the Tudor view of history. Jane Sacheverell's petition is in University of Nottingham Library, GB159 Mi5/168/23.

Bibliography

John Ashdown-Hill, *Eleanor, The Secret Queen* (Stroud, 2009)

——, *The Last Days of Richard III* (Stroud, 2010)

David Baldwin, *Richard III* (Stroud, 2012)

Michael Bennett, *The Battle of Bosworth* (Stroud, 1985)

Annette Carson, *Richard III: The Maligned King* (Stroud, 2008)

Paul Cavill, *The English Parliaments of Henry VII* (Oxford, 2009)

Anne Crawford, *The Yorkists: The History of a Dynasty* (London, 2007)

Sean Cunningham, *Richard III: A Royal Enigma* (London, 2003)

——, *Henry VII* (London, 2007)

Keith Dockray, *Richard III: A Source Book* (Stroud, 1997)

Bertram Fields, *Royal Blood: Richard III and the Mystery of the Princes* (New York, 1998)

Veronica Fiorato et al., *Blood Red Roses: The Archaeology of a Mass Grave from the Battle of Towton* (Oxford, 2007)

Peter Foss, *The Field of Redemore* (Newtown Linford, 1998)

John Gillingham (ed.), *Richard III: A Medieval Kingship* (London, 1993)

Anthony Goodman, *The Wars of the Roses: The Soldiers' Experience* (Stroud, 2005)

Philippa Gregory, David Baldwin and Michael Jones, *The Women of the Cousins' War: The Duchess, the Queen and the King's Mother* (London, 2013)

Ralph Griffiths and James Sherborne (eds.), *Kings and Nobles in the Later Middle Ages* (Gloucester, 1986)

Ralph Griffiths and Roger Thomas, *The Making of the Tudor Dynasty* (Stroud, 1985)

Sarah Gristwood, *Blood Sisters: The Women Behind the Wars of the Roses* (London, 2012)

David Grummitt, *A Short History of the Wars of the Roses* (London, 2013)

Peter Hammond, *Richard III and the Bosworth Campaign* (Barnsley, 2010)

Alison Hanham, *Richard III and his Early Historians 1483–1535* (Oxford, 1975)

Michael Hicks, *False, Fleeting, Perjur'd Clarence* (Stroud, 1980)

——, *Richard III* (Stroud, 2000)

——, *The Prince in the Tower: The Short Life and Mysterious Death of Edward V* (Stroud, 2007)

David Hipshon, *Richard III* (London, 2011)

Rosemary Horrox, *Richard III: A Study in Service* (Cambridge, 1989)

——, (ed.), *Richard III and the North* (Hull, 1986)

Mike Ingram, *Bosworth 1485* (Stroud, 2012)

Michael Jones, *Bosworth 1485: Psychology of a Battle* (Stroud, 2002)

——, *Agincourt 1415: A Battlefield Guide* (Barnsley, 2005)

Michael Jones and Malcolm Underwood, *The King's Mother: Lady Margaret Beaufort, Countess of Richmond and Derby* (Cambridge, 1992)

Paul Murray Kendall, *Richard III* (London, 1955)

Hannes Kleineke, *Edward IV* (London, 2008)

Malcolm Mercer, *The Medieval Gentry: Power, Leadership and Choice During the Wars of the Roses* (London, 2010)

James Petre (ed.), *Richard III: Crown and People* (Gloucester, 1985)

Anthony Pollard, *Richard III and the Princes in the Tower* (Stroud, 1991)

Jeremy Potter, *Good King Richard?* (London, 1983)

Charles Ross, *Edward IV* (London, 1975)

——, *Richard III* (London, 1981)

James Ross, *John de Vere, Thirteenth Earl of Oxford (1442–1513): 'The Foremost Man of the Kingdom'* (Woodbridge, 2011)

David Santiuste, *Edward IV and the Wars of the Roses* (Barnsley, 2010)

Anne Sutton and Peter Hammond (eds.), *The Coronation of Richard III: the Extant Documents* (Gloucester, 1983)

Anne Sutton, Livia Visser-Fuchs and Peter Hammond, *The Reburial of Richard Duke of York, 21–30 July 1476* (London, 1991)

Anne Sutton and Livia Visser-Fuchs, *Richard III's Books* (Stroud, 1997)

Livia Visser-Fuchs (ed.), *Richard III and East Anglia: Magnates, Gilds and Learned Men* (Stroud, 2010)

Alison Weir, *The Princes in the Tower* (London, 1992)

Josephine Wilkinson, *Richard: The Young King to Be* (Stroud, 2009)

Ken Wright, *The Field of Bosworth 1485* (Leicester, 2002)

Index

INDEX

Machiavelli, Niccolò, 214, 255; *The Prince*, 225
McLeish, Andy, 143
Mancini, Dominic, 49–52, 77, 85–9, 106–7, 111–14, 118, 124–7, 151, 156, 159–60, 163, 229, 242, 249
Manuel I, 244
March, Earl of *see* Edward IV
Margaret, Queen, 75, 80
Market Bosworth, 185
Markham, Sir Clements, 48
Mauleverer, William, 149
Mechelen, 9
medieval kings: funeral customs of, 13
Meet the Ancestors (TV programme), 179
Melusina, 120
mercenaries: French, 197, 202–6
Merevale Abbey, 185, 197–200
Michaelmas, 82, 152
Michell, Keith, 2
Micklegate Bar, York, 76
Middleham: church at, 53
Middleham, Edward of, 54, 118, 153, 161, 232, 252
Middleham Castle, 1, 57, 78
Midlands, 55, 80, 110, 165, 173, 187
Milford Haven, 184, 195
Ministry of Justice (MoJ), 12, 15, 103
MIRA scanner, 25
Mistry, Mike, 55
Mitchell, Dr Piers, 169–72
Mitcheson, Graeme, 29
mitochondrial DNA (mtDNA), 8–11, 57, 181
Molinet, Jean, 206
Monasteries, Dissolution of the, 7–8, 39, 166
Montagu, Marquis of, 163
Monteith, Very Reverend David, 182

More, Sir Thomas: 37–8, 45–52, 70, 85, 111–15, 121–2, 146–8, 227–9, 239; accuses Richard III of murder, 45, 231; motivation for study of Richard III, 45; praises Richard III, 45; as source for Shakespeare, 46, 229; describes 'unnatural' birth of Richard III, 70; unflattering physical description of Richard III, 148; suggests Richard III feared witchcraft, 227; *History of Richard III*, 37, 48
Morley, Sir John Sacheverell of, 234
Morris, Mathew, 61–8, 90–102, 129, 132–5, 139–41
Mortimer, Anne, 74
Mortimer, Edmund, 74
Morton, John, Archbishop of Ely, 45–6, 124, 229, 244
Morton, Robert, 151
Moton, Sir William, 15, 144
Mowbray, Anne, Duchess of York and Norfolk, 14–15
Mowbray, John, Duke of Norfolk, 146

Neville family, 72
Neville, Anne, Duchess of Buckingham, 73, 78, 82, 84, 126, 157, 164
Neville, Cecily, Duchess of York, 41, 70
Neville, George, Duke of Bedford, 82, 119
Neville, Isabel, 82
Neville, Ralph, Earl of Westmorland, 69
Neville, Richard, Earl of Warwick, 72, 77–81, 119–20, 163, 192, 225
Norbury Church, 228
Norfolk, 78, 141, 145